A HISTORY AND THEORY
OF THE SOCIAL SCIENCES

Not All that Is Solid
Melts into Air

Peter Wagner

SAGE Publications
London • Thousand Oaks • New Delhi

First published 2001

Published in association with *Theory, Culture & Society*,
Nottingham Trent University

SAGE Publications Ltd
6 Bonhill Street
London EC2A 4PU

SAGE Publications Inc
2455 Teller Road
Thousand Oaks, California 91320

SAGE Publications India Pvt Ltd
32, M-Block Market
Greater Kailash – I
New Delhi 110 048

British Library Cataloguing in Publication Data
A catalogue record for this book is available from the British
Library

ISBN 0–7619–6568–8
ISBN 0–7619–6569–6 (pb)

Library of Congress catalog record available

Typeset by Keystroke, Jacaranda Lodge, Wolverhampton.
Printed in Great Britain by The Cromwell Press Ltd, Trowbridge, Wiltshire

CONTENTS

ACKNOWLEDGEMENTS

This book is elaborated on the basis of previously published articles, which have been edited and revised for the purpose of the overall argument developed here. It has not been possible, however, to fully update the historical analyses in the first part of the book. The original version of Chapter 8 was co-authored with Heidrun Friese. The following list gives the full bibliographical information, including the original titles, on the loci of first publication. Thanks are due to the publishers for permission to re-use the material.

Chapter 1: 'Science of society lost: On the failure to establish sociology in Europe during the "classical" period', in *Discourses on society. The shaping of the social science disciplines*, edited by Peter Wagner, Björn Wittrock and Richard Whitley. Dordrecht: Kluwer, 1991, 219–45.

Chapter 2: 'The place of the discourse on politics among the social sciences: Political science in turn-of-the-century Europe', in *Texts, contexts, concepts. Studies on politics and power in language*, edited by Sakari Hänninen and Kari Palonen. Helsinki: Finnish Political Science Association, 1990, 262–81.

Chapter 3: '"Adjusting social relations": Social science and social planning during the twentieth century', in *The Cambridge history of science*, vol. 7, *Modern social and behavioral sciences*, edited by Theodore Porter and Dorothy Ross. Cambridge: Cambridge University Press, 2001.

Chapter 4: 'Social sciences and political projects: Reform coalitions between social scientists and policy-makers in France, Italy, and West Germany', in *The social direction of the public sciences*, edited by Stuart S. Blume, Joske Bunders, Loet Leydesdorff and Richard Whitley. Dordrecht: Reidel, 1987, 277–306.

Chapter 5: 'Liberty and discipline: Making sense of postmodernity, or, once again, toward a sociohistorical understanding of modernity', *Theory and Society*, vol. 21, no. 4, August 1992, 467–92.

Chapter 6: 'The bird in hand: Rational choice: the default mode of social theorising', in *Rational choice theory: resisting colonization*, edited by Margaret Archer and Jonathan Tritter. London: Routledge, 2000, 19–35.

Chapter 7: 'Dispute, uncertainty and institution in recent French debates', *The Journal of Political Philosophy*, vol. 2, no. 3, 1994, 270–89.

Chapter 8: 'Not all that is solid melts into air: Modernity and contingency' (with Heidrun Friese), in *Spaces of culture. City/nation/world*, edited by Mike Featherstone and Scott Lash. London: Sage, 1999, 101–15.

Chapter 9: '"An entirely new object of consciousness, of volition, of thought": The coming into being and (almost) passing away of "society" as an object of the social sciences', in *Biographies of scientific objects*, edited by Lorraine Daston. Chicago: The University of Chicago Press, 2000, 132–53.

Chapter 10: 'Crises of modernity: Political sociology in historical contexts', *Social theory and sociology. The classics and beyond*, edited by Stephen P. Turner. Cambridge, MA: Basil Blackwell, 1996, 97–115.

Chapter 11: 'Modernity – One or many?', in *Blackwell companion to sociology*, edited by Judith Blau. Oxford: Blackwell, 2000.

INTRODUCTION
HISTORICISING THE SOCIAL SCIENCES

In many respects, the twentieth century appears now, after its end, as the century of the social sciences. It was in intellectual debates, often accompanied by institutional struggles, at the end of the nineteenth century that the social sciences emerged from under the tutelage of philosophy and of history. They gained an independent status and some recognition for their own claim to provide valid knowledge about, and useful orientation in, the contemporary world. From those debates and struggles were then created what is now known as, among other approaches, 'classical sociology', 'neoclassical economics', an anthropology based on participant observation and experimental psychology as well as psychoanalysis, i.e. the whole range of approaches and disciplines in the forms in which we still recognise them today, at the beginning of the twenty-first century. One could be tempted to describe the twentieth century as the history of the emergence and breakthrough of social science.

Two notes of caution are apposite, however. While it is true, on the one hand, that the late nineteenth century can be regarded as the formative period of the institutionalised social sciences, their basic modes of conceptualisation as well as the fundamental problématiques they are addressing stem from much longer-lasting discussions. In such a perspective, it is rather the end of the eighteenth century that stands out as the crucial period in the development of the social sciences. And the 'classical' period at the turn of the nineteenth century is then seen as a period of transformation rather than of foundation. Once the notion of transformation is introduced, however, new questions arise. Can this transformation, which led to the disciplines of the social sciences by and large as we now know them, unequivocally be considered as a process of maturation? Or are further transformations in new historical contexts conceivable? This leads to the second observation.

On the other hand, namely, doubts have arisen during the closing decades of the twentieth century as to whether the social sciences' way of observing, interpreting and explaining the world really brought superior insights into the social life of the human beings. The spectre of 'the end of the social', as such necessarily accompanied by the end of the social sciences, has been raised from quite different perspectives. Some observers were inclined to entirely abandon any attempt to render the social world intelligible in the face of its complexity and lack of evident reason or order. Others, in contrast, see this alleged end of the social as the finally generalised acceptance of the insight into the centrality of individuals and their rationality, so that an understanding of the human world could be based on a rather asocial, individualist theorising. And, finally, philosophers and historians, for a long time on the defensive, have also renewed their time-honoured claim to a privileged understanding of the human condition.

This book adopts neither the view of the inevitable rise of the social sciences after the once accomplished breakthrough nor the alternative narrative of their rise and fall during the nineteenth and twentieth centuries. Neither the epistemological optimism in some periods nor the pessimism in others has necessarily been well founded. But the observation of recurring, or maybe even persistent, challenges to the social sciences, which entail calls for a reconsideration of their form and character, asks for a very reflection about the relation between the history of the forms of social knowledge production and the modes of theory building and concept formation themselves. To provide such a reflection is the objective of this book.

Most generally put, the social sciences are an intellectual response to the post-revolutionary aporias of political philosophy after the American and French Revolutions. The development of the basic conceptual approaches of social theory as well as the emergence of an empirical research strategy in the social sciences – as contrasted to the tradition of normative political philosophy – are means to provide arguments for the form and substance of socio-political orders after the revolutions had initially appeared as melting all that was solid into air. Thus, the history of the social sciences is a history of dealing with a number of key problématiques stemming largely from the onset of political modernity. These problématiques have certainly not been solved, but they have also not been abandoned either. They have, however, undergone historical transformations, of which a history of the social sciences gives testimony. A review of this history, as (selectively) proposed in the first part of the book, is at the same time an exploration of the registers of social and political thinking that are available to us when aiming to understand our current condition. The findings in the course of this exploration will be put to use in the second part of the book.

Part I, thus, portrays the development of the social sciences at key junctures in the history of Western societies and sets their intellectual development in relation to the politico-institutional development of these societies. Two chapters (1 and 2) focus on the turn of the nineteenth century, often seen as a formative period for the 'modern' social sciences as disciplines. They aim at understanding 'classical sociology' and the political discourses during the 'crisis of classical liberalism' as ways of dealing with a first major restructuring of those post-revolutionary societies, a transformation which I have elsewhere proposed to label 'the first crisis of modernity' (Wagner 1994). The next two chapters (3 and 4) discuss the social sciences as participants in the subsequent 'organisation of modernity'; first, in their relation to ideas of societal planning, and second, as contributors to the 'rationalistic revolution' of the 'golden age of capitalism' during the 1950s and 1960s. This part concludes with a discussion of the impact of the postmodernity debate on the social sciences (Chapter 5). It sees this debate as symptomatic of a 'second crisis of modernity'. This view allows me then to compare these debates with those arising during the first crisis of modernity to arrive at a more systematic assessment of such periods of intellectual questioning and restructuring.

This part certainly provides a kind of history and sociology of the social sciences. However, it sees itself not just as a contribution to disciplinary and/or intellectual historiography, but rather as an account in terms of a political sociology which sets institutional-intellectual developments in the contexts of political problématiques. On the basis of this account, conclusions can then be drawn as to the directions which current conceptual debates in social theory should possibly take. This is the objective of Part II.

Overall, the current situation of intellectual questioning (that often goes under the name of postmodernity, or at least used to do so until recently) is here taken to point to a considerable need for conceptual rethinking. However, neither the 'post-modern' conclusion that the intelligibility of the social world is entirely in question nor the opposite view that theorising needs to restart from rationalist-individualist foundations, since there allegedly are no social phenomena, is accepted. The chapters instead take up the reasonings behind key concepts in the social sciences and ask in which way those reasonings have to be seen as historically contextual and possibly superseded and in what respect the concepts still point to important problématiques that social theorising will need to address. In each case, elements for a new understanding of such concepts are provided.

The second part starts out with a discussion of some of the broadest concepts – choice, decision, action and institution. First, the limits of rationalist individualism are discussed in the light of the current trend towards the cross-disciplinary diffusion of rational choice theory. At the same time, the genesis and adoption of such thinking are set into the context of historical situations (Chapter 6). The following chapter (7) turns the question around and asks how the concepts of action and institution can be reconceptualised so as to allow for understanding the situatedness of action under conditions of relative uncertainty and possible dispute. The basis for this conceptual analysis is recent work in the so-called 'new French social sciences' (Luc Boltanski, Laurent Thévenot and others), which stays clear of ontological or methodological individualism without falling into collectivism. The subsequent chapters then deal with those collective concepts that are today often considered as untenable – on either postmodernist or individualist grounds – and discusses the persistence of the problématiques that stand behind these concepts: culture (Chapter 8), society (9) and polity (10). On that basis, the book concludes with observations on the one concept that is currently used to move the social sciences back to a conceptually informed diagnosis of the present: modernity (Chapter 11).

The attempt undertaken here to link history to theory may appear very unusual at first sight. In less explicit form, however, it has been, and continues to be, pursued in a variety of ways. There have been two principal ways of proceeding, both of which need to be avoided, in my view. On the one hand, most of the numerous disciplinary histories of the various social sciences adopt a perspective, in more or less concealed guise, in which all prior debates and disputes gradually and possibly unevenly, but equally unfailingly, lead to the state of conceptual and empirical accomplishment that has been reached in the present. The authors of such accounts are often active practitioners of the social sciences rather than historians of ideas or sociologists of knowledge and the sciences. As such, they find it – understandably – difficult to imagine a higher state of knowledge being attained at times other than their own, be it in the past or in the future.

On the other hand, approaches that we may call, for want of a better term, critical histories of the social sciences insist on the rootedness of intellectual work in the context of its time. Inaugurated, arguably, with Marx and Engels' *German ideology*, such a perspective found a number of important incarnations during the second half of the twentieth century such as Georg Lukács' *Zerstörung der Vernunft* (1954), Göran Therborn's *Science, class and society* (1976), and Geoffrey Hawthorn's *Enlightenment and despair* (1976). Focusing on the rise of the social sciences from the end of the eighteenth century to their own time of writing, these authors rightly connect these developments with the rise of the bourgeoisie, and then mass society, and with the rise of capitalism. However, they have an inclination to work by means of denunciation, which, even though tragic elements are occasionally introduced, stays within the framework of a traditional critique of ideology (see critically Boltanski and Thévenot 1991; 1999). As a consequence, they cannot provide themselves with any means to distinguish between 'what is dead and what is alive' (Benedetto Croce) in the social sciences. Focusing on the contextual embeddedness of intellectual work, they always interpret such embeddedness as a constraint only, which they themselves can identify as well as overcome from a distant vantage-point. The relation between history and theory is conceptualised ultimately in an entirely linear and unequivocal way, in this sense not unlike the way this relation is seen in the histories of the progress of knowledge.

The most recent such critical history of the social sciences is, possibly, Peter Manicas' *A history and philosophy of the social sciences* (1987). As the title already suggests, however, Manicas intends to make the relation between history and philosophy itself problematic. His narrative does not unfold along a straight line, upwards or downwards, but he identifies in the works of authors all along the historical trajectory significant elements for a reshaping of the social science enterprise – which he sees as necessary, and that is why his history can be called a critical one. In this respect, the following book is close to Manicas' way of proceeding as well as to his concern. There are also important differences, though. Where Manicas concentrates on issues of ontology and epistemology, my predominant concern is with what is sometimes called concept formation. In other words, as our titles indicate, his work adopts the language of the philosophy of the social sciences, whereas mine reasons more in terms of social theory (on the problematic nature of these very distinctions see Wagner 2001). Furthermore, where Manicas remains close to the history of ideas, my ambition is to contextualise more thoroughly. This history of the social sciences relates the developments of ideas and concepts to the transformations of modernity (see Wagner 1994). Finally, where Manicas' work culminates in a discussion – and critique – of methodology in the social sciences, my key interest is in the problématiques that underlie and inform both conceptual and methodological choices.

The change in perspective compared with all the above-mentioned works, including even the one by Manicas, has been possible only against the background of the new, or renewed, concern for language in the human and social sciences, sometimes known as the linguistic turn.[1] The implications of such a linguistic turn for the analysis of the languages of the social and the political have been explored in as diverse projects and approaches as those of the 'history of the present', associated with the name of Michel Foucault and subsequent related work; the 'history of concepts', developed by Bielefeld historians around Reinhart Koselleck and others; the study of 'ideas in context', as pursued by Cambridge historians around J.G.A. Pocock and Quentin Skinner; and the 'history of consciousness' of the group around Hayden White. In these works, however, except to some extent in those that followed Michel Foucault's perspective, the 'modern', discipline-based social sciences and their attempt to explain and understand the social world have rarely been at the centre of interest.[2] With precisely such an aim in view, this book provides, first, a critical history of the social sciences in Western Europe (and partly the US) from the late nineteenth to the late twentieth centuries and, second, a rethinking of some key categories of the social sciences in the light of the historical analysis.

PART I

RECONSIDERING THE HISTORY OF THE SOCIAL SCIENCES

1

AS A PHILOSOPHICAL SCIENCE UNJUSTIFIABLE, AS AN EMPIRICAL SCIENCE ANYTHING ELSE BUT NEW

Classical sociology and the first crisis of modernity

Sociologists usually have a clear conception of the history of their discipline. They may disagree on the merits of individual contributions to the development of the subject, but they tend to share the view that there was a first blossoming around the turn of the century, a period which they label the 'classical era'. The era is easily demarcated. While there was a wide diffusion of sociological activity, a limited number of towering figures emerged, often named the 'founding fathers' of the discipline, whose intellectual life-spans coincided neatly. Emile Durkheim got his first appointment, at the University of Bordeaux, in 1887; Max Weber, at the University of Freiburg, in 1895; and Vilfredo Pareto, at the University of Lausanne, in 1893. Durkheim died in 1917, Weber in 1920 and Pareto in 1923. By that time, they had all contributed to the construction of the intellectual field for which two of them had appropriated the name 'sociology'. The third one, Weber, was more reluctant but increasingly used this label after he had been involved in the founding of the German Society for Sociology in 1909. It should probably be no wonder, therefore, that sociologists look back on this period as constitutive for their field. And even to the analytical view of a historian, the era appears as the one of professionalisation of sociology, the setting of standards for sociological work and, consequently, the demarcation of boundaries to other academic fields and to 'lay' non-professional activities (Torstendahl 1993).

   In a significant way, however, such views are rather misleading. While it is true that intellectuals strove to establish a science of society at academic institutions in this period, their project ultimately proved to be a failure. Sociology was not institutionalised at European universities in its 'classical' era. Furthermore, no common understanding on what such a science of society should be was achieved.

Standards of sociological work were developed and proposed but could not be enforced among those who considered themselves to be sociologists. During the inter-war period, the major intellectual projects of this 'classical' period were almost completely abandoned. 'Modern', post Second World War sociology is an intellectual enterprise essentially different from 'classical' sociology. To understand this rupture (which I have discussed in more detail elsewhere: cf. Wagner 1990), it is necessary to look beyond problems of institutional and scientific legitimacy to the different ways in which politics and society were, in part implicitly, conceptualised in these approaches.

'Classical' sociology was, other than a scientific one, also a political project. All variations notwithstanding, it can be called post-liberal thinking. It started from bourgeois liberal assumptions, recognised that societal developments had superseded classical liberalism, but insisted that revisions had to be made in the continuity of that political tradition (Seidman 1983). 'Modern' sociology, however, did away with the liberal tradition from the start and rephrased the relation between the individual and society in completely different terms. A comparison of the fate of both approaches during the first half of the twentieth century cannot be undertaken without looking at the development of political institutions. 'Modern' sociology proved to have greater cognitive affinity to the structures of the interventionist welfare state which emerged in this period; the political legitimacy of 'classical' sociology, in contrast, decayed rapidly.

In the following I shall, first, give an impression of the intensity of the sociological debate and of the social status which the sociological intellectuals enjoyed in wider society during the 'classical' period, and shall point to the decline of this mood in the first decades of the twentieth century. To make these developments understood I shall, second, try to define the project of that science of society in scientific, political and institutional terms. This analysis will allow me, third, to give an account of the failure of the project in exactly the same terms by relating it to the structure of academic institutions and of political institutions and to the transformation of both fields during that period. Finally, I shall give some indications of what happened 'instead' of a continuation of those sociological projects. Attempts to study society scientifically went into different directions during the inter-war years, one of which contained the nucleus of 'modern' sociology as it became dominant after the Second World War.

The rise and decline of early sociology

Between 1870 and the early 1900s, numerous attempts were made to lay the foundations of a science of society, mostly labelled sociology. Programmatic books were published, journals created and academic societies founded, and inside academic institutions moves were made to designate chairs in sociology and to introduce new types of examinations and degrees. A few examples will be given to indicate the breadth and intensity of this sociological movement in continental Europe.

In France, Durkheim's approach was only one among many. Before him Frédéric Le Play had already advanced his action-oriented *science sociale* and had found followers who continued his project. Gabriel Tarde and René Worms, both contemporaries of Durkheim, competed with the latter for the legitimate representation of the discipline to be built. The former advocated an individualist approach based on a law of imitation as the prime mover of society, the latter reasoned in organicist terms. In Italy, the emerging sociological field was even more multifarious and pluralistic. In an attempt at clarification, Icilio Vanni listed no fewer than ten different conceptions of sociology in 1888 (cf. Sola 1985: 136–7). Three years earlier, Vincenzo Miceli had already complained that the field was growing very quickly and had become fashionable to such an extent that whole crowds of *letterati* had entered it:

> Persons who are said to be of common sense or even ignorant speak and write continuously about this science without having at all been engaged in studying it and without, therefore, possessing the preparation which is now necessary more than ever, given the numerous difficulties which the phenomena present. (Miceli 1885)

In Austria, Ludwig Gumplowicz published his programmatic work *Foundations of sociology* in 1885 and Gustav Ratzenhofer followed in 1898 with his treatise on *Sociological knowledge*. In all these countries, the label 'sociology' was used without hesitation and very often with a conscious link to the positivist tradition.

In Germany, in contrast, for the very same reason, that label was untouchable for scholars who had grown up in the humanistic-philosophical tradition of the German university. The relative absence of the word, however, did not indicate the absence of attempts to establish new, or modify old, approaches to the study of society. Whereas Heinrich von Treitschke had rather defined the problem away in his *Gesellschaftswissenschaft* (science of society) of 1859, works by Robert von Mohl and Lorenz von Stein tried to incorporate a new understanding of society into the 'state sciences' during the same period (see in more detail ch. 9). In 1875, Albert Schäffle talked in organicist terms about the *Anatomy and life of the social body*, and in 1887 Ferdinand Tönnies published his influential book on *Community and society* which, however, was newly subtitled *Basic concepts of sociology* only in the second edition of 1912. By that time, the aversion against the word 'sociology' had diminished and Georg Simmel and Max Weber were ready to use it, though in a different mode than their counterparts in Western Europe.

These intellectual activities found their expression also in the creation of social science journals. In Italy, the *Rassegna di scienze sociali e politiche* existed between 1883 and 1890, and the *Rivista italiana di sociologia* was founded in 1892 and continued to appear until after the First World War. In France, Durkheim's *Année sociologique* was probably the most successful, but by far not the only sociological journal. The 'Le Playists' had their own journals and Worms founded the *Revue internationale de sociologie* in 1893, to give only two examples. Worms also created the *Institut international de sociologie*; these were both initiatives to stimulate and enhance international sociological communication and simultaneously means to counteract the emerging dominance of the Durkheimian approach on the national scientific field by enlisting international scholars in his support.

Besides this international academic society, national societies were established. The followers of Le Play in France, for instance, even formed two organised groups, one of a more academic nature, the other more practically oriented. For the Durkheim group, the journal provided a strong organising focus. In the German-speaking areas, the Viennese Sociological Society was created in 1907 and the German Society for Sociology followed in 1909. In Germany, a social science association had already existed since 1872, the *Verein für Socialpolitik* (Association for Social Policy), which showed a broad historical orientation to social science and intended to put its work into the service of the newly founded German nation-state.

Scholarly journals, academic societies and intense publication activities on theoretical and programmatic matters – all the elements required for the building of a discipline seemed to exist in the early 1900s. Sociologists, however, hardly achieved recognition in academic institutions, which is an important precondition for a scientific field to be securely established. Many contributors to the sociological debates were academics who held chairs in disciplines such as philosophy, economics, law, history or medicine. While it is obvious that 'founding fathers' cannot start out from established chairs, it is important to recognise that, though many strove for it, hardly anyone of this generation of sociologists succeeded in obtaining a sociological label for their chairs. Durkheim was one of the few, and by the time of his death three more chairs at French universities carried the sociological denomination. In Germany and Austria, no chairs for sociology were created until 1919, the one at the University of Munich, which Weber had accepted shortly before his death, being among the first. For Italy, Robert Michels – who emigrated from Imperial Germany because he was not accepted in German universities at all – remarked in 1930 that sociology had 'no academic citizenship, and its representatives are either outside the university itself or occupy chairs in economics or legal philosophy . . . So far as my knowledge extends, there is no course in sociology in Italy, with the possible exception of Padova' (1930: 20–1).

By the early 1900s, thus, 'sociology' had experienced a boom of activities which had lasted for about three decades. It had flourished, supported by a 'positive social culture' (Barbano 1985: 68), by a wide interest in new, systematic and 'positive' approaches to understanding social development. Despite this supportive context, however, it had been unable to achieve full academic institutionalisation and, therefore, remained extremely vulnerable to changing circumstances. Around the turn of the century, political and intellectual tides were, in fact, changing. These changes spelled, as I will argue in some detail, the end of classical sociology because of its inability to allow for appropriate modifications of its discourse.

The last three decades of the nineteenth century were, very broadly speaking, a period of construction and consolidation in continental Western Europe. Precarious and unstable socio-political constellations were overcome and the new formulae, after some critical early periods, seemed to work: the lay and socially oriented Third Republic in France; the authoritarian bureaucratic state dominating the society of Imperial Germany; and the unified Italian nation-state based on the interdependence of urban and rural elite groups in the north and south. This was the constellation which bred the self-conscious and self-assuring sociological movements: while these societies surely had problems, they also had the means to solve them by self-inspection through empirical analysis. Especially in Italy, but also in the other countries, one is tempted to speak of an unbound will for knowledge, to use Foucault's terminology.

By the end of the 1800s, uncertainties were returning and were there to stay through the first half of the twentieth century. The rising workers' movement was about to challenge elite consensus; industrialisation and urbanisation not only changed material living conditions rapidly, but also raised uncertainties about social status among many groups, including, not least, the bearers of the intellectual culture. Put in the terms of the historian Stuart Hughes (1958: 41), on all 'levels of intellectual activity, doubts arose as to the reigning philosophy of the upper middle class – the self-satisfied cult of material progress which, in a vulgarised sense, could also be termed "positivism"'. All its heterogeneity notwithstanding, the thought of the early sociological movements was part of this reigning philosophy and went into crisis with it. While the early will for knowledge was based on rather unproblematic, mostly implicit assumptions about the relation between social reality and the knowledge that could be generated by observing it, the new uncertainties were not least of an epistemological character. They raised the question of the very possibility of knowledge about society. The most important contributions to classical sociology reflect the culmination of these crises. Weber, Durkheim and some others doubted the easy claims made by their sociological predecessors. But in contrast to some of their 'culture-critical' and relativist contemporaries they sceptically insisted on, and searched for, the possibility of a science of society.

Over time, in such a changed intellectual climate, the sociological projects were massively transformed, however. In France, Durkheimism remained strong as the basis of a quasi-official republican ideology, but in this function its moral and philosophical aspects were emphasised at the expense of its sociological ambitions. From having been considered a positivist-minded social science, it was turned into appearing to be an idealist philosophy (Heilbron 1985). In Italy, sociological thinking did not survive the onslaught of idealism as epitomised in the cultural dominance of Benedetto Croce's thinking, which has even been labelled intellectual dictatorship (Bobbio 1969; Asor Rosa 1975). As early as 1906 Croce wrote, commenting on a proposal to establish chairs in sociology, that this thinking was a 'chaotic mixture of natural and moral sciences . . . another "new science" which as a philosophical science is unjustifiable, and as an empirical science anything else but new. It is new only as sociology, that is as a barbaric positivistic incursion into the domain of philosophy and history' (Croce 1942: 130). In Austria, sociology continued to flourish for a brief period in the political context of 'red Vienna' but hardly influenced academic debate at the universities and the intellectual debates at large. In Germany, seemingly deviant, sociology was institutionalised at the universities after 1919 with several dozen chairs being created by 1933. As will be shown later, though, this sociology had abandoned most of its earlier ambitions, as its proponents had settled for an institutional strategy which would minimise confrontation with other, well-established academic fields.

In sum, my look at these intellectual and institutional developments between 1870 and 1930 amounts to saying that there was a strong movement for founding and establishing a sociology as the science of society, that this movement culminated intellectually in the proposals known today as classical sociology, but that by the end of that period the sociological project had failed. To substantiate this view, it is required to characterise the main features of that project first.

The project of classical sociology: a science of society

Classical sociology was, first of all, a response to political economy and, then, to neoclassical economics. This feature has been aptly described by Göran Therborn (1976: 170–1):

> In revolt against the deductive, individualist-utilitarian and laissez-faire character of orthodox (above all 'vulgar') liberal economics, new social theories developed in the last quarter of the 19th century which were inductive, social-ethical and interventionist . . . We can distinguish in this respect three critiques of political economy, each in a particular way significant for the development of the sociological project. One centred on liberal economic policies and gave rise . . . to a kind of investigatory practice which is often labelled sociological, but which has increasingly become part of normal administrative routine. The other two were instrumental in . . . constructing sociology as a distinct theoretical and empirical discipline. One of these started from a critical analysis of the epistemological basis of economics. The other was an across-the-board critique of the epistemology, the utilitarianism and policy recommendations of liberal economics. Max Weber may be taken to represent the second and Durkheim the third kind of critiques.

Disentangling this summarising view, one can argue that sociology met with economics in three respects, which can be analytically separated: scientific, political and institutional. In *scientific* terms, it was a response to the individualist methodology of economics and, in part, to its epistemological assumptions. In *political* terms, it reacted against the liberal, non-interventionist implications of a theory, or at least vulgarisations of a theory, that postulated self-regulation and equilibration of economic interests through market forces and, thus, an automatic achievement of maximum welfare without conscious political action. In *institutional* terms, any such project would be faced with the problem that economics was already established in academia and claimed to take the place of a science of contemporary society. This threefold response will be discussed in more detail, taking the examples of Durkheim, Weber and Pareto as the outstanding, but simultaneously typical, contributors to classical sociology.

In Durkheim's view, the economists had taken the first steps towards a science of society; they had been 'the first to proclaim that social laws are necessary as physical laws, and had made this axiom the basis of a science' (1888: 25). They were wrong, however, in seeing in the individual the sole tangible reality that the observer can reach. The constitution of human beings was much more complex than rational-individualist theories assumed; human beings are 'of a time and a place, [they have] a family, a city, a homeland, a religious and a political belief, and all these aspects and others more mix and intertwine in a thousand ways . . .

without it being possible to say at a first glance where the influence of the one begins and of the other ends' (1888: 29). Durkheim replaced the economists' methodological individualism with a perspective which gave primacy to 'social facts'. The economists' view was not completely without value, but limited to the study of very few – for instance, demographic – phenomena. Otherwise, it was to be subordinated to a much more comprehensive social perspective, that of sociology, as he explained immodestly at a meeting of the Society for Political Economy in 1908 (Lukes 1973: 499–500).

Vilfredo Pareto, engineer and economist, had arrived at this very problem, the inexplicability of social phenomena when analysed exclusively with the tools of political economy: 'Arrived at a certain point in my research in political economy, I found myself in an impasse. I saw the experimental reality and could not reach it . . . Driven by the desire to add an indispensable complement to the study of political economy and, above all, being inspired by the example of the natural sciences, I have been induced to compose my *Trattato di sociologia*' (quoted after Freund 1976: 50). His judgement on political economy, however, was not that it was inappropriate to analyse social reality, but that it was incomplete. In his view, this deductive theory and its geometric and mathematical formalisations explained certain parts of society fairly well; the problem was that there were other aspects of society that were not grasped at all. His solution was a division of society, on the ontological level, into the spheres of logical action, to be analysed by economic theory, and non-logical action, to be analysed by sociological theory. Focusing on justifications and rationalisations of non-logical actions, his sociology was mainly an individualistically based theory of ideology. This theory limits the sphere of applicability of economic theory, but acknowledges it at the same time as one of two parts of a comprehensive social science.

The relation of sociology to economics in Durkheim was imperialist domination; in Pareto it was ontological completion of a social science; in Weber it was epistemological reconceptualisation. In contrast to Pareto, Weber stood not in the tradition of orthodox political economy, but in that of the German Historical School. He understood, however, and appreciated attempts, like those of the Austrian Carl Menger, to put the economic and social sciences on a more solid grounding than that provided by the historical scholars who linked empirical studies with notions, of unclear epistemological status, from philosophy of history. While he definitely shared the concern for the fate of the German nation and people with the Historical School, he was unwilling to let notions like the spirit of the people or the realisation of the will of the state enter into his social science as foundational concepts. That is why he disagreed with Gustav Schmoller's rash dismissal of Menger's attempt at giving unequivocal foundations to theoretical sciences of society by drawing on the deductive approach of political economy. To him, the utilitarian categories of economics could well serve, in principle, as cornerstones of a social science, but only if understood as 'ideal types' which render economic behaviour intelligible by naming rationalities of action.

The search for 'ideal types,' a key notion in Weber's methodological work, could provide a way out of the conflict between making regularities of social phenomena understandable on the one hand, and getting at the uniqueness of every event in its historical configuration on the other. Thus, it meant to reconcile the seemingly contradictory ambitions of political economy and the Historical School as sciences of society. The necessity of economic theory was acknowledged, but this theorising was, at the same time, methodologically subordinated to the goal of arriving at historical knowledge. Weber, therefore, concluded that Menger was right on the impossibility 'to come to "laws" in the strict sense by adding up historical observations'. However, Menger was to be told that ideal types could never acquire 'empirical validity in the sense of *deductibility* of reality from the "laws"' (Weber 1973 [1904]: 187, 188). His social science, later to be called sociology, would maintain close links to history and would not abdicate the claim to come to an understanding of real society.

All main lines of sociological thinking during this period stood up against the claim of political economy to be the science of society. And all the major proponents of sociology, as shown, saw their approaches not as an addition, a further perspective on social phenomena, but as a reconsideration of the problems which society posed and as a rephrasing of the analytical requirements to study these problems adequately. The inadequacy of political economy was perceived not only on the terrain of epistemology and ontology but also with regard to the political implications which it carried.

In continental Europe at that time, political economy had hardly been received in its full intellectual sophistication, not to speak of its original philosophical grounding. The most outspoken and popular advocates of this approach in Italy and Germany, to some extent also in France, were vulgarisers who directly linked the theory to their view on the advantages of liberal, market-based societal organisation and the unregulated thriving of private business. They aligned openly with economic interests and it was easy to denounce their reasoning as little more than a political ideology. Sociologists in the late 1800s often rejected this view and themselves took political standpoints in favour of a moderate socialism or conservative, state-oriented reformism. There was, thus, very often a dividing-line between economists and sociologists (or historical economists, to be precise in terminology) on matters of day-to-day policy-making. The political implications of social science theorising, however, went even deeper and acquired the character of a major restructuration of the understanding of society, its development and coherence, in general.

Classical economists, as well as the proponents of sociology in the early 1800s like Auguste Comte and Claude-Henri de Saint-Simon, as different as their theorising was, had shared the Enlightenment optimism about the coming of a society in which the interests of its individual members would converge to thus enhance the well-being of all without any need for major force or complex organisation. These theories of self-acclaimed scientific validity gave an under-pinning to political liberalism. They supported all arguments for a liberation of the dynamic forces of society, a liberation which would lead to new social equilibria on a novel social basis with everyone better off except for the holders of old, aristocratic and religious privileges. By the late 1800s, and in particular due to the experiences of nation building and reconstruction, these convictions had fallen into doubt and were being replaced not only by new ideologies, like *solidarisme* in France and *trasformismo* in Italy, but also by new analytical approaches to society.

To put it in the terms of Pietro Rossi (1982: 198–9):

> After 1870 – a significant date not only because of the changes in European political equilibria, but also for the socio-economic tissue of the continent – it appears evident . . . that the development of industrial society is inadequate . . . to solve the antagonisms which it itself created . . . and that this society would even generate conflicts to a far larger extent than any society of the past. The change of the productive system does not deliver by itself the instauration of a new political organisation; and if [the polity] changes, this occurs in a quite different sense than that of new social 'harmony'.

The classical sociologists were well aware of this constellation of a major political restructuring without a clear objective or guiding ideology. It can easily be discovered as their major political problématique and the basic orientation of the concepts on which they intended to found their sciences. Unable to stick to the idea of a quasi-automatic regulation of interest conflicts, but similarly unwilling to move completely away from the tenets of bourgeois liberalism, they devoted their analytical efforts to the search for those phenomena which might provide for a workable development of society. 'Once the hope to construct (even, to reconstruct) an organic society has proven illusory, sociology turns its attention to the mechanisms which hold the diverse "parts" of the "social body" together, i.e. the groups and individuals of which it is composed and which can secure the continuity or transformation of the specific conditions of industrial society' (Rossi 1982: 198–9). In this sense, classical sociology is post-liberal political philosophy – and ideology.

The different expressions which this post-liberalism found in the works of the sociologists can broadly be related to the specificities of the national societies to the fate of which they felt committed. In Germany the national-liberal movement had failed after 1848, and when the nation-state was built in 1871, after several wars, it was under Prussian dominance, a creation 'from above' by a strong military-bureaucratic apparatus without the broad involvement of a societal movement (see Schiera 1991). Weber had grown up in this state and with the rapid expansion of industrial production which accompanied the early decades of its existence. Whether he welcomed it or not, the bureaucratic state and capitalist-industrial society seemed to be inevitably shaping modern living conditions. Thus, the guiding normative theme of his work became the conditions for the preservation of ways of living for the individuals according to the historical and cultural specificities of their societies. In this sense, and clearly in the tradition of German historical thinking throughout the nineteenth century, he focused on the nation and on the question of which modes of governance might enable a nation-state to fare best under the conditions of modern industrial society. Given the weakness of the liberal bourgeoisie, his thoughts were often occupied with the alternatives replacing it as the hegemonic and leading force in society: bureaucracy, a strong individual or a responsible social democracy. Bureaucratic apparatuses and extended party organisations, large-scale industry and associated rationalised forms of economic activity: these were the phenomena which Weber identified as crucial for the 'life destiny' of individuals in modern society, reflecting the rapid political and economic transformation of Germany during the Imperial period.

Compared with these developments east of the Rhine, the administrative and economic transformations in France appeared to be of lesser importance than the need, under republican conditions, to find new political formulae for a society moving again towards the realisation of the secular, egalitarian and democratic claims of the French Revolution. Consequently, sociologically based political theory set a somewhat different emphasis:

> As in the writings of Max Weber, the problem, not of 'order' in a generic sense, but of the form of authority appropriate to a modern industrial state, is the leading theme in Durkheim's work. But whereas in Germany a different combination of political and economic circumstances helped to establish a tradition of *Nationalökonomie* which led liberal scholars of Weber's generation to an overwhelming concern with 'capitalism', in France the problem was posed within the context of the long-standing confrontation between the 'individualism' embodied in the ideals of the Revolution and the moral claims of the Catholic hierocracy. (Giddens 1986: 12)

Durkheim was always doubtful about any ideas of automatic aggregration of individual interests to a working societal whole. In his view, this was an essentially mistaken view of society. Reversing the question, he looked at existing societies as entities and identified in them social phenomena which served as binding and integrating forces. In traditional societies, this phenomenon is religion; in modern societies, some degree of interdependence is introduced through the division of social labour leading to 'organic solidarity' among the functional groups. However, as these societies have tremendously increased complexity compared with traditional societies, functional interdependence alone would not lead to social integration.

> From the moment when political societies have reached a certain level of complexity, they can no longer act collectively save through the intervention of the State . . . When the State exists, the various motivations that can impel the anonymous crowd of the individuals in divergent directions are no longer adequate to determine the collective consciousness, for this process of determination is the action of the State proper. (Durkheim 1950: 45–6)

While being convinced of this moral role of the state to curb excesses of individual actions and to take account of the general needs of common life, Durkheim was also aware of possibilities for authoritarian abuses of state power, particularly likely in mass societies where direct aggregation of interests was impossible. The measures he designed against such tendencies were, first, well in the tradition of the Enlightenment, moral education towards social responsibility and, second, beyond that tradition, the concept of secondary organisations. These organisations should stand between state and individual, based on the functional division of labour and not on the principle of territoriality.

In contrast to France and Germany, the Italian nation-state did not have socially well-rooted institutions, nor was Piemontese dominance strong enough to integrate society from above. Unification, long desired by the liberals of the *Risorgimento*, was far from leading quickly to the realisation of liberal political ideas. Pareto, himself initially a committed liberal in political as well as in economic terms, observed how a political-intellectual elite came to power with the *Risorgimento* ideas and how this elite compromised its original convictions when building the institutions of the new state and built partial alliances with old elites to maintain its power. While in this process the liberal ideas lost persuasive power, there emerged a new social movement with a different political commitment, the workers' movement and socialism, from which a new elite was pressing into power positions.

A systematic interpretation and assessment of these alternatives was the basis for Pareto's political sociology. He drew on concepts such as, most importantly, that of 'political class' which had developed in earlier Italian political theorising (see ch. 2). The distinction between the political class, the elite and the masses is a universal feature of human societies according to Pareto, and the 'circulation of elites' is one of their important moving forces. Elites attain power through the social dynamics which their political ideologies unleash; once in power, however, they do not live up to their promises. *Malcontenti*, the dissatisfied, start to build an organisation and ideology of their own and will, after some time, be able to succeed the ruling elite in power. 'Aristocracies don't last. Whatever the reasons may be, it is uncontestable that they disappear after a certain time. History is a cemetery of aristocracies' (Pareto 1923: III, 262).

This brief exemplary characterisation of sociological debates was meant to demonstrate that around the turn of the century a new type of social theorising existed which, all differences notwithstanding, had some basically common orientations in intellectual and political terms. It provided responses to the crisis of political economy and of classical liberalism, that, taken together, constituted a first crisis of European modernity. The responses took account of the social and political transformations during the nineteenth century, and thus these theorists saw a need to base the empirical study of society on new foundations. As such, they faced the opposition both of well-entrenched scientific approaches and of different political convictions.

In academic institutions, economic thinking, as political economy or as historical economics, was fairly well established all over continental Europe. Whether sociology tied in with the discourse of economics in one way or the other, as in Weber and Pareto, or whether it took the position of a fundamental alternative, as in Durkheim, it was to be expected that it would not be welcomed by the representatives of the established discipline. Similarly, sociology argued for some break with, or at least rephrasing of, the concerns of philosophy and history. No smooth adaptation could be expected there either. Many, though by far not all, of the early sociologists were aware of this institutional problématique. The attempts to develop both organisational structure and institutional grounding, briefly described above, were a result of considerations to achieve institutional legitimacy for their approach, the scientific and political legitimacy of which they were convinced and which they found, to a certain degree, confirmed in their own intellectual and political environment. The crucial question was that of securing the institutional basis for intellectual reproduction. As this objective was not reached, or in the best case, that of Durkheim, was only partly achieved (Karady 1976), sociology was almost bound to fail once it lost political legitimacy.

The double dilemma of classical sociology and its loss of legitimacy

The period of classical sociology was characterised by a remarkable conjunction of two major long-term developments in European societies. *First*, the second half of the nineteenth century was the time when the research-oriented university reached the peak of its importance, uniting the tasks of advanced scientific research, elite training for all core professions of society and general 'liberal' education (Wittrock 1985a; cf. also Rothblatt and Wittrock 1993). Its organisational structure had a decisive impact on the organisation of knowledge in this phase. *Second*, the institutional structures of the nation-states were either formed in the process of territorial consolidation as in Italy and Germany, or reshaped with the advent of a republic which was born out of deep political crisis in France and was going to have a lasting impact on French society. This conjunction provides the background for the possibility of the sociological approaches to flourish. It allows sociology to emerge as a mode of theorising relatively detached from the day-to-day struggles in politics and oriented towards the advance of general knowledge about society. Simultaneously the sociologists were concerned about the major, long-term political restructurings which were under way and the nature and meaning of which they tried to identify through studying the contemporary situation and structure of their society in a comparative, evolutionary perspective.

The conjunction of these two institutional developments, however, also provides the clue to an understanding of the failure of sociology. Problematic constellations emerged from it, which proved detrimental to the future development of a science of society. They can be termed the *scientific-institutional* and the *political-institutional dilemmas* of social science (cf. Wagner 1989).

The development of the university entailed a weakening of its link to society on the one hand, and a deepening of its internal structuring on the other. The first aspect is mainly responsible for the possibility of a somewhat detached scientific activity to become institutionalised. 'In general, the university teacher has more and more withdrawn from practice and moved into pure sciences', to put it in the terms of a contemporary observer (Paulsen 1902: 78; cf. also Torstendahl 1993). The second aspect is in some sense the precondition of the first. Internal structuring is motivated by the assumption that scientific approaches can be developed for different levels or spheres of reality, approaches which would develop their own object-adequate concepts and would (have to) develop according to their own logic, their standards and norms of valid scientific activity. The nineteenth century had been, in standard terms of 'functionalist' sociology of science, the era of scientification of practices and of differentiation of academic disciplines. Without concurring with the idea of functionality in these terms, one can without doubt assert that a sphere or field of action emerged which developed partially along its own criteria – criteria which influenced the possibilities for action inside this sphere (cf. Bourdieu, e.g. 1975, 1984, for the notion of 'field' of action).

To acquire full scientific status, a discourse had to demonstrate unequivocal standards for the permissibility of statements and to demarcate boundaries to other discourses (cf. Foucault 1971, for related notions of discourse and discipline).

Among the discourses on society, only political economy had approached such a status by the mid 1880s. Its structure, thus, marked a standard which other discourses had to strive for in order to increase their legitimacy. In fact, one can argue that it was the crisis of classical political economy between, broadly speaking, the 1870s and 1890s which opened the space for the various sociologies and other less well-defined discourses to gain ground. The crisis was both an intellectual one, the apparently insolvable value problem, and a political one, the at that time rather undoubted need for state promotion of the economy. Many of the sociological approaches attacked political economy exactly at the points at which its limits could not be overcome but which, simultaneously, were the guarantors of its cognitive coherence and, therefore, scientific standing. These approaches themselves, however, can well be characterised by their neglect of the requirements of gaining institutional legitimacy. Their discourses either moved swiftly across the boundaries established by political economy, or attempted a general redefinition of academic demarcations. The first is the case of Weber and Pareto, for instance, the second that of Durkheim.

The strength of the logics of academic boundary setting can, in contrast, be gathered from the tendencies of formation of other discourses on society, which emerged during the same period or shortly thereafter, and proved to be of more lasting relevance. Thus many economists had opened their theorising to historical and political considerations during the late 1800s and seemed almost ready to acknowledge the inadequacy of the classical theory. Other scholars in their field, however, attempted a modification of the theory, later termed the 'marginalist revolution', which would liberate the discipline of economics of the value problem and restore its coherence on new foundations. Neoclassical economics did not gain institutional ground rapidly in continental Europe (except Austria and Italy; see Gioli 1991), where it had partly been developed by Menger and Walras. Nevertheless it proved to be a solid basis in the long run for an economic science in cognitive terms clearly separated from other discourses on society.

An analogous process of separation was undertaken by legal scholars who formalised the study of public law and the state to put it on, as the argument went, a truly scientific footing. This aim required legal theory to be rid of all impurities which the consideration of political, economic, moral or cultural phenomena might bring with it (cf. e.g. Wieacker 1952; Mozzarelli and Nespor 1981). The legal theory of the state – or legal positivism, as the approach was also called – achieved a dominant position in the faculties for law and state sciences in Italy and Germany (though not in France) towards the end of the nineteenth century. It effectively pushed aside all attempts to establish a science of political institutions and administrative behaviour (see ch. 2).

In countries which had experienced a rapid and more or less precarious process of state building, a theory which constructed a system of legal propositions founded on the personality and will of the state was of obvious attraction to the administrative and political elites. Furthermore, the law faculties trained a core profession of this state, officials who needed 'to act with promptness and precision, clarify the deliberations of the law-maker, and bring unity, coherence and order into the legal system' (Dyson 1980: 111), all requirements which legal positivism fulfilled perfectly. However, it should not be overlooked that much of the dynamics in the development of this theory stemmed from the desire of legal scholars to raise their work to scientific standing. The price was to make the state a pure 'fiction or abstraction' without substantial ties to society, as a critic said (Heller 1931: 610; see earlier, e.g. von Gierke 1915 [1874]), but this seemed not at all undesired for the purpose, in contrast rather a precondition.

Marginalist economics and legal positivism had appropriated the spheres of the economy and the polity for themselves in a radically separated and reductionist way. An open space was, however, left for a science of social interactions, if it was possible to separate them in a similar way from history, culture and ethics, as had been done in the case of economic and public-legal behaviour. Such a science, called sociology, was exactly the project of Leopold von Wiese in Weimar Germany. His 'theory of relations' (*Beziehungslehre*) or 'formal sociology' focused on the form of the relations between human beings and not on the 'substance', the knowledge of which was to come from the neighbouring disciplines (von Wiese 1920: 41). In the context of the university policy debates in Germany after the First World War, this project was the start of a strategic move – highly successful as such – to use a favourable political environment for the institutionalisation of sociology. Given rather adverse attitudes in the universities towards newcomers and potential competitors in the scientific field, von Wiese found it wise to argue for a very limited conception of sociology which would avoid all possible conflicts with other disciplines. The price, however, was a 'dehistoricisation and de-economisation' (Lukács 1954: 461–2; Käsler 1984: 252) of sociology and the abandoning of Weber's project of a comprehensive social science. This concept had some influence on sociological debates in Weimar Germany, not least due to von Wiese's strategic position as a functionary of the German Society for Sociology. It was, however, not very widespread in other countries, except in the United States, where similar debates were held and where the process of boundary setting and of discipline-based professionalisation was much more pronounced than in Europe (cf. e.g. Manicas 1987; 1991).

The process of university restructuring during the nineteenth century pointed to this direction of formal 'scientification' and disciplinary segregation. It was the *scientific-institutional dilemma* of sociology as a comprehensive social science that, on the one hand, it relied on the relative institutional autonomy of the university to develop its discourse on society without being subordinated to political needs, but that, on the other hand, it had to insist on escaping the formalist and segregating logic of 'scientific' development in these institutions. While the university was a necessary condition for such a sociology to develop, it also contributed to aborting these approaches.

The *political-institutional dilemma* of the social sciences stemmed from transformations of the state. The discourses of classical sociology had contributed to a reflexive understanding of state and society, and they had a part in the constitution of the state (cf. Giddens 1985; Wittrock 1988; Nowotny 1991). They had, however, never been the only institutionalised contributors to such a reflexive monitoring; the work of statistical offices and social research done by commissions of inquiry or administrative inspectors of various sorts was pursued parallel to the academic discourses. Throughout the twentieth century, the demand for non-academic research greatly increased and the political institutionalisation reached such an extent that, considerable university expansion during some periods not-withstanding, non-academic researchers outnumbered their academic counterparts in most societies (see chs 3 and 4). Beyond quantitative reasoning, an argument can be made that the discourses of classical sociology proved increasingly inadequate for an understanding of state and society in transformation and that demands for new and different forms of knowledge were raised. The relation between the political and the intellectual crises of the early 1900s, and in particular after the end of the First World War, is, as already argued, crucial for an under-standing of these developments. The outgoing nineteenth century had witnessed the shaking of the foundations of continental European societies:

> After two decades of precarious equilibrium, the institutional arrangements of the major Western European states were again brought into question. The artificial, contrived character of the regimes with which unification had endowed Italy and Germany were reviewed by their malfunctioning – in the one case by the erratic changes in policy that followed the resignation of Bismarck in 1890, in the other by the social disorders and authoritarian government with which the century came to a close. In France the shock of the Dreyfus case acted as a stimulus to the re-examination of the traditional ideologies on which both the defenders and the enemies of the accused captain had rested their case. (Hughes 1958: 41)

The uncertainties and insecurities were exacerbated by the experience of the war and its aftermath. To an unprecedented degree societies had organised for this military endeavour and had thus restructured their economic and political organisations, their cleavage lines and their self-understanding, not to speak of the unforeseen, and by many unwanted, consequences of the outcome of the war.

> The 1914–1918 War was in Europe as decisive a turning point as the revolution of 1789. It perhaps marked the clear beginning of the end of pure industrial capitalism as both the apologists and Marx had described it, and yet also the beginning of institutionalised communism as virtually no-one (not even Lenin) had quite imagined it. It marked the beginning of the refutation of all the progressive social theories of the 19th century. (Hawthorn 1976: 164)

In this perspective, the works of classical sociology can be seen as the last great attempt to save the social theory implicit in the Enlightenment tradition by rephrasing it. Durkheim, Weber and Pareto, as sceptical as they had been (increasingly, in this order), had not completely given up on finding ways to reconcile the individual's objective of realising her/his self with the requirement for societal cohesion, to a degree at least sufficient to guarantee the individual's liberties. Through historical experience they were aware of the problem that no ingenuous mechanism would provide this link. Still they had engaged in the empirical study of their societies in the search for specific phenomena which might enhance or endanger the objective, and had produced comprehensive theories dealing with the interrelations of all phenomena in these societies which seemed relevant for their question. In a very specific sense, this theorising had created liberal capitalist society; it had given concepts to phenomena which had different meanings before those concepts existed. To give a shorthand example of a key nature, social theorising after the mid 1800s had replaced 'mob' or 'rabble' with the notion of 'proletariat'; social theorising after the 1920s tended to replace 'proletariat' with the notion of 'masses' (Maier 1975: 558).

Key features of bureaucratically administered mass society and organised capitalism had been well portrayed and analysed in some contributions to turn-of-the-century sociology. What these sociologists did not recognise was that the development of this society tended to make their type of knowledge, their perspective on this very society, superfluous. The mass worker, organization member and average citizen seemed to require different instruments than those they preferred to develop. The discourse of classical sociology lost its cognitive affinity to the structure of the society which it dealt with, and, therefore, the support of a positive political conjuncture on which it had been thriving for some time.

After the end of classical sociology

What has just been assessed as plausible against the background of political transformations in the early 1900s, the decay of the intellectual tradition of classical sociology, can be analysed in some detail through an account of the 'sociological' field in the inter-war period (beyond the descriptive remarks above). The main tendency then was towards a bifurcation of the techniques, concerns and ways of thinking which classical sociology had been able to hold together. This bifurcation was not just a matter of empirical analysis being separated (again) from theory and philosophy of social science; what is more important is that the two diverging main lines of sociological activity entailed different understandings of the possibility of social science and different basic views on the fabric of society.

One line of thinking, the more traditionally social-philosophical one, responded to the political and intellectual crises of the early 1900s by considering the progressive elements in classical sociological and economic theory as an optimistic error. In the face of rapid social changes it was argued that the development of 'mass society' itself had shown that the requirements for social integration could not be fulfilled. This reasoning was partly rooted in the bourgeois intellectuals' existential anxiety in the face of the dehumanising aspects of the 'factory system' in production and administration and of the growing strength of the workers' movement and its organisations. From such a viewpoint, the turn away from previous social theories took the form of an intellectual and political movement 'backwards'. A moderate version was the emphasis on categories of collective morality in the idealist metamorphosis of Durkheimian thinking (Heilbron 1985); more radical ones were the expectations of an 'authoritarian state' or a 'strong man' (cf. e.g. Gentile 1982; Käsler 1984). Both tried to formulate the conditions under which the re-establishment of a bourgeois-liberal society and its culture along the lines of nineteenth-century models would be possible. It is for this reason that we call this mode of reaction 'backwards'-oriented.

This approach was clearly based in the academic institutions, among the 'Mandarins' (Ringer 1969) of state-oriented European societies, and was thus rather easily identifiable as a transformation of sociological discourse, at least in settings where there was some continuity of institutionalised sociology as in France and Germany. For Italy, it can be argued that the idealist philosophies of Giovanni Gentile, Benedetto Croce and others took the place of legitimate discourse on society which sociology had tried to occupy earlier. The *second response*, however, had rather heterogeneous roots, which have impeded the perception of links and continuities in societal and social science developments. Empirical-descriptive and neopositivistically guided social science was strongly proposed in those intellectual contexts in which the classical sociological orientation had not developed: in the Netherlands as sociography/sociology (cf. van Doorn 1965; Heilbron 1988), in Austria in connection with the 'scientific world-view' of neopositivism. In both cases no linkages to the discourses of classical sociology existed; empirical application-oriented social research either developed in the absence of sociology in the intellectual environment or bypassed those discourses without engaging in conceptual debate. The latter was the case in Germany and, to a smaller extent, in France and Italy, where specific research institutes were set up for applied purposes with the support of interested social groups or foreign foundations and often without the academic *imprimatur*.

The barrier which was cognitively insurmountable between classical sociology and this type of empirical sociology was the conceptualisation of society itself. The latter approach introduced a radical change by circumventing the problem of the relation between society and individual methodologically; mass phenomena were made sociologically accessible by treating the individual statistically and objectifying her/him in a natural science mode. The innovators, who did not share the burden of sociological-philosophical traditions of thought typical of the classical discourses, reconceptualised society as masses who reacted to a stimulus and developed regular patterns of behaviour, a reconceptualisation which was impossible for classical theory.

In political terms, this discourse transformation allowed for the possibility of a planning of societal development by a scientifically informed elite (see in more detail ch. 3). Though this idea is – in modern times – rooted in social democracy, it is obviously ambivalent. There is only a small step from the conception that a reformist elite may act as a transmission belt for the needs of the masses, needs which become known to the elites through social research, i.e. from a conception which intends to retain the emancipatory element of left-wing politics through its 'modernisation', to a model of the will of the ruling elites organised in large-scale bureaucratic apparatuses and using knowledge about the behaviour of the mass worker and the average citizen to improve control and secure domination. In fact, given the weakness, and later the oppression, of the social democracies in inter-war Europe, the latter conception came to dominate the political context of empirical social research, thematically focused first on the factory, later on the territory. Conceptions of an empirical social science which were theoretically and politically more open remained rare and became only weakly organised. After the advent of authoritarian and totalitarian regimes, in contrast, instrumentally oriented, mostly state-owned and extra-universitarian institutes for social research consolidated and expanded. These institutes anticipated forms of knowledge which became characteristic of the full-blown interventionist state of the post Second

World War period (on the notion of 'intra-scientific modernisation' of social science under Nazism, see Klingemann 1981: 483).

Epilogue

Sociologists who believe in the story of the founding of their discipline in the 'classical era' and its fruitful later development even if they were convinced of my argument, might still consider these stories of the past as irrelevant for present sociology. Ultimately, did the good heritage of the founding fathers not survive in the United States, and did not sociologists all over the Western world experience a new blossoming of social theory in the 1950s and 1960s, finally bringing full academic establishment and new legitimacy to the field? These awkward dependencies on hostile institutions and adverse political climates: should they not have been overcome?

Though admittedly many features of the sociological field have changed during university expansion and reform coalitions between social scientists and policy-makers after the Second World War (see ch. 4), the problématique is, in my view, still the same and has even exacerbated. This has also been recognised by reflective representatives of the sociological mainstream, among whom was James Coleman, for instance, who diagnosed a theoretical rupture in modern sociology: 'Concurrently with the emerging dominance in sociology of functional theory at the level of the collectivity came a movement of empirical research that led precisely in the opposite direction . . . The main body of empirical research was abandoning analysis of the functioning of collectivities to concentrate on the analysis of the behaviour of individuals' (1986: 1313–15). At the same time, this research perspective could develop only a very limited understanding of what individuals were actually doing in society. In line with the argument presented here, though then drawing different conclusions, Coleman remarks critically: 'Empirical research . . . was lacking a theory of action, replacing "action" with "behaviour" and eliminating any recourse to purpose or intention in its causal explanations' (1986: 1316; see chs 6 and 7).

Still, one might hold that the 1970s brought the (re-) emergence of essentially different approaches to social science than the instrumental objectivist, empirical ones, namely 'hermeneutical and critical approaches . . . which are epistemologically oriented to *other* modes of utilisation than manipulation and self-manipulation' (Habermas 1985: 321). I am not going to deny this but would argue that, when looking at the structure of the scientific field and not just at the mere existence of some mode of thinking, the picture is different. There was some revival of social theorising in the 1960s and 1970s: the 'second breakthrough of sociology', again thriving on a positive intellectual and political climate just as during the 'first breakthrough' in the late 1800s (these notions have been used by Johan Heilbron). But again, and to some extent analogous to what happened in the early 1900s, this positive conjuncture has vanished and the intellectual alliances have fallen apart (see ch. 5). Social theorising that insists on addressing the problématiques of the classical tradition finds itself, though not threatened in its existence, in an uncomfortably marginal position.

2
TIME OF POLITICS, AND NOT OF LAW
Political analysis during the first crisis
of modernity

'Bastard speculations, half-way theoretical and half-way practical, half-way science and half-way arts': such was the verdict which Emile Durkheim (1970: 225) had for political science in 1890, a strong condemnation without doubt if one considers that, under the name of moral and political sciences, intellectual approaches of this sort had a tradition in France which reached much further back than even the name of 'sociology' and which had achieved early institutional standing in the *Académie des sciences morales et politiques*. Another story, which would consider sociology as the bastard newcomer illegitimately threatening the time-honoured and reputable tradition of political philosophy, seems at first sight at least as plausible as Durkheim's view. However, by Durkheim's time this latter interpretation, though still held by some, had hardly any persuasive power. 'That noble Science of Politics,' as it was once hailed early in the nineteenth century, 'which, of all sciences, is the most important to the welfare of nations' (Thomas Babington Macaulay in 1829, quoted after Collini et al. 1983: V), had lost much of its prestige and intellectual and institutional identity during that century and had obviously suffered from the – relatively and in part itself only temporarily – successful mobilisation for the scientific projects of economics and sociology.

It is no gross exaggeration to say that political science as the discipline that we know today was institutionalised at continental European universities only after the Second World War. In France, the National Foundation for Political Science was then created and institutes for political studies were established at several universities. In West Germany, with the active support of the US military government, a political science was conceived as a 'science of democracy' underpinning 're-education' objectives, and chairs were created at many universities in the early post-war years. In Italy, it took until the 1960s for universities to be reformed and new life given to the moribund faculties for political science. True, institutions had existed before: the Italian faculties are one example, but they were established under fascist rule to serve the training purposes for the regime's higher administrative and diplomatic corps and, consequently, fell into disrepute and oblivion after the war. In France, the *Ecole libre des sciences politiques* existed since 1871 and was often hailed as the first modern political science institution in the world. This was, however, as shall be shown later, not exactly the case. The school was a professional training centre for the nation's administrative and political needs. In Weimar Germany, one major attempt had been made to set up a political science centre, the *Deutsche Hochschule für Politik* in Berlin, created in 1920. Analogous to the French case, this school suffered from its multiple orientations towards education for democracy, administrative training, and political science and research, and developed some momentum towards the latter objective only in its last years before its work could not be continued under the Nazi regime.

There then seems to be a peculiar absence – or weakness, at least – of a discourse on politics among the approaches to study society scientifically between the mid 1800s and the mid 1900s. If it was ever true what Macaulay said, that this science was 'most important to the welfare of nations', this weakness seems, at first sight, the more surprising since the continental European societies and nations got organised or reorganised during this period, in particular after 1870, and underwent major political crises in the early 1900s, in terms both of new internal cleavages related to the rise of the workers' movement and of external challenges linked to increasing imperialist competition and, ultimately, the First World War and its political consequences, a first crisis of European modernity.

This chapter cannot answer all questions connected with the fate of political science around the turn of the century, but it will try to open a perspective which sees the development of intellectual projects, as discourses proposed by scholars drawing on intellectual traditions and modifying them, as doubly linked to their societal contexts, namely through the structure of academic institutions in which they must find a place to secure their reproduction, and through the structure of political institutions to which some degree of cognitive affinity is required for an intellectual project to find support. I shall try to show that 'political science', however it may be conceived, did not fit well either of those two institutional structures in the period under consideration. Doing this, I shall proceed in three steps (for a more detailed account of these developments see Wagner 1990).

First, the non-existence of political science at European academic institutions in the early 1900s was not due to the fact that nobody had tried to establish it. In contrast, the historical constellation of restructurations of the nation-states lent itself to such an interest, and movements for a political science emerged which, however, failed. Their failure can be explained to a considerable extent by the facts, second, that a drive towards 'scientification' in late-nineteenth-century universities bypassed political science, that no scientific language could be phrased, but that instead public law became the codified language in which to talk about the state; and third, that the existing demand for political-administrative professionals in the new states could to some extent be satisfied with exactly this formal legal training and, for the rest, was matched in professional schools whose orientations conflicted with those required for scientific discourses.

The will to political knowledge

Political institutions became problematic in the second half of the nineteenth century, and there was quite a number of concerned intellectuals who found it necessary and worthwhile to devote systematic analytical study to them. In Italy, such a debate intensified along with the first major political shift which the new kingdom underwent with the change in political majorities towards the Historical Left in 1876. The first fifteen years of the unification process had been accompanied by intense empirical social research as a mode of cataloguing and assessing the most important social problems to which the nation should devote itself, but the nature and workings of the polity had not yet moved into the centre of attention. The political changes in the mid 1870s, however, showed that the character of political institutions could inadvertently be substantially transformed while their form remained untouched. Thus, their nature was obviously less unambiguously determined than most political actors had assumed before, and a systematic assessment of the relation between their legal forms, as 'frozen ideologies' (Sven-Eric Liedman) of the national movement, the *Risorgimento*, and their political reality seemed to be called for. The 'parliamentary revolution', as the majority change was labelled by contemporary observers, led to a series of cautiously reformist legislative projects and made the administrative, managerial aspect of power predominate over the ideals and concepts of the earlier post-unitarian liberalism (cf. Sola 1985: 120; see also Are 1974).

These new concerns were reflected in a flood of political science literature. An early contribution was the 1871 volume on *Istituzioni di scienza politica* by Saverio Scolari; in 1881 the *Saggio di politica positiva* by Nicola Di Cagno-Politi appeared, followed in 1884 by Gaetano Mosca's first major work *Teorica dei governi e governo parlamentare*, Attilio Brunialti's *La scienza politica nello Stato moderno*, and Carmine Soro Delitala's *Uffici, limiti, attinenze della politica*, all being published in 1884. Brunialti started editing the *Library of Political Science* as a series with the Turin publishing house UTET in the same year to make, as he said, the most important modern works of political science, Italian and foreign, collectively available to the interested Italian public. His own second political science book *Dell'ottimo governo* was published in this series in 1886. Since 1883 the journal *Rassegna di scienze sociali e politiche* was published by the Florence institute *Scuola di Scienze Sociali*, itself created in 1874 after the model of the Paris school.

More than in any other European country at the time, a proto-discipline under the label of political science emerged in Italy which was pronouncedly empirical in its orientation and showed a rather remarkable degree of coherence in research questions and analytical concepts. Both features were related to the political problématiques which these new scientific approaches devoted themselves to, approaches which were characterised by Pasquale Turiello as 'the new discipline of the coexistence of nation and state', a state which developed very early a specific governing class and a public sector of institutionalised power relations (see Sola 1985: 156). Brunialti was among those who most clearly tried to formulate the programme of the coming discipline and its perspective on political reality. Political science should focus on this public sector and its institutions, it would become a science of utmost intellectual merit: 'the knowledge of the state is a science in the highest sense of the term, an order, an entire system of sciences, a particular scientific encyclopaedia'. It would, at the same time, have the double practical task to form knowledgeable governments and to enlighten public opinion (Brunialti 1888: 62, 68).

Both the theoretical and practical problems specific to this political science had implications for its methodological orientations, namely a break with traditional normative political theorising and an unusually explicit focus on the empirical study of political institutions and their behaviour. These features have since become known as the realist or neo-Machiavellian perspective of political science. They entail some sort of materialism which contrasted with idealistic mystifications of the state as much as with normative conceptions linked to theories of constitutional law. Mosca emphasised this orientation:

> Now we intend to carefully avoid the error that some authors in these matters occasionally commit, to mistake namely in their writings the factual government for the legal government, or at least not to distinguish these two highly different things clearly enough. Let us thus point out that hitherto the object of our study is exclusively the factual government, underlining though, in the course of our work, the main points in which it deviates from, or finds itself even in flagrant contradiction with, the legal government. (1982 [1884]: 366)

The distinction between 'the real country' and 'the legal country', as it was often put, was one of the main concerns of political scientists and required a very fact-oriented, descriptive approach, from which one could move to general concepts of the workings of the polity.

A crucial one of these concepts was that of 'political class', which over time has entered into popular political language in Italy where it still exists today. It was meant to designate the relations between office-holders in the state apparatuses and the remainder of society in terms of a relation of domination between a governing elite, namely the political class, and the governed masses. Mosca (1982: 206–7) formulated this relation very early as necessarily one of a minority towards a majority:

> We cannot conceive of a society, as democratic as it may be, in which government is exercised by all. Even in this case, a governing machine is required, an organisation naturally consisting of a numerical minority, all public functions are in fact exercised neither by one only nor by all, by a special class of persons instead . . . We shall from now on label this special class the political class.

While Mosca has become known as coining the concept in theoretical terms, developing it in later works such as his 1895 *Elementi di una scienza politica*, and Vilfredo Pareto as taking it up as an element of a general theory of societal development (see ch. 1), the basic idea was widespread in other works as early as 1880, such as Pasquale Turiello's *Governo e governati in Italia* (1882), Andrea Cantalupi's *Politica in Italia* (1880) or Michele Turraca's *Politica et morale* (1878) (cf. generally Sola 1985: 155–62).

To understand this commonality of focus and its specificity it is useful to compare it for a moment with Max Weber's well-known concerns about the German state. Both in Italy and in Germany, a centralised state structure had been imposed on a multifariously ordered society with, in part, highly diverse economic, political and cultural orientations. Such a state structure remained almost unavoidably precarious for some time and did not fully meet the demands which social groups raised. In Germany, however, this structure was created and supported by a strong central bureaucracy, building on the structures of a hegemonic Prussian kingdom and drawing support from the old elites. Weber's political thought, therefore, was influenced by the possibility of bureaucracy being used as an instrument for a rationalisation strategy which would be relatively coherent in terms both of social policy and national development and also of finding the social groups to carry through such a strategy in the absence of a strong bourgeoisie. In Italy, in contrast, where the bourgeoisie was almost similarly weak, there was no developed state apparatus either. A dominant social group was only about to be formed, centred on the parliament as a main site of interest articulation, from groupings which in majority shared some bourgeois, national-liberal orientations, but did so on the basis of fairly diverse interests. To complicate the process further, the socialist movement grew in importance before a bourgeois political organisation had constituted itself as the dominant force in society, a movement which acted on the same parliamentary terrain and developed its own political organisation. In such a context Mosca, as most other early political scientists, focused on the nature and formation of these heterogeneous political elites whom they defined in terms of the relations to their clientele as the *classe politica* and whom they saw not just as filling predefined institutional spaces but as drawing on the rules of the *paese legale* to further their interests and those of their clientele, representing different facets of the society. The main tension, in analytical and in practical terms, therefore was the one between the unitary and universal logics of the formal institutions and the diversity of ways they were used in practice.

> The riddle of how to reconcile the unitary and centred model of the legitimation of power with the plurality of sectors and of capacities to translate them into practice constitutes – on the factual more than on the methodological level – the object around which political science was being pursued from the final decades of the nineteenth century onwards. (Schiera 1982: 88)

In France, the creation of the Third Republic gave a similar stimulus to political science debates as did the unification of the nation in Italy. Whereas in Italy, however, the main concern was to determine the relation between state and society under essentially new political conditions, French political scientists could build analytically on greater continuities. An established institutional structure was now differently related to the same society, namely in republican-democratic terms. The inevitable shift in dominant elites had to be reconciled with the continuity of the tasks of political steering and administration; that was the reasoning on which the need for developing a political science was often built. Emile Boutmy, for instance, explained in exactly these terms his initiative for creating a political science institution:

> The new teaching addresses itself to the classes that have an established position and the leisure to cultivate their spirit. These classes have until now predominated politically; but they are threatened . . . Constrained to accept the right of those who are more numerous, the classes that call themselves the elevated classes can conserve their hegemony only by calling upon the right of those who are more able. (1871: 15–16)

Competence should replace inherited privilege in securing the old elites a superior rank in society and should simultaneously underpin political stability in a period of institutional transformation. A politically educated upper and middle class, composed of enlightened citizens, each a competent judge of political questions, capable of discussing them and of guiding public opinion, should be the building block and cement of society (Favre 1981; Leca 1982). Most of the intellectual approaches associating themselves with the label of political science shared this state-oriented, socially conservative view, stemming from much older institutional cleavages in French academia between, on the one hand, the faculty of law and associated institutions (the administration-oriented side) and, on the other hand, the faculty of letters, showing more distance to power and a more critical attitude. In the latter realm, Durkheim succeeded 'halfway' (Karady 1976) in establishing his approach of a sociology as a science of society. This approach clearly had political elements of some analytical weight and was broadly associated with the republican-socialist political project (Lacroix 1981; and ch. 1), but Durkheim consciously rejected the notion of 'political sociology', not least of all because he did not want to associate his sociology with the prevailing concept of political science, and the contemptuous statement quoted in the introduction to this chapter has to be understood in this context (in detail: Favre 1982).

The sociologists' reluctance notwithstanding, there was no doubt in the academic circles of late-nineteenth-century France that a political science was a feasible intellectual project which was well on the way towards constituting itself (Favre 1982: 6). Besides Boutmy's activities, one can cite the publication in 1870 of Esquiron de Parieus' *Principes de la science politique*, in 1871 of Edmond Chevrier's *Les éléments de la science politique*, and of the *Philosophie de la science politique* written by Emile Acollas in 1877. From 1875 onwards the *Année politique* appeared, and in 1894 the *Revue politique et parlementaire* and the *Revue de droit public et de la science politique* both were started.

In contrast to Italy, this movement towards a political science lacked, not so much political, but intellectual and conceptual coherence. Neither was there a dominant intellectual figure who would leave his imprint on the emerging scientific field, as Durkheim did for sociology, nor did the political problématique of the time lend itself to easy agreement on core concepts, as to some extent in Italy. Rather early on, though, the field became institutionally structured by the successful establishment of the *Ecole libre des sciences politiques*, mainly on the initiative of Emile Boutmy. Boutmy himself clearly had a scientific project, one which nowadays would be labelled political psychology. His 'historical and critical' method assumed the determination of collective orientations by physical and social phenomena leading to the constitution of dominant characteristic traits in a people, a national character. These lines of thought can be found in an 1869 publication of his on Greek architecture, and they are elaborated upon in later writings on the political psychology of the English and the American people, to be published in the early 1900s. Basing his approach on psychology, he leaned towards that discipline of the human sciences which already disposed of a solid scientific legitimacy. As early as the 1870s, during the building of the *Ecole libre*, he repeatedly stressed the coherence and scientific promises of his concepts, to be further developed at the institution.

In reality, however, he had already practically abandoned this scientific project of founding a discipline during the 1870s, as it proved to clash with his ambitions as an institution builder. Dependent on private funding from the political and business elites, he was forced to decouple the institutional from the intellectual project. His funders insisted on seeing the training function developed in rather broad terms and having a diversity of courses on legal, economic and historical matters included in the programme. Boutmy responded to the demands, devoted most of his energies for several decades to securing the practical acknowledgement of the school certificates as entry requirements for higher civil service careers, and discontinued the work on his political psychology. The specific feature of the French situation was, consequently, that an institution (more on which below) was successfully established which had a quasi-monopoly on political science but through its very character led to durably imposing a very particular profile on the political sciences (Favre 1981: 461).

If among the continental European countries Germany was the one where least attempts were made to develop political science as a discipline of the social sciences after 1870, this is perhaps because the state was least challenged by the contemporary social transformations. On the contrary, in the eyes of many of the 'Mandarins' – university professors in state service (Ringer 1969) – the idea of the state had ultimately come to realise itself in Imperial Germany, and if there was anything to do for policy intellectuals, it was not to scrutinise the structures and workings of this state but to serve to enhance its fulfilling its functions.

There had been moves towards some concept of a political science earlier, though. Robert von Mohl, for instance, tried to reconcile the policy orientation of the cameral sciences of the absolutist period with more liberal conceptions of a *Rechtsstaat*, based on bourgeois ideas of individual rights. Hans Maier (1980: 232) has aptly characterised Mohl's major work of 1832–3 *Die Polizey-Wissenschaft nach den Grundsätzen des Rechtsstaats* as the product of a transitional period, drawing on ideas of the past and anticipating problématiques of the future:

> Thus, Mohl's policy science . . . as a work of transition looks Janus-headed towards two eras. On the one side, there is the old police state, which Mohl experienced . . . in Southern Germany during the Metternich era – much-governing, regulating from above, busy and occupied with everything, but without any clear objective and without comprehension for the bourgeoisie's striving for autonomy; on the other side, the social movements of the second half of the nineteenth century, which will pose giant tasks to public administration, announce themselves from afar.

While von Mohl's main interest here was in the foundations of the state in terms of legal theory (on his 'sociology' see ch. 9), Lorenz von Stein tried to develop more substantive notions of historically existing states. Though the influence of Hegel's idea of the state and its dialectical opposition to society is visible in his writings, his analyses of social movements led him to focus on the historical reality of the state and to ask concrete questions about limits and needs for state activities in relation to changing societal constellations. He indicated, thus, some steps on the path from the political philosophy of German idealism to a historical-empirical social science of the state, a path which was not taken, though.

Concomitant with the founding of the Imperial German state, the *Verein für Socialpolitik* was formed as a policy-oriented social science association, which proved to have formidable success and to shape social science debates in Germany until the advent of the Weimar Republic. Intellectually, the leading members of the Association belonged to the so-called Historical School of economics, an approach to social science which rejected the formal and deductive reasoning of political economy and preserved the link to historical thinking and analysis which was a major characteristic of German university life in the nineteenth century. Implicitly, the pursuit of such a unified social science also meant a rejection of disciplinary specialisation which occurred towards the end of the century in the US and to which tendencies were also visible in some European countries.

Politically, the orientation of the Association was to state-directed reform policy. Mostly identifying themselves with the project of national unification, the scholars were concerned about the newly formed Empire accomplishing the immense task of keeping the nation together. Gustav Schöneberg (quoted after Schäfer 1971: 286), one of the founding members of the Association, for instance, put the 'social task of the German Empire' as follows:

> The so-called social question is for us, since the national question has found its conclusion, perhaps the most important one for the future . . . Legally, the state of law has today been firmly established. Now the challenge is to let the state come true culturally.

The Association should be the forum where intellectual, economic and political elites meet to find ways and means of policy action towards alleviating the social question.

In the early years, the Association focused its work on assessments of the state of certain social problems like urban housing, factory laws or regulations on work contracts. From the late 1870s on, it increasingly resorted to organise inquiries (*Enquêten*) of its own and devoted considerable attention to methodological questions of empirical research, to the design of surveys, for instance. Max Weber, a member of the Association and – in the perspective of intellectual history – of the so-called Youngest Historical School, the last generation of these historically minded scholars, designed and was involved in several of these empirical research projects.

Seemingly, thus, a strong movement for a politically oriented social science emerged in Germany. The Association was considered by many foreign scholars visiting Germany, among them many of the 'founders' of social science at American universities, as a model on which social science could develop its own identity and institutional establishment. It was widely held that the political, military and economic success of Germany in imperialist competition was not least due to its science: elements of the institutional model were copied in the US, France, Italy and other countries, and part of the fame also went to this type of social science.

However, the policy-oriented social research of the Association was of a very restricted nature, in particular with regard to any conception of political science. Its scope was limited to the assessment of some socially problematic situations in society and to the discussion of policy measures to deal with these situations. There was no room for anything which one might call a sociological or political analysis of contemporary society. In the conception of most scholars the state was something untouchable which could not be exposed to an analytical view from a distance, in striking contrast, for instance, to the political theories of someone like

Mosca in Italy. Weber was the only major exception; Robert Michels, who could have been a second one, could not get a chair at a German university and emigrated to Italy. This exclusion of political institutions and their relations to society from analysis stemmed from the basically complementary nature of this research to the legal theory of the state, as formulated in legal positivism. There was no intention to challenge this doctrine by studying the social foundations of public law or the reality of applications of legal rules; the discourse on the state remained in purely legal terms. The appeal of legal positivism, both in scientific and in political terms, was probably a major reason why something like a political science could not develop in Germany, and why the approaches which were pursued in Italy could not persist.

Limits to the will for political knowledge

> Political phenomena are those that refer to the origins and functioning of the state: these are essentially juridical phenomena . . . This alleged political science is nothing other than constitutional law, that is, a branch of the general science of law. (quoted after Favre 1985: 33)

Leon Duguit's assessment of the hierarchical relation between law and political science, made in 1899, was not an unusual one by the end of the nineteenth century. The law faculties had been one of the cornerstones of the universities: they trained for the legal profession, a key vocation in modern states and societies; and they had increasingly been concerned with developing a systematic body of public law to complement the civil law code. In continental Europe, law had become 'the profession of the state *par excellence*' (Nettl 1968: 584). Two aspects of the centrality of the legal scholar's position in European polities can be distinguished:

> In the first place, the training function of the universities for the state service . . . Secondly, legal scholars sought to provide a doctrine, a body of concepts that were based on elaborate technical distinctions and would enable lawyers and judges to act with promptness and precision . . . Their authority derived from the rationalist character of a legal system that was constructed around the idea of codification and displayed a preference for logical system over the experience of history, for a strict hierarchy of sources of law . . . and for a view that justice was only to be obtained through the strict application of known rules. (Dyson 1980: 111)

We shall turn to the latter aspect first, and discuss the training function later, as they contribute to framing the discourse on politics.

The scientification of public law in the legal theory of the state

The claim of legal scholars to deal with everything that is relevant about the state in a systematic, scientific way can be understood in two divergent ways. Either it was a call for integrating studies of political and administrative institutions into the legal body of knowledge, which would lead to a sociology of law, or to empirically based administrative sciences as subfields of public law; or it demanded the exclusionary systematisation of the legal code so as to impede *a priori* any intrusion of non-legal matters in the scientific theory of the state, which pointed the way towards legal positivism. The first path was mainly pursued in France, and to some extent in Italy, where, however, the newly emerging administrative sciences soon ceded to legal positivism. The latter road was taken in Germany, and increasingly so in Italy too.

Duguit's claim to legal hegemony cited above, arrogant as it may sound, was in fact meant to include, not to exclude the study of politics. Indeed, he saw the danger that law might lose its analytical importance if it did not open up its perspective. According to him, law risked rigidification and the loss of all scientific character if it did not re-establish closer links to social 'reality'. In this sense, sociology could be a means to revive legal science (cf. Pisier-Kouchner 1972: 7). Partly along the lines of Durkheimian thinking, Duguit understood the state pragmatically as the form of political organisation of society and functionally as related to societal objectives, not least that of social solidarity. Demystifying the state, he was opposed both to abstracting the state from social reality in an idealist manner and to identifying it with the law in the Roman legal tradition. Instead of the classical political problem of the basis for the exertion of public power and for sovereignty, he focused on public services as the state's task. The state was mainly seen as an empirically analysable social organisation and not as an abstract legal one. Duguit's theorising, along with other contributions to a sociology of public law, became increasingly influential with the crises of purely liberal conceptions of the state and with the extension of welfare policies. During the inter-war period, however, such views were also heavily criticised for their alleged erosion of the normative foundations of the state.

As in France, numerous proposals were made in Italy in the latter half of the nineteenth century to reform the legal sciences and to open them towards social and sociological issues and analyses. In many cases, some comprehensive, unified and empirical science of the state broadly along the lines of von Mohl and von Stein in Germany was envisaged. Angelo Messedaglia, for instance, made a proposal in 1869 to restructure legal education with the objective to ground this on 'a more complete knowledge both of the institutions of the state and of its historical development and factual situation in general' (1869: 588).

Against the opposition of many legal scholars, steps in this direction were in fact taken and a curriculum of administrative sciences was introduced into legal education in 1875–6 and made compulsory in 1885. In the academic year 1877–8, the first chair in administrative sciences was created at the University of Padova and given to Carlo Francesco Ferraris, who contributed, among others, to developing a historical perspective on legal and state developments which excluded a purely legal theory of the state (cf. Mozzarelli and Nespor 1981). Towards the end of the century, this approach was increasingly criticised for undervaluing the specificity of the state and the distinction between state and society. The legal approach, newly systematised, gained the upper hand, and 'the science of administration finishes at the beginning of the century' (Cassese 1981: 483; on some attempts to develop a sociology of law in Italy, see Ghezzi 1980; Treves 1980–1).

The dominant scientific discourse on the polity in Italy after that time, and in Germany already from the 1870s onwards, was legal positivism. Its main proponents were Carl Friedrich von Gerber and, as the codifier, Paul Laband in Germany, and Vittorio Emanuele Orlando and Santi Romano in Italy. Its emerging and long-lasting dominance can be understood against a background of a conjunction of intellectual-institutional and political developments. In intellectual terms, this theorising was a response to the inability of the Historical School of law to develop its thinking into a systematic body of concepts and knowledge, in the way the internal restructuring of the universities demanded. In political terms, legal positivism provided a doctrine centred on a state which had not to be relativised with regard to society. As such, it appealed to the political elites in the 'late-coming' nation-states in Germany and Italy whose principal objective was to forge a strong state apparatus on a heterogeneous society and who, therefore, had to reason for this state in terms other than societal ones. We shall briefly look at both these aspects of the legal theory of the state and their interrelation.

Gerber's work marks the transition from the Historical School of law to legal positivism. He appreciated the groundwork laid by the historical scholars, but found a systematic inner order of public law missing, an order of the type which the natural sciences had provided for their spheres of analysis. His objective was to collect legal regulations and to interpret them in such a way as to identify their inner nature and hidden relations and, in a next step, to complement the existing principles towards a coherent, all-encompassing system (cf. Bärsch 1972; von Oertzen 1974). In his inaugural lecture at the University of Palermo under the title 'The technical criteria for the juridical reconstruction of public law', Orlando formulated the ambition of supra-historical systematicity in a very similar way:

> For the legal scholar, who sees in law nothing but the reproduction of a juridical principle of which he already needs to have notice and knowledge, [law] cannot be taken account of otherwise than by this juridical principle, through which it is declared, and through which it re-enters into the general system of right. In other words, thus, it is law that presupposes an organic system of right, and not the juridical system that presupposes the law. (quoted after Fioravanti 1982: 94)

In the search for these underlying legal principles, these theorists discovered the central position of the state, its personality and its will. As first formulated by Gerber in 1865:

> We imagine the state (1) as an organism, in which the ethical forces of the people are gathered, and we endow (2) the state, since it is a willing and acting being, with the idea of personality. Its soul is the one of the force of the state [Staatsgewalt], it is the centre of a correct system of state law, the most prominent task of which is answering the question: what is it the state can want and in which way can it announce its volition? (1865: 8)

The theory was systematically elaborated in his Grundzüge eines Systems des deutschen Staatsrechts, which appeared in the same year; it was canonised in the early years of Imperial Germany by Paul Laband in Staatsrecht des deutschen Reiches, published between 1876 and 1882, as the quasi-official legal doctrine of this state, a doctrine of which Laband himself was the most competent interpreter as legal adviser and co-editor of an influential law journal. Public law had, thus, acquired a high degree of coherence, which was often praised as the achievement of scientific status (cf. Meyer 1893; a later detailed assessment is given by Wieacker

1952: see e.g. 253); it did so at the cost of reducing law to the will of the state. In terms of social science discourse it meant the disappearance of any relevant problématique inherent to the concept of the state:

> On the basis of the juridical understanding of the state, the political sciences become the entirely juridical sciences of the state . . . and the others become, residually, social sciences. (Mozzarelli and Nespor 1981: 103–4; see also Mozzarelli 1982: 527)

The stress should be put here on 'residually': the remaining social sciences strove for ontological purity at the cost of conceptual reductionism (cf. Wagner 1989). The German legal theorist Hermann Heller, who attempted to revive a political and sociological analysis of the state in his work of the 1920s, complained in 1931:

> The state . . . however, had become the object of a state thinking that had been handed to the jurists . . . and there it finally turned into a fiction or an abstraction, until at the end this state thinking could do expressly without a state [and] put in its place 'the' order of law. (1931: 610; for an earlier critique of legal positivism, see von Gierke 1915 [1874])

The background to this development lay in political problems as much as in scientific ones, as Heller well knew. He had also recognised that there had been a German tradition of a sociology of the state which had died off after the bourgeois revolution of 1848 had failed. In this sense,

> this state thinking without state is not only a crisis of state theorists but also an indubitable sign of a more profound crisis of the state, a crisis that it in turn aggravates. (1931: 610)

In very fundamental terms, this crisis of the state is a birth defect of the German and the Italian nation, due to the forced superimposition of the bureaucratic apparatus on the state and of its unifying and homogenising norms and regulations on society. Such a political situation seemed to require an extra-societal normative foundation for the state and not one which would be derived from the empirical study of the relations of societal interests to political institutions, types of analysis which a 'political science' could offer. This problem was well recognised by Gerber, whose theorising left its own foundations open to critique. Gerber had argued in 1852, for instance, that the time was not yet ripe for a systematic approach to public law, as this was 'a time of politics and not of law', a time when everything was in flux and in constant threat of change (1852: 12–13). Only after the unification process had been successfully initiated by the Prussian state, did he choose to go further in his theorising. Once powerfully established, the state of Imperial Germany was well served by this theorising, and the crisis of which Heller speaks re-emerges only after political circumstances had changed, gradually first with the rising strength of the workers' movement at the turn of the century (Paulsen 1902: 79), and massively after the breakdown of the authoritarian-bureaucratic monarchy and the advent of the Weimar Republic, the political context in which Heller was working. In Italy, the state was erected on a much more bourgeois-liberal foundation than the German one. Thus, much greater political and intellectual space had existed for a politico-administrative science until the turn of the century. It is only when the societal cleavages seemed to deepen and when the formula of *trasformismo*, of gradual integration of wider societal interests, including working-class interests, into the liberal state, seemed to fail that legal positivism developed to the hegemonic legal doctrine, parallel, by the way, to the decay of positivist social science and the re-emergence of idealist philosophy (Mozzarelli 1982: 526; see ch. 1).[3]

In the conjunction of a critical process of state building on the one hand, and the search for scientific legitimacy of legal theorising in the academic institutions on the other, the legal theory of the state seemed to provide the perfect response for both types of problems. The approach of legal positivism had the capacity to forge a discourse coalition between actors in both the scientific and the political fields. It constructed a cognitive affinity between the two fields, an affinity which laid the basis for its dominance in both spheres, its potential to transform the hegemonic discourses. To the same degree to which the legal theory of the state proved successful, however, the intellectual space in which a discourse on politics could have developed was filled. Legal positivism complemented well the empirical policy studies of the *Verein für Socialpolitik*, which had no interest in the analysis of state institutions, and it pushed aside any attempts for a political and administrative science which had started to develop in Italy (the only exception being the elite theories by Mosca, Michels and a few others which, in the way they were proposed, turned out to well suit the fascist regime).

The professionalisation of politics beyond law

By the mid 1800s, legal training was the basic and main precondition for an administrative career in continental Europe. In transition from the earlier cameral sciences, a 'legal knowledge monopoly' had effectively been established in continental Europe, with the law faculties of the universities providing the necessary credentials. The major exception was France, where the *grandes écoles* continued to train the administrative elite with broader concepts of scientific-technical expertise, and where the law faculties provided training only for those officials following this top group (for Germany see Bleek 1972; for Italy the writings of Cassese e.g. 1974; in general see Aubert 1985). The emphasis on legal knowledge went along with the ideological dominance of the idea of the liberal state, though hardly fully practised, according to which the state should do no more than setting and ensuring the legal framework in which societal interests could be formulated and pursued. With the advent of stronger states after 1870, and in particular with the spreading discourse about welfare measures and the creation of social policy institutions, it could be expected not only that the analytical dominance of legal theorising would be challenged (as described above) but also that the professional structures would be shaken by new demands for practical expertise.

Such demands were in fact raised repeatedly throughout the nineteenth century and they met with some success, in comparative perspective inversely related to the dominance of legal positivism. In Germany, the concept of the 'classical bureaucrat', as aptly analysed by Weber, for instance, was very pronounced. Being a servant of the state that was seen as superior to society, the bureaucrats perceived themselves as a national elite and as the legitimate power basis of the state apparatus. Their superiority drew on the command and application of the body of legal knowledge which would give them an instrument to be of use in all cases.

Even though the increasing demands on the state did not escape their attention, this superiority was hardly shaken, in fact not until the 1960s. Where they did not master the technical expertise which might increasingly be required, they would avail themselves of their competence to sort out the right kind of applicable technical knowledge and draw on case-specific expertise, where necessary, in a hierarchical manner (see Wollmann 1989 for an analysis of changing relations between legal and social science knowledge in Germany). Though somewhat less strictly applied, a similar basic conception of the bureaucrat's role applies to Italy.

Attempts to break up such a development were made in Germany by von Mohl, for instance, when he proposed a special curriculum for administrative training in the universities in 1845 and again in 1869 (Bleek 1972: 249). This proposal headed for a modernised and elaborated continuation of the tradition of the cameral sciences. Related ideas were ventured in Italy by Giandomenico Romagnosi with his proposal for a 'science of public affairs' of 1839 or Messedaglia's initiative of 1851. All these, ultimately unsuccessful, concepts tried to challenge the monopoly of the law faculties as they 'assumed an insufficiency of the traditional juridical knowledge as an instrument of understanding, of organisation and of control in the construction of the new unitary state and of technico-professional preparation of its future leaders' (Mozzarelli and Nespor 1981: 27–8).

The only success was a proposal which bypassed the universities, namely the creation of the *Scuola di Scienze Sociali 'Cesare Alfieri'* in Florence in 1874. It was based on the model of the Paris school and, though it never achieved the importance of the latter, fulfilled its functions as an elitist institution to prepare for higher administrative service. The only case where a major transformation of administrative training was enacted was the French one, with the establishment of the *Ecole libre*. From this experience, one can guess what separate professionalisation of politics and administration would mean for the development of a scientific discourse on politics.

Boutmy's initiative of 1871 was the last in a long series of proposals which headed either for a reform of the university or for the creation of a new school alongside the other specialised *grandes écoles*. Ideas of the former type included the setting up of a new faculty of political and administrative sciences, suggested in 1820 and in 1843 by Cuvier and Laboulaye, respectively. Proposals for the addition of a new school to the system of elite institutions started to be made in 1795 and were repeated through the nineteenth century until 1871 (cf. Favre 1981: 437–8). The most interesting one for the question discussed here was probably the suggestion made by Derny in 1869, to add a section on state sciences to the *Ecole pratique des hautes études*. According to the persistent institutional cleavage in French higher education, such a section would probably have moved away from the professional, administration-oriented pole to the academic pole of this institutional system. This remains counterfactual speculation, however, as this proposal did not come to be realised, like all the others mentioned, not least owing to the resistance of the law faculties.

In the wake of the lost Franco-Prussian War and of the deep crisis of the French state, Boutmy's attempt, in contrast, was highly successful. As early as 1876 his school had achieved such a standing that he could counter a new proposal to set up a state-run elite school for administration by the argument that his institution fulfilled such a function effectively. A move, in 1881, by the law faculties to introduce a doctorate in political and administrative sciences came similarly too late to weaken the *Ecole libre* and was successfully opposed by Boutmy. As described above, however, the survival and career of the institution was achieved at the cost of abandoning the intellectual project of a scientific study of politics and of concentrating exclusively on the professional function instead. As a consequence, the political sciences are well institutionalised in France, but they present a very peculiar image, which Favre (1981: 461–2) summarised:

(1) They are divided, fragmented, in courses that do not at all relate to each other . . .
(2) They are state sciences rather than political sciences: essentially destined to the education of high civil servants . . . (3) They can insert themselves into the *débat d'idées* . . . the political sciences, even though they presuppose research and reflexion, are not always very far from expression of mundane discourse.

A professionalisation of the political role, one could conclude, does not enhance the development of a theoretically well-grounded scientific language on politics either. The legalistic 'scientification' had robbed politics of its contents; the professionalisation had not managed to move beyond mundane elite discourse to a conceptually viable political language.

Epilogue

Spokespersons of present political science may agree or disagree with this analysis. In either case, they could point to its historical character and argue that since the establishment of the modern discipline after the Second World War the problems have fortunately been overcome. My view, in contrast, is that post-war disciplinary developments are hardly less shaped by 'scientification' drives, such as behaviourism, rational choice theory, systems theory or quantitative approaches, and moves towards 'professionalisation', be it of administrative training or of policy analysis, as the defining criterion for the discipline and the institution of 'political science'. As different as the directions of these two movements are, they share the danger of systematically directing attention away from the nature of the political in modern societies. Approaches that have tried to escape both the scientific dilemma and the practical dilemma to which legal positivism and professional policy training have surrendered have been rare and rather unsuccessful. The analysis of political phenomena, however, cannot be decoupled from problems of social theory in general, problems of conceptualising the constitution and restructuring of modern politics and society (see chs 9 and 10; and Wagner 2001: ch. 2).

3
ADJUSTING SOCIAL RELATIONS
Social science and the organisation
of modernity

The preceding two chapters dealt with the emergence (or non-emergence) of social science in disciplinary forms towards the end of the nineteenth century. It was argued that the striving for theoretical coherence in bounded systems of thought was related to internal changes in the research-oriented university, which increasingly demanded such standards and criteria. The specific orientation towards political relevance in those emerging modes of thought, in addition, was connected to the transformation of the nation-state towards mass-democratic forms in what I termed the first crisis of European modernity. This second theme, the reference to the problématique of modern politics, however, had accompanied the social sciences from their very beginning, that is, already before the creation of the disciplines. And a new conception of the usefulness of the social sciences gained ground when the classical approaches had, by and large, failed to become accepted as the valid interpretation of the novel social order. This chapter will focus on the orientation of the social sciences to social planning that leads to what I call the organisation of modernity, a process that is most pronounced between the 1920s and the 1970s. To fully grasp the planning orientation, however, a broader look is required at the link between the social sciences and political modernity.

The social sciences, in broadly their contemporary shapes, emerged after the American and French Revolutions. They offered a variety of ways of dealing with the new, post-revolutionary political situation, which enabled and, indeed, obliged human beings to create their own rules for social action and political order. It has been a part of the intellectual tradition of the social sciences from their beginnings to contribute to making the social world predictable in the face of modern uncertainties, or, in the stronger version, to reshape it according to a master plan for improvement (see some of the contributions to Heilbron et al. 1998).

The general idea of providing and using social knowledge for government and policy was certainly not new at this point. The cameral and policy sciences of the seventeenth and eighteenth centuries were designed for use by an absolute ruler; the very name of 'statistics' reflects the fact of being a science for governmental purposes. The post-revolutionary situation, however, was crucially different in two respects. On the one hand, a much more radical uncertainty had been created by the commitment, even if often a reluctant one, to self-determination of the people, which appeared to limit the possibility of predictive knowledge. On the other hand, this radical openness had been accompanied by the hope for the self-organisation of society and its rational individuals, so that the search for laws of such society and human actions emerged beyond – and partially instead of – the desire for the increase of factual knowledge of the social world.

As a consequence, two competing concepts of social science with different attitudes toward social planning coexisted throughout much of the nineteenth century. Both anticipated a steady increase of valid social knowledge. But such knowledge did not in all views need to be actively translated into planned intervention in the social world. Perhaps the interplay of the free actions of reason-endowed human beings would automatically enhance the well-being of all, as the traditions of political economy and, later, neoclassical economics held; or perhaps a progressive evolution of humankind determined the historical course of societies from lower to higher stages, making interference ineffective and unnecessary. Despite much earlier announcements then, societal planning based on social science knowledge was to be a phenomenon more characteristic of the twentieth, rather than the nineteenth, century.

Ameliorist social science and the social question

From, broadly, the middle of the nineteenth century onwards, the more optimistic views on societal self-regulation proved increasingly difficult to uphold, in the face of rising criticism of poverty and prostitution or a deteriorating medical state of the population. These evils, widely regarded as unprecedented, had at first been seen as transitional problems on the way to a new social order, as the birth pangs of modernity. Now they began to be regarded as persistent and potentially dangerous for the social order, because they were concomitant to other major social changes, such as industrialisation and urbanisation, and because they were linked to widespread discontent.

In this context, explicitly policy-oriented – and, in a loose sense, planning-oriented – forms of social science (re-) emerged in a number of countries. Often, the starting-point of the reasoning was the empirical elucidation of problematic social situations, a strategy employed by activists as diverse as the hygienists and the group around Frédéric Le Play in mid-century France, reformist moralists in Britain, 'mugwump' intellectuals in Gilded Age United States, and factory inspectors in Imperial Germany. Often, the reformism was closely linked to a more comprehensive scholarly ambition and to the creation of semi-scholarly, semi-political associations such as the American Social Science Association and the disciplinary associations that succeeded it, the *Verein für Socialpolitik* of German historical economists, the Fabian Society, and the Le Playist *Société d'action sociale* (Rueschemeyer and Skocpol 1996; Ross 1991: ch. 3; Manicas 1987).

Mostly, the approaches taken were straightforwardly empirical and observational in their methodological orientation, and committed to political reformism of a conservative, ameliorist kind, focused on the safeguarding of order (Wagner et al. 1991). Statistics was often seen as a means to reorder a social reality that appeared to have become recalcitrant (Porter 1986). This was particularly the case in newly formed states, such as Italy or Germany, in which the cohesion and homogeneity of society could even less be taken for granted than in other, more consolidated states.

One outcome of these efforts was to link the work of social scientists directly to state concerns, to orient social knowledge to policy-making in a way which was novel for the post-revolutionary period and to some extent reminiscent of the earlier policy and cameral sciences. Such state-oriented social science defined the major political issue of the time, often called 'the social question', in terms of finding a smooth transition from the earlier restrictive liberalism (or even, as in Germany, old regime) to a fully inclusive order. Politically, the recognition of the salience of 'the social question' spelled an end to any idea and ideology of societal self-regulation. However, the growth of state involvement, while necessary, was generally not seen as a radical break with earlier practice. Social elites just had to be more responsive to the needs of the population than they had been. Empirical social analysis was meant to demonstrate the need for reforms, also against elite resistance, as well as to develop and propose the type of measures that were required (Lacey and Furner 1993; Furner and Supple 1990).

Towards that end, no particular epistemological or ontological issues needed initially to be confronted. Broadly, a sober empirical realism appeared to be sufficient for such a problem-oriented social science. Accordingly, a soft version of positivism prevailed among policy-oriented social scientists after the middle of the nineteenth century, committed to the extension of positive knowledge, and sometimes even evoking Auguste Comte's name, but without the religious fervour of the original project of a positive science of society (Harp 1995; Wright 1986: 269–70).

Social science and the crisis of liberalism

A major transformation in the relation between social science and policy-making started gradually after 1870 and culminated in debates around the turn of the century. The earlier reformism was increasingly regarded as insufficient for the emerging societal constellation, both in its conception of politics and in its conception of social knowledge.

Politically speaking, liberal elites recognised that industrialisation, urbanisation, the emergence of an organised working class and the concomitant demand for full inclusion of all members of society on equal terms posed serious, seemingly almost intractable, problems to the liberal conception of political institutions. Much 'realist' political sociology of the time, including works by Robert Michels, Vilfredo Pareto and Max Weber in Europe and by John Dewey in the US, aimed to identify the required institutional adjustment. At least in the European versions, some elitist conclusions appeared inevitable. More conservative-minded authors, especially on the European continent, understood the same evidence to confirm their view that liberalism was untenable. Even they, however, perceived on the horizon a transition to a new social order, rather than an adjustment of the existing one. In political terms, therefore, what was at stake was an understanding of the transformation of liberalism (Seidman 1983; Wagner 1994: ch. 4).

The political balances tipped toward a strengthening of collectivist orientations, in which the autonomy of the individual was de-emphasised in favour of a voluntarism of the collectivity. Both socialism and nationalism provided versions of such collectivist political philosophy; but even former liberals resigned themselves to social changes that had displaced individual responsibility from the centre of politics. Progressivism in the US, and social democracy in Europe, emerged as new and often quite fragile alliances of socialism and liberalism. With them came a new group of political elites, favouring professionalism and science as opposed to the feudalism and clientelism in the old elites, but often also technocratic and state-centred, and suspicious of the pluralism and democracy of much earlier liberalism (Kloppenberg 1986).

The shift in political orientations, this declining faith in the viability of liberalism, was paralleled in epistemology by a renewed scepticism about the other central tenet of the Enlightenment tradition, the intelligibility of human action and the social world. The period around the turn of the century is now known as an intellectually extremely fruitful, even a classical era in many fields of social science, most notably sociology, psychology and economics. At that time, however, much of the work was driven by a sense of crisis, a feeling that many of the epistemological, ontological and methodological assumptions of earlier social science were inadequate.

In terms of epistemology, social science saw itself forced to largely abandon the idea of representing social reality and accepted the view that conceptual constructions were dependent both on the means and forms of observation and perception and on the interest of the observer in the social world. American pragmatism is the most explicit case of such a reorientation, but similar, often much more tension-ridden, discussions were led in European debates, a prominent example being Max Weber's methodological writings. Key concepts once taken as self-evident were now scrutinised and reinterpreted. This applies both to collective terms, such as society, state, people and religion, and to those referring to human beings and their sense of continuous existence, terms such as individual, action, self, psyche (see in more detail Part II). Certainty about these concepts was especially important, because in some form or other they were indispensable for theorising the political order, in terms of some stable relation between collective phenomena and individual human beings. Epistemological and ontological questionings had repercussions for methodology. Statistical approaches, for instance, always rely on some assumptions about aggregates, mostly states, and their components, mostly individuals or households. If certainty about these concepts was shaken, the ground for any research methodology also appeared insecure (Desrosières 1993).

As a consequence, the turn-of-the-century approaches were more doubtful of the determinist course of human history than earlier social science, and also less persuaded that empirical observation gave direct insight into any laws of the social world. This uncertainty was expected to restrict the viability of social knowledge for policy and planning purposes. The earlier call had been for better knowledge that would lead to better action; according to such a conception, action based on uncertain knowledge should entail uncertain outcomes. And indeed, the turn-of-the-century debates were marked by a chasm between social philosophising that tried to live up to these insights, on the one hand, and empirical research that continued and even expanded, rather unconcerned by such issues, on the other. Through the early decades of the twentieth century, however, were proposed novel conceptions of the relation between knowledge and action that turned out to lend themselves to a greater involvement in policy than before. The world-political crisis of the First World War had the effect of giving such considerations a sense of urgency and of focusing the debates.

Social planning in mass society: the first attempt

The First World War was, among many other things, a giant experiment in social planning. Its unexpectedly long duration and the similarly unforeseen involvement of large segments of the population, as well as trade interruptions and supply shortages, led to increasing government efforts to steer economic and social activities, mostly with but sometimes without the consent of employers, unions and other social groups. At the end of the war, a widespread impression held such planning superior to liberal and market forms of regulation. Direct conclusions were drawn in the aftermath of the Bolshevik Revolution and, less forcefully, by some bureaucrats in the first Weimar administrations, but the impact of that experience was felt throughout the Western world. This enthusiasm for state planning receded as liberal market democracy appeared to recover during the 1920s, but the planning mood revived again after the world economic crisis of 1929. Social science was now directly involved in such planning moves (Wagner 1990: ch. 9).

The Austrian economist Rudolf Hilferding, who contributed to Austro-Marxism but was active in German social democracy during the Weimar period, had developed his concept of 'organised capitalism' even before the war. The notion implied that capitalism was organisable, and that such organisation could be pursued from a reformist perspective. Related ideas were developed by a group of broadly left-wing economists at the Kiel Institute for the World Economy during the 1920s. Some members of the group were also involved in the economic planning debates in the early 1930s when such ideas were found attractive by a range of economists and policy-makers reaching from American New Deal liberals to Soviet planners. A testimony to the range of that debate and its international extension is the Amsterdam World Economic and Social Congress of 1932 (von Bergen 1995; Alchon 1985). The founding of economic survey institutes in many countries, such as the US, France and Germany, during the inter-war period supplied empirical information that could lend itself, potentially, to planning intervention.

While much of that debate was confined to economic terms, some broader conceptualisations of social planning were also proposed. The most comprehensive was probably the *Plan de travail*, developed by the Belgian psychologist and socialist, and professor at Frankfurt University from 1929 to 1933, Hendrik de Man. Presented to the Belgian Workers' Party in 1933, the plan was widely debated in Belgium, the Netherlands and France, where it supported a reformist reorientation of the socialist parties. De Man's case demonstrates particularly clearly the specific reformist-socialist inspiration for social planning, and also its socio-philosophical basis. De Man was well versed in Marxism and social democracy. Yet he gave up social determinism during his German years in favour of a psychologically moderated voluntarism that made reaching socialism a matter of 'will and representation' rather than the development of material forces (de Man 1926). In this respect he was in synchrony with much other social theory. He did not, however, dwell on the possible conclusion that the predictability of social life had decreased but emphasised instead that the malleability of the social world increased once determinism was abandoned.

A related development can be discerned in John Maynard Keynes' economic thinking. Already early in the 1920s, he emphasised the relevance of uncertainty in economic life, in defiance of straightforward neoclassical assumptions about complete information and rational behaviour. His *General Theory*, while formalised to a considerable degree, relied at crucial points on the identification of 'factors' in economic life that were socio-historically or psychologically variable, and so required specific identification rather than general deduction. In France, the Durkheimian economic sociologist Maurice Halbwachs argued for a connection between theorising on conditions for social order and empirical observation of economic life that showed some affinity of principle to the Keynesian approach. Halbwachs supported the creation of a French institute for economic surveys, founded as the *Institut de conjoncture* in 1938, not least with a view to specifying the conditions for the effectiveness of political intervention (Desrosières 1985: 307).

This critique of determinism and emphasis on the feasibility of goal-directed, planned political action was joined to a fundamental and critical epistemological presupposition that the social world is in important respects not found and discovered but made and invented. It constitutes one strand of the planning debate in the inter-war social sciences. The other strand severed its ties with turn-of-the-century social theory entirely and put social science on completely new – some may want to say 'modern' – foundations. The key element here is the 'scientific world-view' of the Vienna School and the unified science movement, which created an unprecedented linkage between positivist philosophy, socialist thought and modern sociological research, or what has also been called a blend of Comte, Marx and behaviourism (Torrance 1976: 459; Smith 1986). In an intellectual and political context of doubt and uncertainty, its proponents hoped to reaffirm the social project of modernity by reintroducing sociology as a science of equal epistemological standing with the natural sciences. They made it part of the very same undertaking, the generation of reliable knowledge that lent itself to prediction and planning.

In both intellectual and political terms, the sources of this approach can be traced to the particular situation of turn-of-the-century and inter-war Austria, and in particular to Vienna, the capital and major city of the Habsburg Empire as well as of the new Austrian Republic after the First World War (Schorske 1980; Janik and Toulmin 1973; Pollak 1984; Gruber 1991). The Austrian socialists and 'Austro-Marxists', who had been confined to theorising during the stagnant years of the Habsburg Empire, gained and held a comfortable electoral majority in Vienna during the Republic, and made it into an experimental space for social planning.

One of the leading activists and theoreticians of social planning was Otto Neurath, author of *The scientific world-view, socialism and logical empiricism* as well as of *Empirical sociology*. A young follower of the same movement was the mathematician Paul Felix Lazarsfeld. The examples of both Neurath and Lazarsfeld can serve to demonstrate the particular connection between politics and social philosophy during this period.

Neurath's conviction that scientific rationality and political improvement went hand in hand was conditioned by his perception of himself and others as united in a struggle against both metaphysical world-views and illegitimate power, a similarly inseparable couple. He witnessed this scientific-political rationality at work in the war economy and participated in the attempts of the post-war revolutionary governments in Saxony and Bavaria to socialise the means of production. Expelled from Germany, he became a leading reformer in Vienna, trying to put rational schemes to work in city politics. In writings on planning, statistics and socialism, he elaborated the view that individual reason, once given the space to develop, becomes essentially identical with scientific reason. As a consequence, 'social technology' could be developed on the basis of an empirical and positive sociology that rejected all metaphysics, and the sociologist could become a 'social engineer'. Crude as the view may now appear, Neurath saw his politics fully in line with the most rational, and thus most advanced, science and philosophy of science of his time, the positivism of the Vienna Circle, to which he contributed. As one observer put it, we may see Neurath's relation to Wittgenstein as broadly similar to Hans Eisler's relation to Arnold Schoenberg (Nemeth 1981: 77).

The young Lazarsfeld, who also had clear socialist leanings, was drawn into statistical work at the psychological institute of the University of Vienna by Charlotte and Karl Bühler, who were involved in youth research for the city administration. He founded the Research Unit of Economic Psychology at Vienna University, which acquired research contracts both from the Austrian Radio Company and from the Frankfurt Institute for Social Research. In this way, Lazarsfeld inaugurated the institutional and operational model of social research for which he and the Bureau of Applied Social Research at Columbia University in New York would later become famous. This was the beginning of survey research on commission at university-based but commercially operating research institutes, a model that soon spread from the US to Europe and then to other parts of the world after the Second World War. Called 'administrative research' by Lazarsfeld himself, this research served the planning purposes of the funder without being involved in setting the objectives.

Lazarsfeld's intellectual biography illustrates again the simultaneously political and epistemological nature of the transition from classical social theory to applied social research (Pollak 1979). Close to Austro-Marxism himself, Lazarsfeld experienced the difficulties of putting reformist ideas into practice in 'Red Vienna'. It was in particular the conception of a preconceived unity between the political actors and the population for which reformist policies were developed – a socialist version of Enlightenment ideas – that proved illusory. In political practice, no such harmonious alignment arose. Indeed, the will of the people was not even known to the policy-makers who claimed to serve them. Empirical social research was designed as a way of transmitting knowledge from the people to the elites, bearing well in mind that the kind of knowledge that was called for was shaped by elite views of political feasibility, as implied by the conditions of the research contract. After his move to the US, Lazarsfeld regretfully accepted the unavoidable decoupling of his political motivations from a research conception that remained otherwise unchanged.

This empirical positivist sociology was one specific, and highly articulate, response to an increased demand for social knowledge in the crisis of liberalism. It found a number of other, much more loosely formulated expressions else-where. In the Netherlands, social planning emerged in connection with the draining of the Zuiderzee polders, wetlands that could be made usable for agriculture and settlements. Dutch sociology, known as 'sociography' between the wars, had developed a very empirical and applied orientation. H.N. ter Veen, one of its main spokespersons at the time, elaborated proposals for the Zuiderzee colonisation and used them to demonstrate the possibilities of sociologically guided social planning. In the US, the report on *Recent social trends*, commissioned by President Hoover and delivered by William F. Ogburn in 1929, is a major example of a social-statistical attempt to grasp the main lines of social development as a guide to government action. And the New Deal, with the foundation of the National Resources Planning Board and the longer-lived Tennessee Valley Authority, made attempts to base planning on social knowledge.

From the late 1920s onward, we can recognise the contours of an empirical positivist social science, oriented to application and developing in special institutions, which subsequently shaped the image of those sciences in the second post-war era. This social science liberated itself from the doubts of the 'classical period'. Its particular form of empirical social research circumvented the problem of relating the individual to a mass society. Doubts about epistemological and conceptual issues could not be entirely removed, but they could, it was supposed, be contained by starting from the most secure elements one could find, the empirical observation and collection of data on the preferences and behaviours of individual human beings. Conclusions referring to the larger scale of society and politics were reached by aggregation of those data; and the organising questions were derived from policy needs for 'social control'. Thus, a 'soft' behaviourism aligned with a similarly 'soft' pragmatism (Ross 1991: ch. 9).

Such behavioural social research recognises the individual human beings and their doings as a methodological starting-point. It mostly rejects any prior assumptions about behaviours as 'unfounded' or, in Vienna Circle terminology, 'metaphysical'. Thus, it may be seen as drawing one crucial premise, and not an unproblematic one, from a basic tenet of political modernity, the primacy of individual autonomy (Shklar 1987: 346). However, it is a very different kind of individualism from that assumed in either liberal political theory or neo-classical economics, where individual rationalities are postulated. In behavioural social research, social regularities can only be discovered through the study of the utterances or behaviours of individuals, not in any way derived. But after such regularities are identified, they may be reshaped by altering the possibilities of action – for example, in terms of products or party-political programmes on offer.

Neoclassical economics is a post-Enlightenment doctrine – a doctrine of liberal modernity – in the sense that it assumes the self-regulation of a society of reason-endowed (read: rationalistic) individuals. Behavioural social research is a post-liberal technology – a tool of the organisers of modernity, of the planners of 'modern' society – in the sense that it constructs individuals to make them amenable to policy action and planning. The basic cognitive move in this approach was to isolate individuals from each other, to ignore whatever social relations they may have and then to counterpose this atomised mass to the state. 'The underlying assumption of social statistics and social research . . . is that singular human beings can be treated as externally related individuals. The State and its individuals are notions from which both social statistics and social research derive' (Österberg 1988: 44). Here sociology echoed Balzac's novelistic social analysis: 'Society isolates everyone, the better to dominate them, divides everything up to weaken it. It reigns over the units, over numerical figures' (*Le curé de village*, quoted after Gigerenzer et al. 1989: ch. 2; Desrosières 1993; Wagner 1994: ch. 7).

Planning and freedom: the social philosophy of planning

While the implementation of this form of social knowledge and planning was yet far from certain, doubts were already voiced as to whether the longing for planning and organisation, as well as the forms of social knowledge that accompanied it, were indeed compatible with liberal democracy. Especially in the light of the experiences with totalitarian regimes, which turned out to be the earliest and strongest promoters of social planning, the model of a direct transmission between masses and elites, mediated by empirical social science, was unpersuasive. Reservations were particularly strong in the US, where the values of individualism were firmly rooted, and the necessity of planning accepted most reluctantly.

By the mid 1930s, whatever enthusiasm there had been about entering a new age had waned, giving way to a more reflective debate about the social and political implications of the move toward planning. The 1935 meeting of the American Sociological Society, devoted to the theme of the 'Human side of social planning', provided an occasion to review recent developments in the political philosophy of pragmatism and to rethink 'social control'. There was widespread agreement that a more interventionist state had emerged since the First World War, one heavily involved in planning. The sociologists debated how a commitment to autonomy and democracy could nevertheless be maintained. Ernest W. Burgess could not resist the conclusion of a Carnegie Foundation report on schools, that 'American society during the past hundred years has been moving from an individualistic and frontier economy to a collective and social economy'. He insisted, however, that any planning in the US had 'to accord with mores of individualism, democracy and humanitarianism', the moral bases of American society (1935: 33). By contrast, William F. Ogburn, in a much more technocratic vein, asserted that 'some loss of liberty under the predicted conditions is to be expected, for such is the implication of any high degree of organisation' (1935: 37). Lewis Lorwin put the recent developments into the long-term perspective of a 'continuous enlargement of organised groups through which the individual has to act in order to shape public policy'. But he saw those changes less as an unequivocal loss or gain than as a transformation of the political issue: 'Not regimentation versus freedom, therefore, but social control versus unlimited economic power of individuals and minorities is the issue.' In theoretical terms, he identified a fundamental transformation of the concept of rights:

> As planning develops it will shift emphasis in our political thinking from the idea of formal rights to the concept of 'real rights' based on capacity; from the notion of the state as a protector of property to that of a leader in the utilisation of our natural and economic resources; from the concept of law as a balancing of individual rights to that of a process of adjusting social relations; from theories of atomistic individualism to those of social solidarity and cooperative action; and from reliance on an assumed metaphysical benevolence of self-interest to a demonstrable hypothesis of the potentialities of scientific guidance of economic and social forces. (1935: 42, 44, 47–8)

By putting the issue as a historical shift between formal rights and substantive commitments, Lorwin captures a basic ambivalence of liberal political modernity which, though often much more implicitly, had characterised socio-political debates since the French Revolution and which is currently again in the forefront of discussion (Sewell 1986: 60; Donzelot 1991: 171).

While the move towards social planning did not develop the same momentum in the US compared with some European countries and met more principled criticism on grounds of the American tradition of individualism, the emergency situation of the Second World War saw the social sciences nevertheless drawn into planning activities of a large scale, not least with a view to improving the efficacy of military operations and to limit and mitigate their social implications and 'side effects'. The volume *The policy sciences*, edited by Harold Lasswell and Daniel Lerner in 1951, gives testimony both to the involvement of social scientists from all disciplines in war planning and to a willingness to reconsider the possibility of using social knowledge for planning and policy in the light of those, by and large deemed successful, experiences.

In Europe, the most profound reflections on social planning, in terms both of the underlying conception of social knowledge and of the related political philosophy, were written by Karl Mannheim. In his early works, while living on the European continent, he developed a sociology of knowledge and a theory of the role of intellectuals which aimed at a principled reformulation of those issues for an emerging mass society. The earliest version of *Man and society in an age of reconstruction*, which appeared in German in 1935, characterised the major transformation of Western societies in familiar terms as a 'crisis of liberalism and democracy' in a highly organised mass society. To rely on *laissez-faire* would lead necessarily to 'maladjustment'. When the considerably enlarged English version appeared in 1940, he thought he had sufficient experiences with planning under democracy while living in English exile to conclude that 'freedom and planning' might possibly be made compatible through some 'synthesis of democratic planning' (Mannheim 1940; 1943; 1951; Loader 1985; Kettler and Meja 1995).

A synthesis of sorts: the second attempt at social planning

After the war, the operating modes of those liberal democracies that appeared to have managed a successful transformation toward inclusive mass societies – above all the US, the UK and Sweden – were (re-) imported to continental Europe. 'Democratic planning' and 'modern social science' were two key elements of those modes of operation, and strong efforts were made to implant them firmly on continental soil (Wagner 1990: part IV).

The United Nations' cultural organisation, UNESCO, and US-based private foundations were active in promoting a social science oriented to the empirical study of contemporary policy problems with a view to applications. Paul Lazarsfeld himself was involved in building social research institutes in Austria. *The policy sciences* was translated into French by leftist reformers and published with a preface by Raymond Aron, who, having earlier already made arguments for a more 'inductive' rather than philosophical sociology, thus lent his reputation to the development of applied and planning-oriented social science.

Key areas of the social sciences acquired a cognitive affinity to social planning. In economics, Keynesian theorising stimulated research on those economic indicators that were seen as the key variables of macro-economic steering. In sociology, theories of modernisation and development were elaborated on the basis of functionalism and systems theory and were 'applied' to societies in alleged need of development. Quantitative social research flourished. Although academic sociology, economics and political science also took a 'quantitative turn', this kind of social knowledge was increasingly produced on demand of government agencies, business organisations and political parties with a view to their own policy and organisational planning needs. Specific methodologies of policy analysis, such as cost–benefit analysis and planning, programming and budgeting systems (PPBS), were developed.

Such efforts also met resistance. Theodor W. Adorno, for instance, criticised the transformation of sociology into statistics and administrative science as the knowledge form of an 'administered society'. Hannah Arendt's comprehensive study of *The human condition* included a fundamental critique of statistics and behaviourism as undermining any conceptualisation and understanding of human action. However, between the 1950s and the 1970s American and European social science became more and more policy- and planning-oriented. This perspective can be characterised by its substantive focus on issues of policy, strategy and administration, and its conceptual focus on the functioning of goal-oriented organisations, both public and private, and their leaders.

In terms of philosophy of social science, Karl Popper's neopositivism offered a softer version of the inter-war proposals for what was then often a quite technocratic social science. His conception of 'empirical social technology' that could be used in 'piecemeal social experiments' was explicitly based on 'trial and error' and directed against 'Utopian social engineering'. While he offered a new linkage of epistemology and politics, this was one that showed much greater modesty and hesitancy than some inter-war proposals (Popper 1945: 162–3, 291). Popper and Adorno debated their views at a 1961 meeting of German sociologists.

By that time, the reflective social philosophising of both had been overtaken by the flourishing of empirical, often application-oriented, social research.

In the public realm, the new shift towards policy-oriented social sciences was brought about by reformist discourse coalitions between the younger generation of social scientists and modernisation-oriented politicians aspiring to power. In the US during the 1960s, the reform drive of the Kennedy administration was translated into the Great Society and War on Poverty programmes during the Johnson administration. While these social planning initiatives were soft in the sense of being based on incentives and encouragement rather than on command and restriction, they aimed at a major process of planned social change (Davies 1996; deHaven-Smith 1988; Aaron 1978; van Gunsteren 1976).

Similar discourse coalitions formed in many European countries during the 1960s and 1970s, often also in the context of government changes towards more reform-minded majorities (see ch. 4). In many respects, these coalitions were not unlike those the socialist-leaning scholars and reformist administrators had entered into after the First World War. While the more recent alliances were somewhat tempered by historical experience, they had a much more sustained effect both on the social sciences and on policy-making.

Again, prevailing convictions held that potentially violent strife and conflict, in which one group could gain only at the expense of others, could be transformed into cooperative positive-sum games with the help of social science knowledge (Massé 1965: 18; 1981: 38). In comparison with the earlier effort, this second broad movement for social planning was shaped by the historical experience of totalitarianism, whose recurrence it aimed to avoid by emphasising democratic consensus. This would prevent planning from becoming the enemy of freedom (Oulès 1966). On the other hand, however, the new generation had a markedly higher opinion of advances in social science than the first planning movement. Intellectual progress, especially methodology, was deemed to have allowed a much firmer cognitive grip on social reality. Together with the apparent 'end of ideology', this meant that social-science-based social planning appeared ultimately truly achievable.

Looking back from the early 1980s to the 1960s, a French research administrator, Robert Fraisse, spoke of a pervasive 'optimism with regard to the exhaustive cognitive mastery of society'. He continued:

> This research is led to endow itself with an aura of the all-comprehensive, owing to the functional use which administration wants to make of its results – and without doubt owing also to the optimism which gives responsible administrators the idea of a strong and continuous growth [of knowledge]. One speaks in terms of knowledge gaps, which are now to be closed. In a certain sense, the objective is the exhaustion of the real, as is evidenced in the requests for proposals of the time which underline the relevance of comprehensive inquiries about consumption, income, life-styles; about regional and national economic accounting; about global modeling of public action systems etc. (1981: 372)

This planning optimism reached its zenith when it made the social sciences themselves one of its objects. During the 1970s, the Organisation for Economic Co-operation and Development (OECD) proposed a 'social science policy' in order to optimise its contributions to policy-making. OECD also commissioned country analyses of the state of the social sciences in various countries (France, Norway, Finland, Japan) to detect deficiencies and enhance their efficiency. Some observers spoke of an outright 'planification of the social sciences' (Pollak 1976).

After the planning euphoria

From the mid 1970s onwards, it became increasingly evident that social planning had fallen short of these high expectations. The master example for the crisis of planning was the arrival of unmanageable economic downturns with the simultaneous occurrence of rising inflation and unemployment. This discredited Keynesianism, which had seemed to rule out 'stagflation'. In economics, this experience led to intellectual shifts towards monetarist and 'supply-side' approaches, with a much reduced emphasis on public intervention and a return to market regulation. A similar reorientation also occurred in the other policy- and planning-oriented social sciences. In part as a response to the results of applying social science knowledge to policy practice, attention was directed to such apparently novel phenomena as 'unintended consequences', *effets pervers* and 'implementation problems'. Social reality proved recalcitrant to planned intervention.

Though the precise relation between these two phenomena needs further exploration, the crisis of the policy sciences seems to have been deepened by a turn away from objectivist epistemology and the overemphasis on quantitative methodology in the academic social sciences (Fischer 1990; Dryzek and Torgerson 1993). The 'interpretive turn' or, more broadly, the 'linguistic turn' in the human sciences has had strong, though unequal, effects in the sciences devoted to the study of contemporary society. Emphasis on the linguistic constitution of the social world and on the interpretive openness of social representations brings the social sciences back to a period of epistemological, ontological and methodological reconsideration which shows many parallels to the 'classical era' at the beginning of the twentieth century (see ch. 5).

A century ago, those doubts were temporarily resolved by a faith that the social world was indeterminate and for that reason malleable, allied to the search for an actor powerful enough to transform the social world according to a conscious will. This combination made possible the emergence of the planning-oriented social sciences. Under current conditions, the argument for the indeterminateness, or contingency, of the social world is possibly even more strongly voiced than a century ago. But the belief in the existence of a strong actor appears to be much more decisively shaken. For the time being, the double reorientation in both the planning-oriented and the academic social sciences has entailed the abandonment of the idea of comprehensive social planning. With it, the strong figures of the state as an all-pervasive power centre, and of the intellectual committed to universalist values and to the search for generally valid knowledge, have also almost disappeared from public debate (Lyotard 1984b). If one looks for alternative conceptions that may have replaced these strong views, the only contender seems to be the neoliberal and rationalist belief in the optimisation of human interaction without a conscious planning subject. A version of such thinking, with almost opposite starting assumptions, can be found in theories of autopoietic systems. Over the long run, however, 'weaker' versions of the traditional concepts may emerge, with the state as a 'moderator' and, as Zygmunt Bauman (1987) suggests, the intellectual as an 'interpreter'.

Nevertheless, the current lack of fully convincing sociological representations of society and the absence of societal planning do not entail that cognitive representations of society are less regularly put forward or that planning has been abandoned. On the contrary, business and other organisations depend on strategic planning, for which they commission expertise on an unprecedented scale. The proliferation of market assessments and opinion polling in current politics and commerce attest to the continued vitality of planning. The relative weakening of nation-states and national markets has created this growing need for planning-relevant knowledge. And in the course of such knowledge production, representations of the social world are incessantly produced. However, such plans are less comprehensive and coordinated than the social planning of the 1960s, and they are mostly produced in contexts lacking the commitment to public validation which, despite all criticism and ongoing transformations of those institutions, still characterises universities and academia. It is not the idea of planning that is currently in crisis but the ambition of comprehensive social planning under conditions of public exposure and validation.

4
THE MYTHICAL PROMISE OF SOCIETAL RENEWAL

Social science and reform coalitions

In the post Second World War history of the social sciences in France, Italy and West Germany, a distinct period can be detected in which a policy orientation was (re-) introduced into these disciplines, as briefly discussed in the previous chapter. In this period major research efforts were undertaken, either on specific policy areas or on the politico-administrative processes themselves, with a view to improving policy-making by putting it on a 'scientific' or 'more rational' basis. These processes took place in the 1960s and early 1970s and thus followed previous developments in the USA where the term 'policy sciences' (Lerner and Lasswell 1951) was coined, but they differed significantly from the US experience. The specific nature of the confrontation between the innovative approach and the established national science traditions and the interaction of the emerging policy researchers with actors in different politico-administrative systems had a significant influence on the shape the process took.

The key actors were groups in the political and economic elites who saw the need for an encompassing societal modernisation process, including the introduction of rational planning procedures and the formulation of reform policies which would enable all social groups to participate in economic and societal progress (see Marin 1982: part III, for Austria). Social scientists sometimes joined outright reform coalitions with these groups, shared their basic political convictions, and saw their own task in designing the required political innovations on the basis of social science expertise. In Germany and Italy, the scientists' interlocutors were mainly members of groups in those of the major political parties that had not yet reached power positions; in France social scientists were more oriented to the process of *planification*, which as such took a more long-term perspective on social developments and seemed more open to heeding scientific advice and to initiating social reform. These intense interactions between academics and non-academics, however, proved to be of a short-term nature. Recognising political and scientific deficiencies in their approach to a science–politics interaction, researchers turned away from these coalitions in a learning process which was speeded up by social developments. Some then started to search for new social actors to engage in research-based political action.

As in the case of university–industry relations analysed by Stuart Blume (1987: 34), the emergence of a policy orientation in the social sciences can be characterised as 'the construction of a research programme in relation to a particular sort of social network, which consciously embodies the goals, needs, interests or aspirations of actors within this network'. The following analysis is devoted to such coalitions between social scientists and political actors, 'common social projects' in Blume's terms, and to their demise and the related emergence of new coalitions and research programmes with different political orientations. As an analysis of the social sciences it thus deals with struggles over the production and imposition of legitimate representations of the social world, and will have to pay particular attention to political actors and their positions within the different societal contexts (Fridjonsdottir 1987; 1991). The importance of the political context will already become clear from a short description of the situation of the social sciences before the policy orientation emerged.

The social sciences in an early phase of institutionalisation

The processes under analysis here, through which a policy orientation emerged in the scientific fields of sociology in France and Italy and political science in West Germany, took place mainly between the late 1950s and the early 1970s. In the 1950s the social sciences in these three countries were characterised by a low degree of academic institutionalisation, by strong links to philosophy and to normative thinking and by lively debates about the consequences to be drawn from the first experiences with modern, allegedly methodologically rigorous empirical research techniques (see chs 1 and 2).

In France, sociology formally received early recognition as an academic subject when Emile Durkheim became the first regular professor in social science at the philosophy faculty of Bordeaux University in 1896, and more significantly when in 1913 the chair at the Sorbonne to which he had moved was renamed 'education science and sociology', thus recognising the notion of sociology. This success in terms of institutionalisation, however, must be ascribed mainly to Durkheim's personal endeavours. He had purposefully worked to institutionally secure his scientific approach (Geiger 1981; Clark 1973). Although his school remained moderately influential in different fields in the inter-war period, no further steps towards full institutionalisation could be made. In the mid 1950s in the whole of France there were only four university chairs in sociology plus three chairs in ethnology (Drouard 1982: 66–7). The post-war debate over the central importance of the social sciences in rebuilding French society had raised high expectations, which, however, materialised only to a small extent. The most important organ-isational innovations were the creation of the Centre for Sociological Studies (*Centre d'études sociologiques*, CES) in the National Centre for Scientific Research (*Centre national de la recherche scientifique*, CNRS) and of the Sixth Section of the School for Advanced Studies (*Ecole pratique des hautes études*, EPHE, later the *Ecole des hautes études en sciences sociales*, EHESS), which were soon to become the most important social science centres in France (Pollak 1978: 30). These academic institutions remained outside the universities, which is a typical feature of the French research system but was also significant for the low academic reputation of the discipline. A decisive change resulted only much later from the full recognition of sociology as a university subject by the introduction of a specific full degree, the *licence*, in 1958.

The situation in Italy before the 1950s was even less impressive. Neither the intense empirical research of early positivist sociologists, such as Enrico Ferri or Cesare Lombroso, nor the more theoretically oriented works of Roberto Michels, Gaetano Mosca and Vilfredo Pareto, had any lasting impact on the academic organisation of the social sciences. Before the Second World War there was no university base for social science research except for some teaching in social philosophy and some social psychological research at the Catholic University of Milan (*Università Cattolica del Sacro Cuore di Milano*) – if we exclude the Statistical Institute under the directorship of Gini and the faculties of political science created at a number of universities during the fascist regime for the purpose of training future diplomats and high-level administrators to deal with social facts on the basis of an elitist ideology (Lentini 1974; Leonardi 1967; Mieli 1983: 66–7). In the early 1950s there was just one university chair in sociology in Italy, in Florence, and not until the mid 1960s was sociology – after long disputes – fully recognised as a university subject leading to a separate degree.

The academic tradition of sociology is much stronger in Germany, with the early inquiries of the *Verein für Socialpolitik* around the turn of the century, the foundation of the German Sociological Society (*Deutsche Gesellschaft für Soziologie*) before the First World War, the important research institutes in Cologne and Frankfurt during the Weimar period, and about a dozen chairs in sociology by 1932 and again by 1955 after the re-establishment of the discipline (Lepsius 1979: 33; Kern 1982). Political science had a predecessor in the cameral and state sciences which were designed to fulfil analytical functions for the absolutist state. But the rise of liberal ideology and industrial capitalism caused this quasi-interdisciplinary approach to decay as political aspects lost their importance in favour of legal ones.

After the Second World War, West German political scientists were influenced by the double experience of witnessing the breakdown of parliamentary democracy and the establishment of a dictatorial regime, on the one hand, and, on the other, by witnessing in American exile the capacity of a different political system to deal with enormous economic, social and military problems without abandoning its institutional order. Consequently, priority was placed on the study of institutional systems of government, in particular Western ones, with special regard to the stability of formal democracy and with an explicitly normative orientation in this direction. In addition, the study of the history of political thought was considered a precondition to a debate on democratic values. Philosophical reflection on political developments was seen as the specific task of the discipline, one which would distinguish it from the other social sciences and from law and would turn it into a somewhat superior subject (Kastendiek 1977: 185ff).

A high degree of political involvement and strong philosophical orientations were also characteristic of French sociology after 1945, but in a very different fashion. Because of its historical links with the philosophy faculties, sociology in France had a permanent point of reference in the ongoing philosophical discourse. From this perspective, the orientations of the intellectually dominant philosopher-sociologists of the immediate post-war period, such as Raymond Aron, Maurice Merleau-Ponty or Jean-Paul Sartre, can be regarded as a revolt against the routinised and institutionalised sociological approach of the Durkheim school (on the origins of this attitude during the 1930s see Heilbron 1985). Historicity, class consciousness and commitment (the consecrated words of the philosophical semantics of the time, to use a phrase of Pierre Bourdieu and Jean-Claude Passeron) could not easily be linked either to the Durkheimian tradition of thought or to modern research techniques. In this intellectual climate, sociology proper had little chance of attracting the most enterprising minds; this attitude 'thereby helped to hold back the development of the human sciences and especially the social sciences' (Bourdieu and Passeron 1967: 179). The attitude of the *intellectuel engagé*, which doubtlessly had been furthered by the experience of the Resistance, anchored the intellectual debate firmly in the political environment of the time and thus in some sense prepared the ground for a more practical orientation of the social sciences than was the case during the inter-war period. Given the presence of a strong communist party as the major force of opposition in society, intellectuals were under a virtual obligation to clarify their position towards Marxism and communist politics.

In this latter respect, the intellectual atmosphere in post-war Italy resembled the French one. Many intellectuals were attracted to a strong communist opposition, which was soon almost totally excluded from political power and from the process of societal restoration. In this environment, the rejection of modern sociological approaches was so strong that the word 'sociology' was used with the pejorative connotation of an American imperialist instrument to secure bourgeois domination. This attitude was in accord with the still culturally dominant idealistic philosophy mainly represented by Benedetto Croce, whose influence had even increased by virtue of his anti-fascism. Throughout his life, Croce had opposed empirical social science research as unable to 'understand' society, which he believed was possible only through historical-philosophical intuition (Ferrarotti 1981: 149ff; Pinto 1980: 234ff). Sociology gained its first foothold in post-war society in intellectual environments which were both non-Marxist and anti-idealistic: groups in and around the Catholic University of Milan and in the modern industrial city of Turin.

It was mainly in Turin that the first generation of sociologists found an opportunity to do empirical research supported and financed by industrialists such as Olivetti. Industrial work organisation – and to a certain extent also urban and regional planning – became the early thematic focus of sociological research related to topics such as modernisation, rationalisation and technological progress, and their consequences for societal development. Similarly, French sociologists at about the same time began to engage in empirical research on demand and with the support of non-academic actors. The research in industrial sociology pursued by Georges Friedmann, Alain Touraine and others, although partly based at CES and EPHE, was financed by sources such as the European Productivity Agency or the European Coal and Steel Community, and was encouraged and made possible by industrial companies such as the Régie Renault (Durand 1980: 5; Drouard 1983: 89–90, 126ff). In the same period, Jean Stoetzel, who was strongly influenced by Paul F. Lazarsfeld, tried to spread the use of quantitative empirical methods at CES and in French sociology in general (Stoetzel 1956). In Germany as well, the debate over the relevance and necessity of sophisticated modern methods and, following this, of the relation between theory and empirical facts, was led primarily by sociologists who had more experience in this area than political scientists. Normative attitudes and the emphasis placed on the study of ideal-type workings of institutional systems of governments, rather than the empirical distribution of power and influence, made the latter a marginal issue in political science until the 1960s.

In spite of all the differences in the national situations of these social sciences in the 1950s, there emerges a common picture of these disciplines as hardly possessing secure legitimate roots in academic institutions; as strongly linked to philosophical discourse, at least partly as a result of the lack of consensus on basic conceptual matters; as disputing imported methodologies with which they were as yet unable to cope; and as firmly tied to developments in the political environment as a point of reference for their normative intellectual self-image.

Social transformations

By the end of the 1950s the initial room for economic expansion – which had resulted from reconstruction needs, the influx of labour and changed consumption patterns – had been filled in the three countries. Comparatively high rates of employment had been reached; internal migration or immigration increased, which led to social tensions; inflation rates rose rapidly; and growth rates, though still high, showed a tendency to decline. The response to these signs of crisis in the political and economic system was to strengthen those forces which sought to modernise both the economy and the politico-administrative apparatus, which should then become capable of supporting economic restructuring as well as the planning and implementing of reform projects to prevent or mitigate social tensions.

One of the early topics of this emerging modernisation debate was the need for a science and technology policy. Public funds for research, which had traditionally been considered a consumption expenditure, were now seen increasingly as a national investment, the returns from which would come from improved international economic competitiveness based on technological progress and increased productivity. The creation of science policy institutions, such as ministries, research councils and commissions, dates from the mid and late 1950s in all three countries (Brickman and Rip 1979 for a Dutch–French comparison). The social sciences, however, were rarely the subject of science policy debates in these early years. A similar debate concerned the need to improve and expand the educational system in order to increase the qualifications of the workforce. However, this issue had a second and equally important political focus in the discussion over social reform and the equality of educational opportunities.

This 'reform mood', common to all three countries in these years, found different expressions in changes in the political majorities. However, in all three cases, reform policies were based on the concept of sustained economic growth, harmonised and regulated by government intervention and linked to a set of social reforms through which the increase in welfare would be more evenly distributed in society and the external costs of growth would be diminished. The government apparatus had to be adapted to this new and more demanding style of policy-making. Such measures as ministerial reorganisation, the introduction of improved techniques for monitoring administrative activities and efficiency control, and the creation of new institutions were designed to allow for purposeful and effective intervention into economic and social developments (for more detailed analyses see for example Lapalombara 1966; Cohen 1969; Altvater et al. 1979; Hayward and Watson 1975).

In the following section the development of the social sciences will be sketched against this background of a pronounced 'reform mood' in the political system. The interactions between social scientists and actors in the political system were not part of a 'top down' social science policy: this did not yet exist. Moreover, although the non-scientific actors involved in these interactions can doubtless be considered part of a larger societal elite, most of them were in political opposition and strong advocates of change.

The policy-oriented social sciences: the rush to relevance

Although remaining almost completely outside the academic institutional framework, Italian sociology since the 1950s had developed a strong social position – Pinto (1981: 676) even spoke of 'cultural centrality' – closely linked with the emerging so-called centre-left politics, the entry of the Socialists into government, which was previously dominated by the Christian Democrats. In theoretical terms, the American functionalist approach provided a comprehensive and coherent framework under which social phenomena could be subsumed, and it allowed the steering capacity of specific political actors to be made the central point of reference in theoretical reasoning. It can be plausibly argued that the absolute reliance on private funding sources with specific policy interests, namely on private and public enterprises, was crucial in establishing the predominance of the functionalist approach in Italian sociology which was stronger and imported more easily than in other European countries (Rossetti 1982: 284–5).

Modernisation was the thematic and conceptual focus of almost all sociological research. The basis of the modernisation process was seen in technological innovation; the major task of sociology was to analyse the impact of technological change on work organisation and productivity, on social mobility and the class structure, on urban and regional developments and, more generally, to focus on the possibility of harmonising and controlling the social processes set in motion by technological development.

One year before the long-awaited centre-left coalition would shape politics at the national level, in 1961, the Italian Association of the Social Sciences chose as the topic for their meeting in Ancona a problem of central concern to most sociologists seeking to become socially relevant: 'Sociologists and the centres of power'. The main thrust of the Ancona debates can be summarised by saying that most of the social scientists felt that their field had now been consolidated; they possessed the analytical tools to interpret social developments; and they were at the point where they wanted to translate their findings into practice (Treves 1962).

In fact, the period of centre-left dominance brought sociologists increased importance in defining reform policies. In disciplinary terms, these developments even increased the dependence of sociology on a policy model, since academic institutionalisation proved to be a much slower process, beginning in 1962 with the establishment of the Institute for Advanced Studies in Sociology at the University of Trento (a move which was also politically motivated), but bringing full recognition of the subject only in 1968.

Italian sociology outside academia was thus influenced by a politico-scientific constellation to such an extent that one may speak of the absolute predominance of a functionalist approach in scientific terms, and one oriented toward modernisation and reform in political terms. By contrast, in French sociology, with its modest but more secure institutional basis, changes in the socio-economic environment led to divergent approaches in the sociological community rather than a complete and unanimous orientation towards reformist policy-making. This latter position was clearly represented by Michel Crozier (1964), who explained his view in terms of a profound change in the role of the intellectuals from the immediate post-war period to the early 1960s. Following Raymond Aron's version of the 'end of ideology' theorem, which emphasises steady economic growth, internal stability and cumulative progress in the sciences and in technology as factors allowing for a new form of rationality and for knowledge eliminating the need for force, Crozier argued that intellectuals had to move closer to action, and their thought needed to become much more pertinent and applicable in a direct way. In political and intellectual developments beginning with the late Fourth Republic government of Mendès-France, he traced the emergence of a new elite which brought the whole sphere of political and social action and the strategy of reform into the intellectual domain. For the social sciences, this would lead to increasing the influence of those groups who 'form a sort of link . . . between the intellectual tradition seeking to reform itself and the world of action which is trying to renew itself through a process of more scientific reasoning' (1964: 537).

Seeing himself as a representative of this new type of social scientist, Michel Crozier had already contributed to this approach by elaborating an analytical model for the study of bureaucracies. His book on 'the bureaucratic phenomenon' (Crozier 1963) generated a French school in the sociology of organisations at the *Centre de sociologie des organisations*, which was set up in 1966 under Crozier's directorship and has been innovative in opening up private and public administrations to empirical research. Reluctant to give policy advice in this book, Crozier in his later publications came closer to the new role of the intellectual as he conceived it, and offered more direct policy recommendations. During the post-1968 government he took up the role of informal policy adviser to Prime Minister Chaban-Delmas.

Basically sharing Crozier's view on the desirable future position of sociologists as policy intellectuals, Raymond Boudon voiced a different perspective on a strategy for the development of the social sciences. In his opinion, the way to achieve both a greater utility of sociology for societal practice and greater scientificity lay in methodological advances and, concomitantly, in the extension of the research infrastructure which this would necessitate. In spite of profound differences, Crozier and Boudon can be grouped together with some other sociologists under the heading of a politics–science interaction model in which the role of the social sciences is to provide knowledge for the socio-technical steering of societal development by government and administration.

In contrast, Alain Touraine's sociological approach, although it also sought to break with traditional philosophical discourse and to be more empirical, tried to maintain a greater distance from politics. Touraine acknowledged the legitimacy of the call for societal relevance and recognised the pressures to produce knowledge instrumental to political and administrative needs. But his reaction was a refusal to make the analysis of the functioning of social systems his primary research objective. Instead, his 'sociology of action' analysed the commitment and engage-ment of individuals and collective actors, by which they create situations and establish meanings (Touraine 1965). Consequently, he saw the possible application or utility of sociological knowledge not necessarily and not primarily in the politico-administrative system, but in terms of other social actors, such as social movements. He was later to elaborate this approach in greater detail.

A third group of sociologists around Pierre Bourdieu was not centrally concerned with the potential practical use of their sociology. Linking up with the Durkheimian tradition and to structural analyses of society, their work on the educational system and on intellectual milieus tried to relate micro-level analysis to macro-sociologically conceived developments. Refusing a 'voluntarist orientation towards knowledge application' (Michael Pollak), their analysis of the reproduction of social structures in and through the educational system (Bourdieu and Passeron 1970) has in fact played a part in the gradual disillusionment with the possibility of social reform through educational policy.

Compared with developments in Italy, a rather similar socio-economic environment in France did not lead to an identical reaction among sociologists. Strong incentives to produce politico-administratively relevant knowledge accompanied the emergence of policy-oriented sociological approaches, but at the same time brought about different 'non-governmental' reorientations in French sociology. Comparable processes took place in the West German political science 'community', although along different lines of debate.

A debate on the need to reform the governmental apparatus began in West Germany in the early 1960s, when the political system was increasingly considered as malfunctioning, in particular with regard to harmonising economic and social development. As earlier in France and Italy, this debate centred on the issue of modernisation understood in terms of adjustment to world-wide technological and economic change. Unlike in the other countries, however, the German debate concentrated on the issue of restructuring the politico-administrative system and did not really widen to include societal modernisation in general. This political focus may have been decisive for the turn toward political science instead of sociology to deal with this problem.

Around 1965 the issue of political reform began to be discussed in the social sciences. In the following years a number of different programmatic positions emerged alongside the traditional administrative/juridical one, which proved unable to encompass the empirical analysis of policy-making. In addition to the sociological approach of Niklas Luhmann and an attempt to widen the scope of the traditional administrative sciences (e.g. W. Thieme and F. Morstein Marx), at least three different conceptions emerged within the framework of political science (Ellwein 1982; Hirsch and Leibfried 1971: 236ff).

Very much in the tradition of normative political philosophy, Wilhelm Hennis sketched the task of a *Regierungslehre* (government science) as the study of 'the manner in which the steering, governance and co-ordination of a policy can be effected given the challenges to the modern state' (1965: 24). In a similar way, but more willing to deal with the concrete policy issues of the time, Thomas Ellwein argued for studying the processes of political decision-making and their transformation into policy programmes. Third, a rudimentary alternative research programme was emerging as a reaction to the government-centred approach. At its core was the analysis of the entire political process, including the way in which changes in the economic system prestructure and define the government's capacity to act in an anticipatory way (Hirsch 1968; Grauhan 1970: 591).

The breakthrough from this programmatic debate to a broad range of empirical research projects occurred at the end of the 1960s and was made possible by the Volkswagen Foundation, a major social research funding institution, and by a whole set of research contracts issued by the newly formed project group on governmental and administrative reform and mainly given to the 'reform university' in Constance.

This emerging policy orientation is best exemplified by the work of Fritz W. Scharpf. His understanding of administration in terms of political actors, who thus need to be studied within the framework of political science, is sketched in a paper published in 1971 in which he explicitly refers to the advancing policy research in the USA and advocates this approach as a promising new direction in political science (Scharpf 1973: 34). His publication on the 'organisation of planning' (Mayntz and Scharpf 1973) collects a number of papers written on political demand for the reform of the federal politico-administrative apparatus, and can be considered the centrepiece of the early phase of policy-oriented research in Germany. The emphasis of the authors on intra-administrative organisational factors provoked the criticism of a number of researchers who considered themselves politically to the 'left' of social democratic reformism, and who argued that Scharpf and others failed to recognise the decisive importance of external, mainly economic factors which limited the effectiveness of governmental reform policies and the scope of reformism itself. From this position emerged a 'critical' approach which agreed on the need for empirical studies of policy processes. One strand of this approach sought to integrate the viewpoint of the citizens concerned, while the other, a much stronger neo-Marxist current in political science, concentrated on determining the extent and manner in which external constraints limit the autonomy of the political sphere (Holloway and Picciotto 1978; Fach 1982).

Political innovativeness as a topic

Following that brief sketch of the scientific positions which developed during the 1960s, the task of this section will be to trace the politico-scientific interactions which lay behind the successful appearance of new research programmes. The changes which occurred during, broadly speaking, the 1950s and the 1960s and which amounted to the emergence of a policy orientation were conceptually least significant in Italian sociology. With no real change in theoretical and political assumptions, the shift from industrial relations to policy issues is mainly to be explained by a growing debate in this period on the need for public intervention into various policy fields. To understand why political influence could reorient the entire scientific discipline so strongly, one has to remember the low degree of academic institutionalisation and recognition. 'Sociologists constitute a reference group of yet low relevance and cohesion, and thus Italian sociologists address themselves only in part to a public of scientific colleagues, but value much more highly the reference group formed by the larger cultural environment' (Martinotti 1972: 143–4).

Around 1960 a striking convergence of interests emerged between social researchers and policy-makers in the 'cultural environment' of the North, especially in Milan and Turin. Left-Catholic, socialist and modernisation-oriented lay groups transcended party boundaries on the basis of the common idea of politically regulated and planned social change. Social scientists offered their support as scientific experts able to analyse social problem constellations and to indicate the necessary political interventions: 'In these years, sociology identified completely with the social project of changing Italian society' (Martinotti 1984: 3). Political and intellectual elites from the North joined forces to achieve this project. A number of initiatives flourished in the late 1950s providing contacts between people from different professional groupings and political orientations. The cultural and political association *Il Mulino* in Bologna was one of the most important of these initiatives, starting mainly as the editorial committee of a journal and later on expanding to include one of the most important social science publishing houses and a research centre. Another one was the *Centro nazionale della prevenzione e difesa sociale* (CNPDS) in Milan which gave birth to the most important sociological research institute of the 1960s, the *Istituto Lombardo per gli Studi Economici e Sociali* (ILSES). The CNPDS was instrumental in founding the Italian Association for the Social Sciences in 1958 and in organising and financing its first conference. In 1960, debates at CNPDS led to the idea of setting up a research centre after a congress on the impact of technological progress on society. Informal talks in Milan with leaders of the new centre-left coalition sufficed, and ILSES developed into the place where almost all sociologists of the first and second post-war generations worked and which gave an enormous impetus to sociological research in Italy. To grasp fully the close relation between science and politics, it is useful to quote Alessandro Pizzorno, one of the founding fathers, describing the project in retrospect: 'It was a study centre of the anticipated centre-left government, where political forces met with a group of independent scholars. The ILSES was to be the symbol of a new politics which should be based on analyses and research' (quoted after Giacomoni 1970: 105). This concept was transferred to the national level after 1962, when the centre-left alliance was formed in Rome and again brought about a number of ambitious political reform initiatives and the setting up of policy-oriented research institutions.

In her analysis of the relation of sociology and politics in Italy, Diana Pinto asserts that the interest in modernisation was translated in this period into a recourse to American political, economic and social models, and as such, into an interest in American social science. This science model was a precondition for enabling sociology to become the new *lingua franca* of the centre-left, capable of bridging the historical and cultural gaps which separate the Christian Democratic tradition from that of lay socialism. Ahistorical and international in scope, the social sciences smooth out any major conflict between the two political traditions, primarily by treating Italy's problems as the product of qualitatively new social and economic transformations, for which past solutions (and therefore conflicts) would be of little use (Pinto 1981: 20). More sceptically, Franco Ferrarotti (1966: 29) saw as one of the insidious dangers for Italian sociology in the mid 1960s its being considered as a '*deus ex machina* for evidently complex social problems'.

Much of this analysis would also hold for Michel Crozier's political and sociological ambitions. His article on 'the cultural revolution', cited above, can be read as an attempt to present his conceptions of the political advances required in French society and the role of the intellectuals engaged in these processes. From a different standpoint Lucien Goldmann (1966: 6) wrote: 'Future historians will probably identify the years 1955 to 1960 as the sociological turning point in France between crisis capitalism and organised capitalism, accompanied by a transition from philosophical, historical and humanistic sociology to the ahistorical socio-logical thinking of today.' But in France it proved much more difficult to get this position accepted in and against a much stronger and more self-conscious intellectual life. Thus, sociologists intending to adopt the prescribed new role of the intellectual had to look outside academia for support and acceptance.

Personal contacts were vital, and the main reference group was high-level administrators and managers, in both the public and the private sectors. As in the Italian case, a major catalytic influence can be traced to the private associations which organised around journals or simply as meeting places such as the *Club Jean Moulin*, the *Association d'études pour l'expansion de la recherche scientifique*, or the journals *Esprit* and *Prospective*. Unlike in Italy, these groups could not yet refer to a specific emerging political project, but in a less clearly defined way they assembled members of the political, economic and intellectual elites (Drouard 1983: 68; Bourdieu and Passeron 1967: 187; Pollak 1978: 54).

Looking back, Jacques Lautman has recently recalled the importance of the 'personal connections which played a capital role in the formation of the spirit of state patronage' (in Drouard 1983: 78) for social science around the Fourth Plan. He notes that Alain Touraine maintained close relations with Claude Gruson, the head of the statistical institute INSEE between 1962 and 1967. In fact, Gruson, who argued in 1964 for the integration of sociological expertise into the planning process – though on a position subordinate to economics (Gruson 1964) – seems to have offered Touraine the post of director of a new sociological section to be created at the INSEE, but these plans did not materialise due to a lack of financing (Gruson in Drouard 1983: 147). Michel Crozier's research profited from the patronage of Jean Ripert, at that time a high functionary in the Planning Commissariat, and was conceptually oriented strongly towards the sociological analysis of the planning process (Crozier 1965). Touraine himself later regarded the constellations around the colloquium at Caen in 1956, one of the major science policy initiatives of the Mendès-France government, as a confused coalition of all modernisation-oriented elements. 'This coalition of the Mendès-France type for a number of years constituted the universe in which the social sciences developed' (Touraine in Drouard 1983: 180). Its strength even increased with the return to power of de Gaulle and the reformism which then set in; after a great number of more or less informal meetings, one major event in this phase of intense interaction between social scientists and modernisation-oriented administrators was the 1965 congress of the French Sociological Society, in which a group of high-level bureaucrats participated, among them Gruson, P. Massé, the director of the Planning Commission, and R. Grégoire, who was active in economic policy-making.

The orientation and behaviour of individual social scientists must be seen against the background of a changing socio-economic and political situation in which a strong demand for certain types of social knowledge exercised a major influence on the social sciences. But they have to be understood also as individual strategies to achieve or secure a reputation in a scientific field which was under-going rapid transformations. The importance of the traditional Parisian intellectual community diminished, and political recognition gained in significance. This development has been described as the emergence of a second pole of reference for social scientists, the pole of power as opposed to the intellectual pole (Pollak 1975: 36).

The social processes which lay behind the emergence of a policy orientation in German political science seem to suggest that here the pole of power predominantly structured the field in which different scientific approaches competed (see Hirsch and Leibfried 1971). Without doubt, the launching of the initial research projects and the opening up of the administrative apparatus towards empirical research were closely linked with the political intentions of the Social Democrats who became a minority partner in government coalitions in 1966 and the majority partner in 1969. A key figure in this process seems to have been Horst Ehmke, himself a professor of law, state secretary in the Ministry of Legal Affairs, and minister in the Chancellor's Office after Willy Brandt, a close friend of his, became Chancellor. Ehmke was among the programmatic thinkers of the SPD, who wanted to develop long-term perspectives for Social Democratic government, and who saw a primary task in restructuring the politico-administrative apparatus to increase rationality and efficiency in political processes. His preparatory work led, after some political compromises, to the formation of a reform cabinet which soon created the Project Group on Governmental and Administrative Reforms, still under the Great Coalition government in 1969 (Schatz 1973: 29ff).

The inter-ministerial group, together with the Department of Planning established in the Chancellor's Office by the subsequent Social Democratic govern-ment, drew a great many social scientists into the policy process as advisers. In a second stage, and largely due to this advice, a demand was voiced for social science analyses to be pursued in the ministries. Many of these research tasks were contracted out to the newly formed 'group for comparative administration research' at the University of Constance. Given the political interest, it is not surprising that the research group followed the 'government-centred' approach closely, dealing with issues such as internal control in planning administration, medium-term budgetary planning, or reform of the ministerial organisation. However, this was only one step towards changing the political science agenda. In 1969, similarly influenced by the political debate on reform needs, the Volkswagen Foundation raised the issue of funding concentrated research efforts on public administration. After long discussions about the appropriate conceptual framework, a research committee was created to review funding applications. This group included representatives of the traditional administrative sciences, the reformist political scientists, and the emerging neo-Marxist current. In this way, a funding source came to exist whose decisions were not dominated by purely political criteria (Friedberg and Gremion 1974: 8ff). Both the reformist proponents of an 'active policy-making' (R. Mayntz and F.W. Scharpf) and the neo-Marxists presented their research at meetings of the political science association. Given the state of the discipline, which was not homogeneous, no integrative effects could be expected. Rather than the search for a common research programme or paradigm, a polarisation of the discipline occurred.

The emergence of scientific currents critical of the policy orientation which for some years either was or appeared to be dominant is a common feature in the social sciences of the three countries analysed here. Guido Martinotti suggests for the Italian case (and with some qualifications this holds also for France and West Germany) that the social scientists were for some time guided by a mythical figure, the 'innovative policy-maker' (Martinotti 1972: 146). A subsequent disillusionment and the occurrence of social revolt against the policy model they had advocated led to a reorientation not only of political conceptions but also of scientific approaches.

Political crisis and social revolt: social scientists in search of a new coalition

In the changed political environment of the late 1960s and early 1970s a process of rethinking conceptual approaches started or accelerated among social scientists. The revolts of 1968–9, the abandonment of economic planning in Italy, dis-illusionment about the capacity to steer economic and social developments in France, and emerging financial and political restrictions on the reformist capacity of government in West Germany, all helped to destroy the political and 'epistemological optimism' and brought about or strengthened less directly policy-centred conceptualisations. In Italy, the sociologists had begun to withdraw from the modernisation project in the early 1960s, but this movement became generalised at the end of the decade with increased working-class militancy, the student rebellion, and the observation of political impotence in the face of an aggravation of social problems. Of great significance was the concept of action research, *conricerca*, as developed by the *Quaderni Rossi* group. *Quaderni Rossi* was a leftist political group organised around a journal which criticised the traditional workers' organisations for their integration in the capitalist system and their class collaboration. In the first half of the 1960s – six issues of the journal appeared between 1961 and 1967 – the concepts developed by this group had considerable influence on strategic debates in the reviving workers' struggles. Central to these discussions was the notion of autonomy, which indicated not only a dissociation from the established organisations for the representation of workers' interests, but also a rejection of the entire capitalist state, society and way of life, and an attempt to organise self-determined spheres of work and life.

The concept of *conricerca* was considered by *Quaderni Rossi*, which consisted mainly of intellectuals, as an essential instrument to establish contact with workers on the shop-floor and to intervene in industrial relations. The group was aware of the American origins of the idea of action research, but intended to redefine it politically (de Palma et al. 1965). Drawing on Marx's workers' inquiry worked out in 1880, the aim was to use such sociological techniques for a number of purposes. First, the responses would allow an assessment of the development of capitalist work organisation and thus help to refine the theoretical analysis of the capitalist system. Second, it would make the workers aware of the exploitative conditions under which they were living and working, and would initiate or advance their reflections about counter-strategies. Third, it would establish or improve contacts between revolutionary groups and the workers (Lanzardo 1965). The actual research pursued by members of *Quaderni Rossi* hardly reached the high theoretical and methodological levels which were sought; but these reflections were important in preparing the ground for a reorientation in the sociologists' work concerning both the users of research findings and theoretical developments. In a cultural environment where in particular the (communist) left was suspicious of modern sociology as an instrument of class domination, this approach reconciled Marxism and sociology by defining Marxism as sociology: 'Marxism . . . originates as sociology, what is "Capital", as a critique of political economy, if not sociology? . . . In my view . . . sociology is not a bourgeois science . . . we can use and criticise sociology in just the same way as Marx did with classical political economy' (Panzieri 1964).

Among the first generation of Italian sociologists, who were established professionally in the early 1960s, the impact of the rising political and social tensions can best be exemplified by the work of Franco Ferrarotti. Acting as a sort of spokesman for Italian sociology, he proclaimed as early as 1966: 'It is necessary to advance from sociology as a palliative to sociology as a means of participation' (1966: 31). In the early 1970s, a programmatic essay on 'the alternative sociology' summarised his critique of sociology, and he published the findings of a study of the victims of modernisation in the shantytowns around Rome (Ferrarotti 1972; 1971). An organised expression of irritation and the desire for a new conceptual orientation among sociologists was the 1971 conference on 'Sociological research and the role of the sociologist' in Turin, which focused exclusively on attempts to clarify past errors, assess the development of the discipline in Italy and abroad, and define a new role for the profession in society (Rossi 1972).

The problem of an adequate interpretation of the notion of 'society' now emerged as a central conceptual issue. Society in the early 1960s had been seen in a very restricted sense as a 'force to be moulded and regulated by planners and technicians from above' (Pinto 1981: 680; also Rossetti 1982), whereas through the revolt it had come to constitute itself as an actor in its own right. Similarly, at the Second Congress of the French Sociological Society in 1969, Robert Castel argued that the methodologies adopted in sociology had strengthened the importance of empirical statements, of formal schemes of organisation, and of superficial equilibria, and had tended to misconceive the social significance of change and of social conflicts. This was thought to have led to similar concepts of political action now reduced to the management of social order and the manipulation of subjects to adapt them to this order. Alain Touraine summarised the significance of the social crisis for sociology: 'The intellectual problem which is posed to the sociologist is the political problem which is posed to society; and the political awakening of society . . . or at least the calling into question of its orientations and its forms of organisation allow the sociologist to rediscover the unity of the object he studies and thus of his own approach' (quoted after Scartezzini 1972: 257; also Touraine 1969). In his own work since 1968 Touraine has continuously tried to draw conclusions from this diagnosis.

The approach which he had set out in *La sociologie d'action* in 1965, seeing social actors as transforming society by creating instead of merely responding to situations, is further developed by his turning to social movements as the principal agents of history. In this analysis of the French May revolt (Touraine 1968) he not only chooses to study different social phenomena but links them to a concept of sociological intervention. The interventionist sociologist, as an analyst in interaction with social actors, seeks to stimulate the auto-analysis of groups acting in social movements. This auto-analysis, it is assumed, enables the actors to give meaning to the confrontation and their position in it, and thus contributes to advancing the movement as a whole.

Politically motivated action research was also a topic in German sociological debates in the wake of the student revolt. Compared with Italy and France, it was, however, seen less as a new and alternative political and scientific approach than as a critical reorientation, complementing and adjusting existing research programmes and reform strategies, which were still being pursued by the social-liberal government at that time (Fuchs 1970–1; Haag et al. 1972; Horn 1979; Kern 1982: 261–72). In the field of political science, which is traditionally focused on institutional analysis, the latently counter-institutional approach of action research had no influence. The politicisation of the research environment strengthened the 'leftist' position in political science, but very few studies tried to advocate participatory approach. Most research efforts were meant to counter the 'policy-oriented' researchers on the system level by developing the concept of systemic limits to state action in capitalist society based on a reconstruction of the Marxian critique of political economy. In its extreme versions, this neo-Marxist current virtually denied intra-organisational factors in the politico-administrative system all relevance for the outcome of (reformist) policy-making. By contrast, the proponents of 'active policy-making' laid almost exclusive emphasis on the study of these intra-organisational factors, thus, at least by implication, placing a high value on their importance. This dispute can partly be described in terms of a too restrictive conceptualisation of the political system, and especially of the notion of 'policy', which had been stripped of its historical and societal context. As with the influence of functionalism on Italian and parts of French sociology, this approach in German political science was shaped by the American understanding of policies as institutionally discrete and temporally exactly defined actions pursued by an independent political system. This concept easily lent itself to the support of voluntarist reformism. During the 1970s, the experience of increasing difficulties and the partial withdrawal from reformist policy-making on the one hand, and the exhaustion of increasingly barren attempts to determine purely theoretically the restricted nature of the state's autonomy under capitalist conditions on the other, led to a convergence of both approaches on the field of an empirical and theoretically more open study of policy processes.

After these periods of high engagement and dispute, intra-scientific discussions became less conflictive in all three countries. This may be in large part due to the fact that such intense alliances involving the merging of political and scientific goals no longer attract large groups of social scientists. But that the question of how to develop the interaction of social science and politics remained on the agenda can be seen for example from the debates at a round table of the German Political Science Association on the topic of 'policy studies and traditional political science'. At its centre was the fear of a fragmentation of the discipline due to the rising political demand for specialised analyses in different policy fields (Hartwich 1985). Similarly, at the National Colloquium in January 1982, which was to inaugurate a new and better era in science policy after the coming to power of a socialist-led government in France, a strong resistance on the part of the social scientists could be observed, rooted in their memory of the tendency towards subordination to political interests in the 1960s and 1970s.

Conclusions for a political sociology of the social sciences

This chapter has described and analysed the emergence of an intense collaboration between social scientists and political actors, a reform coalition, its demise, and the search for a new coalition, a new definition of social relevance on the part of social scientists. The term 'reform coalition' in this context has first been used by Wollmann (1984: 44; and 'discourse coalition' by Wittrock and Wagner 1987). The much nicer term 'honeymoon' was employed by Guido Martinotti in an interview with me, and I rediscovered it in Fridjonsdottir (1987). The advantage (or disadvantage) of the latter is that it may be considered to contain the implicit assumption of an early end.

Coalitions are joined for certain goals. In very broad terms, the aim of the reform coalitions discussed here, their 'common social project' (Blume 1987), can be described as modernisation and social reform (Beck and Bonß 1984), while the goal of the action research projects which followed was support for the victims of capitalist modernisation and the construction of a societal alternative. The following remarks explore some of the implications of these processes in terms of the interaction between scientists and non-scientific groups.

The social demand for knowledge, and in the case of the social sciences, also for interpretations of social reality which are adequate and necessary for some actors' interests, can be considered as a general condition for such forms of collaboration. Since the end of the Second World War, the 'mythical promise of social renewal through the social sciences' (Lentini 1974: 21) has been one of the most important motives for becoming a social scientist. This promise was not only unfulfilled by 1960, but became even more urgent, as the political restoration had left many social questions unanswered. The pressure on the social sciences to become societally relevant stemmed from a larger socio-political environment and certainly was internalised by many social scientists. Their identification with the political project thus went far beyond the mere acceptance of a social task, and can only be explained in this larger context.

But the social scientists also had an academic project. In all three countries, although more in France and Italy than in Germany, the degree of institutionalisation of the social sciences was insufficient for expanding research activities and for consolidating the disciplines. The promise of immediate political utility could be used to claim resources and to facilitate academic establishment. In France and Germany, the phase of intense interaction between social scientists and policy-makers paralleled the expansion and the full institutionalisation of the social sciences at the universities. In Italy, delays in a planned university reform due to resistance by the representatives of established academic interests meant that the full recognition of sociology as an academic subject did not occur before 1968; but with the Committee for the Political and Social Sciences (COSPOS), other institutional solutions could be found to bridge this gap. From the viewpoint of disciplinary interests, then, the interaction with influential non-scientific groups served this aim of achieving full academic institutionalisation.

A third consideration concerns the role of the disciplinary community as a reference group for the individual scientist and the implications for innovative strategies. In West German political science the normative commitment to Western parliamentary systems was initially shared by almost all the members of the community, since it had been a constitutive element in the (re-) emergence of the discipline. The policy orientation of the late 1960s introduced an unfamiliar perspective into the disciplinary debates: the focus was now on the empirical study of substantive policy issues, and to a number of the 'traditional' political scientists, this 'modern' viewpoint overemphasised technical issues and disregarded the central political problems. It can thus be argued that without external support providing research funds and influencing science policy decisions (besides providing the necessary access), the new approach would have faced much greater difficulty in gaining acceptance.

In France, the intellectuals in Paris doubtless formed a sort of community in which every member had to refer to the works of other members and to write and act according to certain standards. These intellectual circles, however strongly they may have shaped the re-emergence of sociology, did not, however, themselves form or intend to form a scientific discipline. Thus, much of the sociological work of the 1960s bears signs of the tensions between the strong grip of the traditional reference group and the attempt to build up one's own position by distinguishing oneself from the philosophies of the past and by establishing a real 'science'. The issue of 'scientificity' as a precondition for becoming a discipline had the least relevance in Italian debates about sociology in the 1950s and early 1960s. The sociological approach accorded almost perfectly with political reformism, and not much care was taken to emphasise the differences between science and politics. For sociologists it could be as important – or even more important – to establish close links with relevant centre-left party politicians as to engage in intense discussions about scientific progress in the field.

In this last case it is obvious that the degree to which a self-referential disciplinary community existed was connected to its degree of external orientation. While in Italy the absence of a scientific community was connected with the extreme importance assigned to external political processes, the two factors are not necessarily identical. In France, on the contrary, it was a key feature of the intellectuals that while being self-referential in their interactions they were also highly engaged in commenting on social developments and taking political stands, their ideal being that of the *intellectuel engagé*. Direct and utilitarian contact with political, economic and administrative elites was considered a breach of the traditional ideal, endangering the critical function of intellectuals by reducing their distance from power. It seems in large measure to be the definition of their relation to society that emerged in the 1960s which has distinguished the different 'schools' in French sociology, which have mainly been grouped around dominant individuals (but see ch. 7 for more recent developments).

The interference of these disciplinary and individual considerations in the macro-politically influenced desire to conduct socially relevant research, in my view, considerably modifies the notion of 'shared social purpose' which Stuart Blume assumes to be the basis for such interactions between scientists and non-scientists. In part, the different actors use a common situation for their *different* purposes.

One such feature in these coalitions – one might call it the 'honeymoon syndrome' – is at the root of their demise. Coalitions are entered into with high expectations, and programmatic statements at the beginning of a collaboration are usually enthusiastic. Regarded in retrospect, both the political and the scientific outcomes are highly exaggerated, and sometimes it seems as if a more sober contemporary might well have recognised this overstatement. But exaggerating the opportunities of the coalitions might have served as a useful way to strengthen the position of the collaborators in both fields. However, once an innovative scientific approach has been established with the help of external support, or once a group of political actors has come to power proclaiming rational policy-making on the basis of social scientific advice, the different logics in the two fields reassert themselves and interests begin to diverge (Wittrock 1985b).

In the above analysis it has been suggested that the demise of the modernisation-oriented reform coalitions led to the emergence of the critical action research approach. This shift, of course, should not be regarded as a clear sequence. As can be seen most clearly from the discussions about *conricerca* in Italy, this conception emerged while modernisation-oriented sociology was still at full strength. But a second differentiation has to be made regarding the success and the stability of such coalitions. The policy-oriented social sciences addressed themselves to identifiable actors who would ultimately dispose of large resources; the interaction between social scientists and policy-makers might become institutionalised in social science policy and thus achieve a certain continuity and stability. The action researchers, by contrast, had much greater difficulty in identifying their relevant public and, even when they could, in maintaining a stable relationship of communication and interaction. Their involvement very much depended on the existence of active social movements or other social groups having a definable political perspective and interest. Moreover, even when these conditions were met, continuity could only be expected if institutional settings were available which allowed researchers to concentrate on these issues. In the absence of these pre-conditions, the action research approach as a broad movement of social scientists proved to be very short-lived, though it survives in other forms.

Finally, the problem of the epistemological consequences of the coalitions between social scientists and non-scientists needs to be mentioned briefly. This problem cannot be fully analysed here on the basis of the previous analysis, but our discussion of the changing concepts of 'society' and 'policy/political system' clearly suggests that significant epistemological shifts in the social sciences can be observed depending on the type of actor orientation which is dominant at a specific time (Diesing 1982). Although these shifts cannot be measured against any baseline (of purely internal scientific progress), the concept of 'epistemic drift' introduced by Aant Elzinga (1985) seems to be a valuable one. The task of a political sociology of science would thus be to specify in detailed analyses the character of specific 'drifts' by studying both the socio-political environment and the potential audience of a discipline and the structure of its scientific field as a precondition to understanding the behaviour of specific actors in this field.

5
OUT OF STEP
The social sciences in the second
crisis of modernity

Seeking a response to the question 'Can modernity survive?', Agnes Heller once described the state of the social sciences as follows: 'Social science has promised certitude and self-knowledge as the result of a new, rationalist quest for meaning. This promise has not been kept. Where there was certainty, there was neither meaning nor self-knowledge; where there was meaning and self-knowledge, there was not certainty' (1990: 40). No sensitive observer of contemporary reality will deny that there is what some have called a deep-seated 'crisis of representation' (Jameson 1984: VIII; Eagleton 1985: 70; Boyne and Rattansi 1990: 12) which reaches far beyond the academic discourses on society into all major societal institutions.

Some of the analyses of these crises have been cast in terms of stories claiming that the end of something has occurred and that we therefore live in a post-something era. The most widely known terminations are the end of history, the end of the social and the end of utopia. Among the labels for what happens after the end, the notion of postmodernity has long been a clear favourite.[4] This concept suggests, if read sociologically, that those societies that were forming in Europe, and later elsewhere, in the wake of the scientific, industrial and French revolutions have reached their historical end and are being transformed into something else. In fact, where historical dates are given, modernity is often referred to as the two centuries after the French Revolution, and postmodernity is deemed observable in the last two or three decades (for broader discussions of the temporality of modernity see Wagner 2001; Yack 1997).

There are only fragments of sociological argument in writings of postmodernity. What I do in the following is ask, if a sociology of postmodernity existed, what it could sensibly look like. Briefly, I follow Agnes Heller both in acknowledging the deep-seated crisis of representation and in insisting on the possibility to strive for an understanding of entire social formations over long periods of time.

I start by highlighting two features of this 'end of an era' literature. First, in describing contemporary society the ephemeral, the fugitive, the fleeting, the contingent nature of the postmodern condition is emphasised. The present is distinguished from the past by being more in motion, less fixed: what was bound is set free, what was orderly and perspicuous becomes chaotic and undecipherable, what was taken for granted and for undoubtedly real has to be questioned and, often enough, assumes an air of 'pervasive unreality' (Norris 1990: 127). I give just a few examples. Jean-François Lyotard (1984a: 17) speaks of the ' "atomisation" of the social into flexible networks of language games'. In Jean Baudrillard's work, there is a thesis on dedifferentiation, on the collapse of the social into the economic and political, or vice versa, or in the collapse of all three into something completely different (e.g. Baudrillard 1982). Claus Offe, Scott Lash and others speak about the disorganisation of capitalism. And the books are legion that discuss the shifting boundaries of state and society, public and private, social and individual (Offe 1987; Lash 1990; Lash and Urry 1987; Maier 1987).

Second, there is a peculiar theoretical ambivalence in this literature. In line with the general idea of fleeting openness, one type of reasoning emphasises the liberation of the individuals from the bondage of institutional iron cages. Postmodernity is the ultimately victorious challenge of a historical resistance against social determination, a resistance that leads to the very destructuration of society (Baudrillard 1982: 28, 45–8). In a poststructuralist vein, the key to this reading is the ultimate end of any possibility of representation (also Rorty 1989: chs 1–3).

Having experienced the inadequacies of any cognitive representation of societal reality in social science and of all political representation of societal interests by parliaments and parties, the subject liberates herself from any of these demands by 'pushing into hyperreality' (Baudrillard 1982: 50) Many works are variations on the theme of difference, plurality, multiple realities and the like. Often pursuing deconstructionist analytical strategies, they may be accompanied by a normative stress on wide constructivist openness. Even if basic differences are granted, there is a surprising proximity between such discursive arrangements and pluralist and subjectivist theories of the individual in society, as conventionally held by the ideologies of liberalism. Often enough, though, they sound much less committed.

The other line of reasoning, however, points to the very destruction of the subject in contemporary society. Disregarding, for the moment, any epistemological argument on the death of the subject, I look here at the postmodern notions of the constitution of the subject and the self rather as sociological questions and try to assess their heuristic value and contemporary plausibility. In such a perspective, the most recent social transformations put an end to whatever there may have been of the subject in modernity. To quote from a summarising critique of such reasoning, what is left of the subject may just be

> a dispersed, decentred network of libidinal attachments, emptied of ethical substance and psychical interiority, the ephemeral function of this or that act of consumption, media experience, sexual relationship, trend or fashion. The 'unified subject' looms up in this light as more of a shibboleth or straw target, a hangover from an older liberal epoch of capitalism, before technology and consumerism scattered our bodies to the winds as so many bits and pieces of reified technique, appetite, mechanical operation or reflex of desire. (Eagleton 1985: 71)

This line of reasoning, too, has a long intellectual tradition. Where liberal thinking asserted that the revolutions of modernity would enable the individual subject to form and realise herself according to her own will and preferences, the critical tradition emphasised that new social phenomena would emerge, not least as a result of the liberating revolutions, that would constrain the subject, first, with regard to knowing herself and her real will and interests and, second, with regard to pursuing these interests. She would be alienated by the markets, subjugated by the bureaucracies and instrumentalised by science. What would remain would be a multiply reduced, fragmented and disciplined object without identity. The main modification in postmodern thinking as compared with this critical tradition is that, quite apart from merely not being realised, the very idea of the identity of a subject might well have been a fiction.

Neither of these two types of reasoning on the social subject is, thus, entirely new. If the theory of liberation in postmodernity sounds like liberalism without commitment, the theory of disciplinisation and fragmentation reiterates familiar left-wing criticism, only it is without hope. What seems specific to the discourse on postmodernity is the unusual combination of these two themes. This combination is related to the postmodernists' own views on contemporary society and on the position of their own discourse in comparison with more conventional social science. In both its variants, the sociology of postmodernity links a historical claim, the end of a social formation, to a theoretical claim, the inadequacy of the established concepts of social science to account for these recent social transformations. In the remainder of this chapter I discuss both claims critically.

An assessment of the historical claim requires a brief sketch of the social transformations during the past century with a view to reconsidering what modernity was, and, if it is over, how the present could be seen to differ from it. The main argument will be that postmodernity theorists are likely to be right in identifying a major, real-world, societal restructuring, but that their 'end of an era' discourse tends to exaggerate the dimensions of change. Indeed, many analogies can be drawn between theories of postmodernity and theories of a crisis of modernity that were put forward broadly around the turn of the nineteenth century.

This tendency toward exaggeration itself, however, has its own intellectual context, which, at least in part, should be appreciated by social theorists. The theoretical claim of postmodernity namely should largely be seen as a response to reductionist and reified conceptions of the modern in conventional social science and social theory. The second part of this chapter, therefore, is devoted to an assessment of the theoretical significance of postmodernity. As in the case of the historical claim, I argue that there is a considerable significance, though often less in the exact terms of such works and more in terms of a sensitising with regard to issues that are neglected or repressed in a social science that often was all too modern.[5]

The historical claim of the sociology of postmodernity

The journey through modernity will start in the continental Europe of the second half of the nineteenth century. This is where, a point on which many contemporary accounts converge, the experience of modernity, of life in a modern society, was reflected upon early and most consciously. This is the Paris of the *flâneurs, fin-de-siècle* Vienna, and the Berlin that gave birth to Georg Simmel's sociology of the city (Berman 1982; Schorske 1980; Pollak 1984; Frisby 1985; 1990; Harvey 1989: e.g. 28). Quite a number of labels are available to us for characterising these societies. Among them we find 'organised capitalism',[6] 'early welfare state',[7] societies of 'transformism',[8] each capturing a specific aspect of social organisation. My brief description starts with the notion of 'post-liberal society', focusing on the elites' reflective understanding of their society.

This late-nineteenth-century European society is post-liberal not merely because it came after the climax of liberalism with the national-liberal revolts and revolutions of mid-century, but also because its most sophisticated self-reflection was, more or less explicitly, guided by the question of what needs to be done to save as much as possible of the liberal and Enlightenment ideals, given that *in toto*, as everybody knew, they would not work. Emile Durkheim's concern about education and religion can be understood in this context as can Max Weber's struggles with notions of legitimacy and domination. This was a period of intense sociological activity but, if compared with earlier optimistic empiricism, it was much more sceptical about the possibility of knowing. The question of the adequate political representation of the people gained prominence simultaneously with the question of the adequate cognitive representation of society (see ch. 2).

If we look briefly at the self-reflective discourses on society at the time, we can distinguish three grand critiques. The first was the critique of political economy as developed mainly by Karl Marx. Its starting-point was the critique of alienation in an economy based on market exchange and forced sale of labour power, driven by laws of abstract value. The second was the critique of bureaucracy and large-scale organisation, as analysed most prominently by Max Weber. Its focus was on the construction of iron cages subjecting human beings to the dominance of instrumental rationalities. The third was the critique of science, put forward in very different forms, for instance, in the German debates on the natural and cultural sciences, by Friedrich Nietzsche and, later, by Max Horkheimer and Edmund Husserl. Let me summarise these latter highly varying analyses under the label of a rejection of positivist, empiricist and determinist science as incapable of reflecting the essential of human action.

All these grand critiques share some important features. They identify over-arching structures in modern society, and they focus on the ways these structures work on the individual. They even share a concern for the subject, whom they see threatened, and for her possibilities of self-realisation. If the perspectives of the contributors to these critiques differ widely, they were united in the diagnosis that some drastic changes in society are required to reverse tendencies toward the self-extinction of humankind as societies of self-reflective and active individuals.

And most of these critics tried to develop some sense of the possibility for change, too. Marx, optimistically, tended to argue that the development of capitalist economic interaction itself would breed the agent who would overthrow the system and replace it by a more humane economy. This agent would be a socially homogenised and politically united working class. Weber, much more sceptically, saw the nation-state as the only viable form of polity and desperately looked for agents in it who could at least safeguard the minima of civil life. And the critics of science, weak as their voices were, worked on socio-philosophical conceptions that allowed for a science of society without falling into objectivism.

I tend to see these analyses and proposals as the grand critiques of modernity at the time and the turn-of-the-century European societies as shaken by a crisis of modernity. These critiques were grand in the sense of Pascal's dictum that one does not show grandeur by being at one extreme point, but by touching two extremes at the same time. And the crisis of modernity was the deeper, the more the elites abandoned such a position and went to one extreme. Touching both extremes, in my sense, means voicing a radical critique of the existing aristocratic-bourgeois society and its institutions while maintaining a commitment to the liberal-humanist ethos of the Enlightenment. Moving to one extreme, in these times, meant mostly to abandon this ethos, favouring instead collectivist political arrangements, which would be based on some assumption of group priorities and would show only limited openness to free argumentation.

In Europe, the First World War provided an opportunity for major political restructuring. It entailed the downfall of the 'old regimes' and opened a limited time-span for experimenting with institutional alternatives (Mayer 1981; Maier 1975). In the view of many participants of the most diverse political leanings and beliefs, the experience of wartime economic and social management meant that the full establishment or re-establishment of the liberal institutions was neither possible nor desirable. The entire period from the beginning of the First to the end of the Second World War can be seen as one long and protracted struggle over societal reorganisation. Almost all proposals for reorganisation that were made during the inter-war period headed for a greater degree of social organisation than any liberal political or economic theory prescribed. Now the ingenuous idea that atomistic individuals might autonomously achieve a viable organisation of society was widely seen as flawed and replaced by notions of more class-, culture- or ethnicity-based collective polities.

The reorganisation proposals reached from class-based Soviet socialism through French People's Front and Swedish people's home to Vichy regime, fascism and, most clearly ethnicity-based, German national socialism. The theoretical positions were not mutually exclusive, and it is worthwhile to analyse how, for instance, the Swedish social democratic welfare state and the German national socialist warfare state shared ideological roots (Wittrock and Wagner 1996). What seems important to me is that all these proposals are responses to the perceived instabilities of the post-liberal regimes. In terms of the proposed opposition of liberty and discipline, all these conceptions restricted the notion of individual liberty in the name of some collectivity, some collective liberation. New homes were to be built, so to say, for the liberated individual who often felt homeless, more set out than set free (Berger et al. 1973). All differences notwithstanding, the approaches shared, in theory and practice, the search for new homes.

If we divide these concepts along the lines of conventional political terminology, we can say that most of the more left-wing proposals were domestically defeated before the war, at the latest when fascist or national socialist organisations seized political power. The only major exceptions in Europe were the emerging social democratic states of Sweden and, later, Britain, and state socialism in the Soviet Union. The right-wing proposals were militarily defeated in the Second World War. Restoration after the war occurred in the political and economic terms of the victorious nations, the two Germanies being the best example of the restructuring of the European continent along divided lines (Wittrock 1991). One of many consequences of these developments was the formalisation and limitation of political discourse. In the West, the experience of Nazism and the portrayal of state socialism as something of an equivalent to Nazism allowed the limitation – often gradually and by persuasion, but often also by means of legal and police repression – of the debates about political, economic and social restructuring to a kind of modernised restoration of the pre-authoritarian institutional structures. Only what is still known as liberal-democratic capitalism was regarded as both normatively acceptable and politically viable.

At the present point in history, it seems easy to write this story as the gradual resurgence of an effectively superior mode of social organisation (forgetting, though, the abundance of 'end of liberalism' literature from the 1940s, e.g. Schumpeter 1947; Hallowell 1971). The fall of the remaining openly authoritarian regimes in the West (Greece, Portugal, Spain) during the 1970s and the collapse of state socialism at the end of the 1980s would provide the material. Such an account, however, would remain faithful to the limited political discourse of the post Second World War era that (in the West) knew only right- and left-wing authoritarianism beside liberal democracy. In my view, it is essential to see that the survival of allegedly liberal capitalism hinged on another major transformation during the post Second World War period. Not too dissimilar from all other defeated previous projects, this transformation involved an increase in the degree of organisation of society. But it had some peculiar features that I shall carve out, after first briefly portraying the societal constellation of, say, the 1960s in comparison to turn-of-the-century societies.

Not only under attack from the three critiques, the turn-of-the-century societies had shown strong inherent contradictions, too. A profit-driven economy of large-scale enterprise had a mass-production apparatus at its disposal that was far too powerful to be satisfied with given domestic demand. This is what the economic debate on imperialism around the turn of the century was all about. A *de facto* increasingly bureaucratic and interventionist state pressed by competitive mass parties continued to be based on an outdated liberal ideology, neither giving any rationale for most of what it did nor, vice versa, imposing any limits to further increase of activity. The debate on the 'rule of law' state and on its theoretical foundation in legal positivism focused on this problématique (Heun 1989; von Oertzen 1974; and ch. 2). Social science derived its respectability increasingly from scientistic formalism, but because of the way it did so it could decreasingly account for any changes in contemporary society (Lukács 1954; Käsler 1984; Wagner and Wittrock 1991).

If the critics had argued for conditions allowing the self-realisation of the subject, the transformations that were achieved during the first half of the twentieth century, while often retaining the notion of individual liberty, meant a further reduction of the meaning of the subject itself.

Economists tend to term the developments of the late 1920s and 1930s a crisis of overproduction or underconsumption. The main distinction between the capitalism of the early 1900s and that of the 1960s in this respect is that consumption has developed extraordinarily. It has been supported by wage increases and it has been oriented to goods that did not exist a century ago and that were luxury items half a century ago. Consumption not only increased rapidly but took on a particular mode, usually short-handed mass consumption, that is: demand for standardised products by a large number of consumers who essentially were at the same time the producers of these goods by means of mass-production technologies or, increasingly, their distributors by means of large-scale technological networks.[9]

In nineteenth-century political thinking, political parties were free associations for the formulation and expression of political wills. The emerging mass party, especially on the socialist side, was just one specific example of this concept. By the 1960s, when the mass party had become an overall model for political organisation, the understanding was quite different. Parties were not merely to express but rather to channel the will of the electorate into the representative institutions, thereby transforming it into whatever the organisational elites deemed negotiable and advantageous in the competitive struggle. Parties were to educate the voters in terms of democracy, directing them to the viable political choices. Rather than expressing, party elites formed and shaped the political discourses and struggles.[10]

By the early 1900s, the complex relation between individual and society was the key concern of social science. By the standards of the modern social sciences of the 1960s the problem had disappeared, if only because it had been circumvented. Mass phenomena were made sociologically accessible by treating individuals statistically and objectifying them in a natural science mode. 'Society' was reconceptualised as masses who reacted to a stimulus and developed regular patterns of behaviour (see ch. 3).

According to postmodernists, this society should probably be labelled the society of late, or high, modernity. In institutional terms, it can be conceived of as a Keynesian, or interventionist, welfare state cum competitive party democracy (Offe 1983). It is based on a mass-consumption mode of economic organisation, large-scale technological systems connecting all members of society, regularly recurring mass expressions of political loyalty to the elites, and objectivist, empiricist social analysis. At this point, I want to stress two historical-comparative features of this society. First, all major tensions of the post-liberal society seemed resolved. The critical tendency toward overproduction was overcome by developing the mass-consumption mode. The problem of political representation of an uncivilised, potentially irresponsible and radical electorate was solved by the emergence of a restricted field of elite competition. And the representation problems in social science were solved by conceptual and mathematical aggregation.

From this characterisation follows, second, that there is a pronounced rupture between the societies of the early 1900s and those of the 1960s. In the early period, one could say, observers clung to some notion of naturalness of the problems. This was no naive realism. Most observers were aware of the problem of finding and, indeed, constructing categories to analyse a social situation. But still there was something obstinate, something independent about reality: the brutal force of economic dynamics, for example, or the resistance of large groups to comply with an orderly path of political development, such as that of revolutionary socialists, or the still incalculable relevance of religion and ideology. The political objective in social analysis, as in Weber's or Durkheim's for instance, was to find ways to live these stubborn realities. By the 1960s none of these problems had completely disappeared, but the view was quite different. In the epistemological optimism of the time, society was not an autonomous, incalculable force, but something to be shaped and moulded from above. This thinking found its most clear-cut expression in social and political theories based on cybernetics and systems analysis. If there was a problem it was complexity, but that could be handled technically. Society was no given anymore, however difficult to know; it has to be transformed according to the enlightened will of the knowing elites and ultimately in the interest of the better of all. It is in this view of society that postmodernity comes in, slowly but inescapably.

By some of its members, the society of the 1960s was referred to by the notion of post-industrial society and by the theorem of the end of ideology (Aron 1968; Bell 1973). Both concepts bear some family resemblance to the notion of post-modern society and the slogan of the end of history.[11] But there is a difference. The post-industrialists would probably see themselves best described as political realists. Limiting political strife to contests between civilised elites would impede a regress into the bad old times. Stepwise increase of technological knowledge would allow the growth of material well-being. And with the help of social science, material abundance could be increased to enhance the redefined goals of freedom and equality. Many of the contributors to this debate would not struggle long with the notion of liberty. Post-industrial society was probably not really liberal, but it was as liberal as it could get under conditions of modernity.[12]

The post-industrial argument did not go uncontested though. Throughout the 1960s we find an abundance of plausible accounts on disciplinisation in contemporary Western societies, too. Foucault's well-known work on medical and penal institutions provides a good example of one critical genre; Adorno's notion of the administered society is, in a sense, a radicalisation of the Weberian thesis. In the same theoretical context, we find Herbert Marcuse's account of one-dimensional society. And one can add, from a quite different genre and perspective, Pier Paolo Pasolini's reflections on the truly fascist character of the Italian consumer society of the 1960s, a phenomenon which he sees as much more destructive to society than the historical fascism of the 1920s and the 1930s (Foucault 1973; 1977; Adorno 1969; Marcuse 1964; Pasolini 1975). While not everybody will share the exact terms of these critical analyses, there is clearly something to them, something that contradicts the notion of the ultimate triumph of liberty.

After that came the political contestations of the late 1960s, the economic downturns of the mid 1970s, and the environmental debates throughout that decade. A number of unexpected, new or resurgent tensions arose. And ideology, in the sense of the end-of-ideology theorists, revived.

What triggered the debate on postmodernity was that this revival of older themes and struggles did not lead to anything. Almost everybody came to agree that technology is often more hazardous than beneficial; that science is unfounded, arbitrary and often politically compromised; that democracy does not work, given that we are governed by incompetent, prestige- and stable-income-seeking bureaucrats at best or competing cliques of arms traders at worst, and cannot do anything about it. And that all that can go on for quite a while. *Rien ne va plus*, but anything goes; such is the experience of the postmodern analyst.

From this starting-point, postmodernists endorse some of the theorems of post-industrialists and radicalise them. Where the latter spoke of endless growth of good knowledge to be applied for social betterment, the postmodernists see an arbitrary variety of intervention-oriented concepts evaluated purely according to their performance. Where post-industrialists identified enlightened steering elites in the top positions of an organised society, postmodernists see neither top positions nor any steering worth that name but a diffusion of activities in an ocean of simulation. And the masses are not functionally tied into social subsystems giving readable signals of approval or disapproval, but are an amorphous whole that through its very hyper-conformism undermines any quest for legitimacy.[13]

The postmodernity theorists relate to post-industrial society and the modernisation theorem of sociology like the crisis-of-modernity theorists of the turn of the century to liberal society and liberal political theory. It is compelling to compare Simmel's sociology of fragmented life with the resurgent interest in micro-sociology and in the sociology and anthropology of everyday life; Weber's iron cage of bureaucracy with Foucault's disciplinary society; and Pareto's transformation of democracy with Baudrillard's mass society in the shadow of silent majorities. In both cases, theorists see that societies are not as they are described in the dominant discourses. They oscillate between two interpretations of this divergence: either the societies have changed, or the discourses were flawed in the first place.

In many respects, such works contain elements of an effective critique of the political and sociological theories and practices of representation in contemporary societies. But at this point, many of the postmodernity theorists give up. Their analysis leads them, in their own views, to a negative response to any quest for intelligibility, meaning and agency. What is interesting, though, is less this (temporarily) negative response than the persistence of the quest. To pursue this point is to search for a sensible theoretical claim in the sociology of postmodernity.

The theoretical claim of the sociology of postmodernity

Some postmodernity theorists declare the end of social science. This may be premature, but one basic point is undeniable: social science, as we know it, developed in modernity, as a part of those societies' self-reflective knowledge. Its categories are deeply permeated by modernity, possibly to an extent that may render them incapable of grasping anything else, including the transition from modernity itself.

The radical nature of this question can hardly be underestimated. The easy distinction, for instance, of state, economy and society was one of the cornerstones of the societal self-understanding and indeed was at the root of the disciplinary subdivision of the social sciences. The differentiation of societal entities into those three relatively autonomous subspheres is an essential element of liberal thinking. And it is true that with the political success of that ideology, in so far as it occurred, it acquired some analytical validity throughout the latter part of the nineteenth century and some way into the twentieth. Until the present day, this distinction informs most theorising on society like the neofunctionalist differentiation theories, structuralist or functionalist Marxism, and the Habermasian counterposition of colonising social systems with an asystemic life-world (Alexander 1985; Münch 1984; Hirsch 1974; Habermas 1981).

But what has happened conceptually to these subspheres over time? Once, in liberal political philosophy, they were a normative proposal to secure spheres of freedom for the individual in society. Then, in the grand critiques of modernity, they were identified as emerging institutional structures disciplining the individual and endangering the project of modernity. Ultimately, in modern social science, they became reified as some superhuman phenomena to which human beings are subjected, without any action or choice. Where Marx and Weber were still concerned about, as the latter said, the 'life destiny' of the human being under modern conditions, later social science came to be rather one more wire of the iron cage than a means to push that cage open through self-reflection.

Astonishingly enough, this holds true for both mainstream, functionalist modernisation theories and many critical theories of society. Whereas the former develop a complete system of interlinked subsystems, the latter either introduce contradictions between subsystems, between politics and the economy, for instance, or conceptualise one specific sphere from which critical intervention could start out, like the life-world in Habermas' case. But the reified, non-agential conception of society is essentially the same.

More recent postmodernist theorising removes the world even one step further from any potential human agency by introducing hyperreality or autopoiesis of systems. Both the cognitive grip on reality and the political grip on some powerful actor are made theoretically even more unlikely, if not excluded. Interestingly, the reasons given for this conceptual move are often more historical than theoretical and display an astonishing realism. Both a systems theorist, Niklas Luhmann, and a postmodernist, Jean-François Lyotard, tend to argue that any broadly humanist, agential conception of society is quite simply 'out of step' with reality. It may have been appropriate at some earlier point in time, but evidently no more today (Luhmann 1971; Lyotard 1984a: 14).

This is a fundamental misconception of both social science and society. Social theory and historical social science, as I would like to see them, could not else but start from the question of the constitution of society in the interaction of social, knowledgeable and capable human beings, and from the question of the constitution of selves in that very social interaction (Giddens 1984; Bourdieu 1990). Key categories could be the types of knowledge human beings develop about themselves, technologies of the self, as Foucault (1988: 18) has put it, and the structures of everyday life, as seen in the perspectives of Agnes Heller (1984) or Dorothy Smith (1987), for instance. This could be no micro-sociology, as we know it; it is impossible to get at the conditions of human life in modernity without conceiving of social phenomena that are widely extended in time and space. But these phenomena would not be seen as superhistorical and superhuman, instead as produced and reproduced in everyday human practice.

It is indeed a very characteristic of modernity that individuals relate strongly to such widely extended institutions – abstract systems, as Anthony Giddens (1990) calls them – by trust, trust in the convertibility of money into goods or services, or trust in the reliability of expert knowledge. Numerous of our everyday interactions are based on trust in abstract systems in this sense. And, as Wall Street crashes or the political demise of nuclear energy programmes after Chernobyl show, such systems can collapse quite simply by the collective withdrawal of trust.

If trust is one important individual aspect of widely extended modern institutions, its reverse side is dependence and disciplinisation. Increasingly, one would be unable to sustain one's life or, at least, one would suffer heavy disadvantages, if one did not relate to those systems. And one would be excluded from access, if one did not master and apply their rules, like complying with repayment of debts or following the driving rules on the highway. Often, no local communication brings one back to social life, after having, even unknowingly, violated such rules of widely extended, highly technically arranged systems. The spread of abstract systems is an immense collectivisation process, which enables individuals to undertake actions that could never be organised locally; it is enabling, though under the strict and often non-negotiable precondition of following disciplined lines of behaviour.

The extreme organisation and collectivisation inherent in these systems go along with an equally extreme individualisation of their use, a use that after disciplinisation no longer requires communication. It is a common deficiency of normative liberal theories of modernity not to acknowledge that the social conditions for the formation of the self themselves have been transformed throughout the period commonly labelled modernity. Slightly exaggerating the point, one could even say that disciplinisation always preceded liberation. One had to learn work discipline before the benefits of the market could be reaped. One had to be educated before participating in collective decision-making. One had to show reasonable behaviour before being set free from the asylums. Or, in social (and social science) terms, people had to learn to behave predictably like orderly organised masses, before the benefits of social planning could be reaped.[14] The liberated being obviously has to be assumed quite different from the being before liberation.

The social transformation, therefore, which was conceived by many of its protagonists as liberating the subjects from traditional bondage, entailed a transformation of the very conditions in which subjects can form themselves. Untying them from being subject to rulers, religion and restrictions of expression, they were inescapably subjected to new forms of constraint, to disciplining rules and institutions. A good liberal would say here: subjects tied themselves into those new and possibly necessary and worthwhile restrictions. But that would do strong injustice to the highly stratified nature of means for active expression of one's intentions (see Lindblom 1990). By most members of nineteenth- (and also twentieth-) century societies, these transformations were experienced as something coming from outside, against which one could try to defend oneself, but which one could hardly shape and influence.[15]

The simultaneously enabling and constraining character of abstract systems together with the highly stratified nature of enablement and constraint are the key to the ambivalence in both everyday experience and distanced interpretation of the modern world that I tried to identify earlier. The simultaneity of enablement and constraint is one of the roots of the ambivalent accounts of liberation and disciplinisation. The turn-of-the-century writing about the crisis of modernity was often torn between being impressed by the immense possibilities offered by urban social technologies, world-scale economic organisation and the like, on the one hand, and being scared of the loss of the identity of the subject and the machine-like workings of such collective phenomena leaving no place for individual volition, on the other. Similarly, current postmodernity theorists often seem undecided between an outright appraisal of the new time and a tragic feeling for a further drifting away from any possible realisation of human objectives.[16]

Often, however, the question of the stratification of modern experience is sorely neglected in such analyses. It is often a very naively realist view on the development of social knowledge and of social reality that many theorists display, as I argued earlier. I think we have to be very careful in assessing what happens to whom and who is talking about it. If modernity, for instance, as many sociologists would say, is science, industry, democracy and bureaucracy, very few turn-of-the-century Europeans had much direct access to it. Inhabitants of rural areas and many women had not more than occasional touches of these phenomena. But what, then, was the turn-of-the-century discourse of modernity about; what were its specifics, especially if compared with the present debate about postmodernity?

Generally speaking, all aspects of the discourse of modernity, all problems of political philosophy and epistemology inherent in the liberal and Enlightenment tradition, have been discussed for long time. I do not really see any recent contribution that has added something significant in this respect.[17] What has changed over time are the social conditions under which human beings try to implement (or transform or abandon) these traditions according to the experiences they and their contemporaries have made. It is mainly in this respect that there are fundamental differences between the turn-of-the-century crisis of modernity and the present debate about postmodernity.

The turn-of-the-century debate followed on, or went along with, a disembedding process of giant scale (cf. Giddens 1990). Industrialisation and urbanisation transformed the big European cities and the life of a large part of their population. I do not dare claim that this was a disembedding process of unprecedented dimensions; historical comparisons of scale are often difficult to sustain. But what was probably unprecedented was that such a process happened before the open eyes of an enlightened, literate public guided by Mandarin intellectuals (Bauman 1987). In the latter's views this disembedding was likened to an unleashed force of nature that could not be tamed, but whose consequences could and had to be dealt with. All subsequent proposals, which I have discussed earlier, can be regarded as attempts at *re-embedding* the individuals by organising them into quasi-natural (that is, not fully reflected) institutions. Thus, it was held to be in the objective interest of workers to organise themselves along class lines given that the economic dynamics had forced them into this fate. Others held it to be a cultural (spell: natural) predeterminant to gather linguistic groups into political entities and make these entities the prime vehicles to solve social tensions. Thus were born the nation-state and the 'social question'. Throughout the first half of the twentieth century, organisation of society's individuals as members of a class or a nation was more or less successfully or disastrously tried.

In more recent decades the doubts about modernity are again related to a major process of disembedding. In some countries, such as the former two Germanies after the Second World War, there was an enforced radical break with any unambiguous idea of nationhood. More important in international perspective, though, are the transformations of social positions and orientations during an extended period of material growth. Any number of instances can be cited, such as the physical reshaping of city and countryside during the 'age of the great programmes', or the unprecedented growth in higher education reshaping the outlook on one's own future from one generation to the other.[18] It is difficult to assemble systematic knowledge about the consequences of this transformation in terms of social experiences. But my hypothesis is that it was profound indeed and that this transformation can, until now, largely be conceived of as a *disembedding without re-embedding*. Nothing comparable to the organisation of society's individuals during the first period happened. While class and nation-state remain of importance, they are hardly a resort for unconditional hope anymore.

The responses are many and manifold. Religious fundamentalism, be it in the allegedly modernised societies or in those seen as on the threshold to modernity, appears to remain at odds with the workings of societies of global interaction and exchange.[19] Liberal intellectuals in the West, including many postmodernists, try to design societies without universalist discursive foundation. I do not venture into speculation here. I simply argue that the analogy to the turn-of-the-century period that I propose here underscores the need to understand the present as a time of major societal restructuring, a contested process with a very open outcome.

Conclusions

It is this major restructuring that postmodernity theorists struggle with, too, I think. And many of their texts are highly sensitive accounts. Two points of key importance, however, need to be stressed.

First, although this constellation has to do with the self-reflexivity of social knowledge, there is no fundamentally new epistemological question (see in more detail Wagner 2001: ch. 1). What postmodernists refer to when they talk about the all-pervasiveness of simulacra, the disappearance of reality and, as a consequence, the end of social science, is the fact that – following this second major process of disembedding – many more people have become, often painfully, aware of the always transformed nature of society. Modernity, so to say, has gained many more citizens. What more could one say about economic harmonisation after the crisis of Keynesianism? How else could one talk of social solidarity after the alleged 'crisis of the welfare state' and its expertise-based, administered social policies?

In their members' practices these societies were (and are) permeated by social scientific knowledge. Such success of the scientification of social processes has entailed unintended and unforeseen consequences. Growing awareness of the lack of any Archimedean point has put social science knowledge into question, not least in the view of the many hitherto pretty unreflective social science practitioners themselves. This is probably a historically new social experience, but it requires no new epistemology.[20]

Second, this constellation certainly shows features of fragmentation, but at its roots is not less but more, and more widely extended, organisation. Fragmentation and dissolution may be seen to appear in two different forms, in the realm of the personal organisation of lives and in that of 'modern' political structures. The former, the experience of disunity and incoherence of life projects, is the more or less direct consequence of disembedding, that is the possibility or necessity of dealing with a number of abstract systems, often quite differently organised and occasionally conflicting, and having to integrate them into a one and only personal life (see Wagner 1994: ch. 10; 2001: ch. 3). The spreading of such experience, however, more common as it may evidently get, should not be overstated either. Often, it may well not go far beyond the social analyst and his or her fellow elite intellectuals. Many people for most of their lives manage efficiently to bracket a however fugitive outside world from their lives. The main means to do this is to personalise access points to abstract systems, to create new quasi-local contexts. What anthropologists have called favouritism and clientelism, for instance, is ultimately the sum of many people's attempts to secure their relations to abstractly organised providers of goods and services. Thus, one hardly needs to trust in abstract expertise but can rely on personal skills, acquired in non-modern ways. The experience of modernity may for many people still be limited to a few extraordinary occurrences, be they of the nature of personal crises or of the sudden intrusion of world-scale events.

In the other form, too, fragmentation and dissolution are not often experienced directly, except for some elite actor and some social analyst. What is termed the 'disorganisation of capitalism', the 'decline of the nation-state' and the 'changing boundaries of the political' are all very real processes. And they do entail that many of the concepts social scientists have developed for industrial-capitalist society do not work well anymore. But they do not entail that no new social and political boundaries will be established, or do in fact already exist, or that it would not be possible to come up with adequate concepts for an emerging societal constellation. One can even assume that, unless major disasters occur, new social structures will be more extensively organised rather than more local. There will be difference and plurality, but most likely in the context of abstract systems reaching out widely over time and space.

These remarks, however, do not in any way intend to downplay the critical nature of the present societal constellation – even apart from the lasting consequences of the massive political turmoil of the early 1990s that is problematic enough on its own. Normatively speaking, the farewell to agentially conceived social class and sovereign nation-state robs many social scientists of dear friends, incorporations of political agency. They should indeed not overlook that these phenomena have historically been as disciplining as liberating, as totalitarian as beneficial. Unidimensional hopes were misdirected from the start. Analytically as well as normatively, theorems on postmodernity tell us that the link between the dynamics of overarching political and economic institutions on the one hand, and the life destinies of human beings on the other, was and is much more complex than modernist social science had conceived of.

Unfortunately, however, and in contrast to what some postmodernity theorists seem to think, we cannot rest content with the falling apart of the idea of this linkage, or with the way in which the reality of it is being restructured. Even if the beneficial workings of class or state may have in large part been a modernist fiction, there is no reason to assume that some beneficial collective guidance is not needed – unless one wants to return to the idea that the interaction of a multitude of individuals would automatically secure positive collective results. In reality though, the effective globalisation of social phenomena will entail that individuals are more and more exposed to their effects, while being less and less able to exert significant influence according to their volition and practices. In such situations, there is a great likelihood of a real loss of intelligibility, meaning and agency.

Postmodernity theorists often seem to argue either that this loss cannot be remedied (because of the fictitious character of any 'modern', Enlightenment-style solution), or that it does not matter much (because, ultimately, individuals will cope). Radical theorists of modernity will continue to think that it matters (because deprived, constrained individuals cope badly), and they will continue the search for points in collective social life where a renewal of historical agency could start out – even if this programme may sound utterly 'out of step' at times.

PART II
RETHINKING KEY CONCEPTS
OF THE SOCIAL SCIENCES

6
CHOICE AND DECISION-MAKING

Of sparrows and doves

There is a saying in the English language that holds one bird in the hand to be worth two in the bush. The recommendation for choice and decision-making presupposes an order of preferences in which, first, a 'bird' is considered to be a good worth having and, second, the possession of this good in increasing quantities has a positive utility attached to it. There is nothing extraordinary about this assertion thus far; economic theorising of rational choices under conditions of scarcity has long formulated such propositions and elaborated them further. The interesting part of the recommendation comes with the comparison between actually having a certain quantity of the good, on the one hand, and having a greater quantity in view, on the other.

In the metaphorical language characteristic of everyday wisdom, 'hand' stands here for actual possession, whereas 'bush' refers to present unavailability and potential, but uncertain, future possession. From the point of view of the preference-holder, the difference in the spatial location of the goods is one of accessibility. For reasons that will become clearer in a moment, let me underline that a difference in quantity of the good is here related to a difference in accessibility, and that the question of accessibility itself is confined to 'having' and 'not (now, or yet) having'. On the face of it, there are no further significant connotations that come with 'hand' or 'bush' in this context.[21]

Before moving on, an observation on the status of this proposition is in order. The recommendation is clearly one of prudence, but this does not necessarily imply that the social world in which it is uttered and accepted is one in which prudence reigns. In general, everyday wisdom is known to be internally contradictory. A counter-recommendation, for instance, is contained in the proverb 'Nothing ventured, nothing gained.' The existence of such contradictions can be interpreted in a variety of ways. Often, it is assumed to be inappropriate to expect coherence and consistency from a body of knowledge which has been accumulated naturally, such as everyday wisdom. This is precisely what is considered to distinguish scientific-philosophical reasoning from common sense. Alternatively and more interestingly, however, one can see everyday wisdom as working with a plurality of repertoires. In that case, its single maxims would not be meant to be applicable across all kinds of situations; rather, their application is situation-dependent, or more precisely, dependent upon the interpretation of the situation.

In the German language, there is a saying that at first sight seems to make precisely the same recommendation as the English one just cited. Its literal translation is: 'The sparrow in the hand is better than the dove on the roof.' In this proverb, having a bird is also better than only hoping to obtain one. But this saying moves beyond triviality, not by increasing the quantity of the birds not possessed, but by introducing a qualitative distinction – between a bird of lower utility and one of higher utility. At the same time, the metaphor chosen to mark the distinction between that which is accessible and that which is inaccessible is also cast in different terms. While 'hand' (in lay Heideggerian terms?) stands here, too, for what is available, conversely that which is not accessible is moved, we may be justified in saying, to a higher, a superior plane – using the philosophically time-honoured and linguistically almost unavoidable association of altitude with value and importance.

If, just for a moment and for the sake of developing the argument, we worked with a standard cultural-linguistic theory of social life and assumed that linguistic forms express cultural values, would there be an important difference between an 'English' society and a 'German' one, using these names as shorthand for societies whose members understand and accept, in principle, the one or the other maxim? Moving beyond the shared emphasis on prudence contained in these particular sayings, rather different registers of evaluation can be identified which stand behind the construction of the choice and decision-making situation.

The 'German' choice is between goods of different quality, whereas the 'English' one is between different quantities of the same good. Some may want to say that this aspect should not be exaggerated: after all, a bird is just a bird. And the fact that the one is larger than the other and that the one is widely considered edible and the other is not do not make much of a difference – or only a difference that makes the preferences assumed in these proverbs plausible, as is necessary for their proverbial status. If those points exhausted the differences between a sparrow and a dove, this objection would be valid. In one view the difference is located on a common scale of size, that is large/small (or more/less), and the size of a 'good' equals its value. Alternatively, the difference is translated into the ability of the good to satisfy a universal human need, i.e. the need for food.[22]

Such a reading, however, would miss some significant interpretive possibilities. First, it ignores the irony that often occurs in common wisdom. For all intents and purposes, a sparrow is no good at all, and this observation means that the proverb should possibly not be read as advice in a situation of choice and decision. Instead, the German saying may indeed be telling us that there are moments in which one has to resign oneself to quite a miserable life in spite of high-flying ideas and ambitions. Among the latter are peace, and also love and freedom, for all of which the dove can stand as a symbol. Because of that, we may also find explanations for why the German dove is on the roof, while the two English birds are in the bush. That which is inaccessible in the English saying is just in a different place, a site different from that of the subject and one which he or she could only reach by making an effort. In the German saying, by contrast, inaccessibility refers to a higher plane, where ordinary life does not take place, and from which one would look at life from a different perspective.[23]

Third, the suspicion that there may actually be no choice or decision to be made in this situation can be read in the opposite way. If the saying is taken to mean that a sparrow in the hand is *obviously* better than a dove on the roof, then it may call for a halt to further inquiries. By digging further into what one's preferences actually are and how they can best be satisfied, one may destroy any possibility of satisfying them. Ultimately, there may be no way to avoid the connotations of intimacy, since it is here that this aspect is most evident. If one keeps questioning oneself about whether the person you are with is the one you love, then one precondition of love and friendship, namely their existing unquestioningly, will cease to hold. Theorists as diverse as Maurice Merleau-Ponty, Hannah Arendt and Jon Elster (1986: 13) have discovered this insight.

I will call a halt here to further inquiries in comparative cultural metaphysics, since this is not the purpose of this essay – worthwhile as such an effort could be, if it were pursued on more secure grounds than one made up of two proverbs. This little comparative exercise was meant to direct attention to some features of 'decision-making' which are often neglected, and which I will now explore in more technical language.

Of rags and riches

Two observations have been made about the relation between the two proverbs (and it will have become clear that they are indeed two proverbs and not, as they appeared to be and as dictionaries treat them, two versions of the same proverb). First, I have suggested that they vary in their construal of the goods at stake. A qualitative difference in the one case turns into a quantitative one in the other. This raises the issue of the commensurability of these goods. If there is a situation of simple increases in marginal utility, then inhabitants of the 'English' world could probably indicate for which number of birds in the bush they would give up the one bird in the hand. But could 'Germans' conceivably give the sparrow up for, say, an eagle – i.e. for (collective) power and glory instead of for peace and love? Possibly, but there would be no formal method, at a level comparable to marginal utility theory, of approaching the question. Eagles (as well as doves)[24] may belong to a quite different order than sparrows, and one could not be traded against the other. This observation leads into a discussion about what Charles Taylor calls 'hyper-goods' as well as 'irreducibly social goods' (e.g. 1989b: ch. 3, 1995), both of which are difficult to conceptualise from a rationalist-individualist point of view.

Second, pursuing that kind of observation further, one could argue that a world in which there are sparrows, doves and eagles is a world quite different from one in which there are only birds existing in different quantities. In other words, the 'Germans' and the 'English' use quite different registers of evaluation when interpreting and judging the world in which they find themselves. The theoretical conclusion that follows here is that there may be differences between registers of evaluation such that they cannot be reduced to differences of preferences, at least not without further implications. Such a conclusion can be related to a Wittgensteinian emphasis on languages rather than on words or concepts, and to the idea of the 'form of life' that emerges from there. More recently, Luc Boltanski and Laurent Thévenot (1991) have attempted to show that disputes in contemporary Western societies are indeed approached from a number of different registers of evaluation, many of which have their own internal consistency and coherence, but which are incommensurable and thus mutually irreducible.[25]

At this point, we may ask what happens if one tries to make goods commensurable or to translate from one language or register to another, say from 'German' to 'English'. This would be an effort at redescription, which, in Richard Rorty's (1989) understanding, changes the world. In other words, when moving from 'German' to 'English' one may indeed make different goods commensurable and reinterpret differences in registers of evaluation as differences in preference orders, but at the same time the situation is altered for those human beings who face the choices. Arguably, this is precisely what the application of rational choice theorising does and what such theorists normatively recommend human beings to do.

To broaden the view on rational choice theorising as a mode of social theory still further, I shall take up the two other observations made briefly above. I have claimed that with some kinds of 'preferences' it is essential for satisfying them that they should not be revealed in the situation of 'decision-making' – without this being a question of deception of others or even of oneself. Reasoning against the background of an ideal state of complete information, rational choice theorising holds information to be a good, of which it is always preferable to have more. This good is weighed only against the cost of obtaining yet more information, which is conceptualised as a form of transaction cost. In contrast, the example developed above held that acquisition of further information may make a certain good unobtainable and a given preference unsatisfiable. Thus, it undermines the general validity of the concept of grounding rationality in information.

As in the earlier two cases, following the advice from rational choice theory would considerably alter the situation of 'decision-making'. This alteration, however, may be highly undesirable; and the degree of such undesirability might be untheorisable from the point of view of rational choice theory. A final observation relates to the question of the 'situation' itself. Building on the insight that singular human beings may avail themselves of more than one register of evaluation, the interpretation of a situation gains crucial significance. To elaborate further on one example, the relation to another person may be one of justice, e.g. between colleagues at work, or it may be one of love (see e.g. Boltanski 1990). The observably different registers of evaluation which human beings apply would have to be interpreted as a violation of the need for consistent preferences as presumed by a rational choice theorist. The only alternative, in order to avoid strongly counter-intuitive outcomes, is to claim that situations can unequivocally be defined as 'given', i.e. as one of justice or as one of love, and can then be treated unproblematically as the 'context' of decision-making. The rational pursuit of preferences 'under constraint' could thus again be made consistent. Situations, however, are often not unequivocally defined, and the interpretation of a situation may be exactly what is contested or in doubt. In this case, then, rational choice theorists would apply the maxim of scrutinising both one's preferences and the situation, since this is seen as the only maxim that is applicable to *any* situation. But it would invariably favour the calculating individual. This, however, means preferring a *particular* register of evaluation, and transforms the situation to make it amenable to this register.

Four problems of decision-making have now been raised: incommensurability of goods, a variety of registers of evaluation, inconsistent preferences across a variety of situations, and situation-dependent rules of application. Already at first sight, they pose enormous difficulties for theories of the rational chooser. Rational choice theorists have pursued two different strategies to deal with these complications. Accordingly we can group those theorists into two categories, the doves and the hawks.

Doves and hawks are equally convinced of the superiority of rational choice theorising. Thus, a major spokesperson for the doves, Jon Elster, claims un-equivocally that this approach is unrivalled as a normative theory. But let us see what price, to use hawkish language, he has to pay for that assertion. He and his fellow doves allow their individuals all kinds of preferences: they may follow social norms, engage in collective action, accept institutions as bounds of their rationality, or forgo the best outcome for an inferior one because they are satisfied with it. In short, they appear like quite ordinary and reasonable human beings. But what is their claim to rationality and in what sense is this normatively superior behaviour? Technically speaking, all particularities of human lives are assimilated into either the preferences of the actors or the context of the decision-making situation, both of which are outside the realm of the rationality of the choice. The claim to normative superiority ultimately boils down to an understanding of rationality in which to be rational, *pace* Hegel, means to do what you think is good for you. While this is quite agreeable, it leaves all the tasks of social research and social theorising to others – namely to find out how preferences emerge and change and what the social contexts are in which human beings happen to find themselves.

Hawks, in contrast, keep their eyes firmly on the calculating individual. In their view, reason-endowed atoms are what the social world consists of, and the more this fact is recognised the better everything will be. Rather than accepting the particularities of human social life and trying to adapt their theorising to it, as the doves do, they recommend ways of acting and behaving. Summarised briefly, in the light of the above observations, their advice runs as follows. Consider yourself an individual who knows what you want before you enter into any situation of decision-making. When in such a situation, aim at establishing cognitive control over it, i.e. provide yourself with as complete information as is available (or as much as you can afford). Systematically relate the information gathered to your preferences. Design strategies to see which preferences you can satisfy to which degree. Weigh your preferences, i.e. make them comparable, so that you can establish a hierarchy of strategies. Decide.

Looking back at the decision-making problems discovered by interpreting the proverbs, we see that the following happens here. If commensurability of goods was not given, it is now established. Any diversity of registers is reduced to one. Preferences are being ordered in a consistent way throughout. The situation is now unequivocally defined. The two presuppositions that are needed for this procedure to work are the assumption of an individual with fully established preferences and the assumption of the possibility and desirability of absolutely context-independent judgement. Rather than always already being in some world full of strange birds and other animals, the human being is seen here as initially standing outside the world and only moving towards it with some intention and purpose. Or more precisely, since it is a theoretical operation we are talking about, the distancing from a context is seen as the precondition for rational action of the individual. However, this specifically entails an alteration of the situation, in the sense in which I referred to such an occurrence above. It is inappropriate to say that a rational choice approach allows a different (read: superior) way of dealing with a given situation. Rather, a rational choice approach changes the way in which a human being is situated in the world. It is an intervention in the world rather than an analysis of it.

A number of rational choice theorists will not be at all unhappy with such a diagnosis. After all, some may see themselves as engaged not only in knowing the world, but also in improving it. And there can be no doubt that a rationalist-individualist approach, in a broad sense, has enabled human beings to gain insights and possibilities, many of which they would not want to miss (though space is too short to go into detail, I will implicitly provide some illustrations below). However, the action that is performed is one of reducing that which is not reducible. Translations introducing commensurability and unequivocality lead to an impoverishment of the available repertoires of evaluation. The messy richness of the world is exchanged for some clean rags. While hardly any reasonable being would prefer rags to riches as a matter of principle, there may be situations in which one has reason to believe that one cannot do otherwise.

Of wars and revolutions

As a mode of social theorising, rational choice theory is, or better relies on, a theory of modernity. It works with a postulate of autonomy: human beings have wills and are, in principle, able to act according to them. And on this basis, it takes the pursuit of their strivings, with a view to accomplishing their objectives, as that which human beings will want to do, i.e. as expressions of rationality. In terms of Enlightenment philosophy, rational choice theory takes a version of the combination of freedom and reason as its basic philosophy. It thus relates closely to what I like to call, in somewhat broader terms, and following Cornelius Castoriadis (e.g. 1990: 17–19), a commitment to autonomy and mastery as the double signification of modernity.

However, rather than merely situating itself within modernity, rational choice theory provides a very particular interpretation of modernity. As I have tried to argue at some length elsewhere (Wagner 1994; 2000), both of those meaning-providing terms (autonomy and rationality) are underspecified and ambivalent on their own, and tension-ridden as a double-barrelled concept. The social signification of modernity is widely open to interpretations. Autonomy, for instance, can be understood predominantly on individual terms, but it can also be read as collective self-determination. Rationality or mastery can be conceived of in purposive, instrumental and then procedural terms, but it can also be related to substantive concerns. And these formulae for ambivalence – individual/collective, instrumental/substantive – do not yet capture anything approaching the richness of possible interpretations, nor are they even necessarily the best way of framing the issue. Rational choice theory, in contrast, proceeds from an unequivocal starting-point. Its social entities are individuals, and they behave according to instrumental rationality.

If rationalist individualism (from now on I will use this broader term because moving on to historical considerations) is a theory of modernity, but a very particular one, the question arises as to the grounds on which it was preferred to others. To approach an answer to that question, a rapid survey of the history of this thinking is useful.[26] Rationalist individualism initially emerged in social contract theories, as first spelt out unequivocally in Hobbes' *Leviathan*, and was emphatically developed as a basic theoretical approach by thinkers such as Condorcet in the context of the French Revolution. In parallel to the latter, Smith's moral philosophy provided a space for rationalist individualism within the confines of the economy, an approach which also inspired Marx. Abolishing the elements of a separate moral-political philosophy, this thinking was radicalised during the marginalist revolution in economic thought, which led to what is now the dominant thinking in this field, namely neoclassical economics. During the inter-war years of the twentieth century, European cultural critics identified a degraded version of rationalist individualism, in the form of a conjunction of atomism and conformism, as the prevailing attitude in mass society, in particular the North American one. Weber, though not a typical proponent of this thinking, laid many of its foundations. After the Second World War, rational choice theorising gained the form in which we now know it and spread from economics to the other social sciences.

With the help of these few historical reference-points, elements of a contextual understanding of the way in which the particular, rationalist-individualist interpretation of modernity imposed itself can be provided (the following draws on Wagner 2001). I will anticipate the general argument and will then situate it in various contexts. Rationalist individualism may emerge and find acceptance, or even impose itself, as a social theory by default. By default I refer to a move that is made in situations in which other interpretations of the modern condition, while they may be available in principle, cannot be utilised. The default situation may arise as a consequence of the exigency that all other such interpretations have to make stronger social presuppositions or, in other terms, would need to assume more substantive social prerequisites than the individualist-rationalist one. To relate this idea to the signification of modernity: *not* to interpret autonomy as purely individual autonomy requires, if not a coherent and stable collectivity, then at least socially rich ways of relating to others, that is both singular others and networks of others. *Not* to interpret mastery or rationality in instrumental terms requires other substantive value orientations, which again need to be, if not shared with, then at least communicable to and acceptable to others.

If this consideration is generally acceptable, the next task is to identify the conditions under which such other interpretations become difficult or impossible so that the default situation arises. Very abstractly speaking, such conditions prevail in times of destruction of a social configuration, in particular rapid and forceful destruction, and in times of the founding or refounding of social configurations, especially if this occurs under pressure or comes from a great diversity of sources. Destruction may be caused by imposed social change, such as was the case historically due to the capitalist revolution and through the building of bureaucratic state apparatuses. Here we recognize Marx's theory of alienation and Weber's theory of rationalization as responses to such experiences; and now we would also need to include the experience of totalitarianism. But destruction of a social configuration also occurs through warfare and revolutions. And in this context it is significant that individualist-rationalist modes of theorising made early breakthroughs in the context of the seventeenth-century religious wars and the eighteenth-century revolutions. In such situations, no other way seemed available to conceptualise the return to peace and order.

To the present day, Hobbes' *Leviathan* is one of the key references when the attempt at grounding political order on an abstract conception of the individual human being and its rationality is discussed. The abstraction from any concrete situation, later to be called the hypothesis of the 'original position' (John Rawls), would then provide the required distance and make rational-scientific knowledge possible. However, rather than reading Hobbes' *Leviathan* as the inauguration of scientific method in political thought, it can also be interpreted as a contribution to solving an urgent socio-political problem, namely how to bring an end to violent religious strife.

In such a contextual perspective, Hobbes' attempt shows a clear awareness of an inescapable dilemma. On the one hand, there is a deep intellectual consciousness of the lack of stability and certainty. Radical doubt is indeed the starting-point of the reasoning. On the other hand, Hobbes was also driven by the conviction that humankind could not live well without some categories of social and natural life which impose themselves on everybody, and such categories would only impose themselves if and because they were considered as undeniably valid. The uncertainty that was experientially self-evident in a situation of devastating religious and political strife had to be overcome by appeal to an instance that, in his view, could only be found outside such experience. The coexistence of these two apparently incompatible convictions gives his work a character which one might label as dogmatically modernist: radical in the rejection of unfounded assumptions, but inflexible in the insistence upon some definable minimum conditions of cognitive and political order that could, and would have to be universally established. After the religious grounding of unity had been irretrievably lost, it could in his view only be replaced by individuals and their rationality. All other categories could be contested, and strife would be renewed.

Rather than giving intellectual support to the idea of a strong state, Hobbesian thinking opened the way for an increasingly consistent derivation of political power from the combined will of the individuals in a given collective. The American and the French Revolutions marked attempts to implement such a conception. Thus, they revived the theoretical problem and gave it a new urgency. Edmund Burke (1993: 8–9), sceptical observer from across the Channel, issued an early warning in his reflections on the French Revolution: 'The effect of liberty to individuals is, that they may do what they please: We ought to see what it will please them to do, before we risque congratulations.'

In this situation, the rationalist-individualist approach reaffirms itself, alongside the other emerging social sciences, as one way of finding out 'what it will please them to do'. The hope and aspiration was that the moral and political sciences should and could now achieve 'the same certainty' as the physical sciences (Baker 1975: 197). Certainty was a requirement of some urgency, since the new political order needed assurances of its viability. But it was also regarded as a new historical possibility, since political action was liberated from the arbitrariness of decisions made by rulers of doubtful legitimacy and given into the hands of the multitude of reason-endowed human beings. The 'blend of liberalism and rationalism', which Keith Baker (1975: 385) observed in Condorcet's convictions, can thus be explained as stemming from the Enlightenment linkage of freedom and reason.

In such a view, the rights-endowed individual became the only conceivable ontological as well as the methodological foundation of a science of political matters after the revolutions. Once the rights of man had been generally accepted as self-evident and inalienable, it seemed obvious, to Turgot and Condorcet for instance, that they were also 'the logical foundation of the science of society' (Baker 1975: 218). In rights-based liberalism, the individual is the only category that need not and often in fact cannot be contested. The individual is simply there, whereas everything else – for instance, what criteria of justification are to be applied when determining the collective good – is subject to argument. Substantive aspects of human interaction are dependent upon communication and consensus. And it is even uncertain, to make the issue more complicated, with whom should one enter into communication, because the boundaries of the community are not themselves given, but subject to agreement.

Once this assumption was accepted, basically two avenues for constructing a science of the political had opened up. One possibility was to try to identify by theoretical reasoning the basic features of this unit of analysis, individual human beings, and their actions. Since this unit was conceived of as an ontological starting-point, devoid of all specific, historical and concrete ties to the world, its characterisation had to proceed from certain inherent features. From earlier debates, those features had often been conceived of as twofold, namely as passions and as interests. In the late Enlightenment context, the rational side of this dichotomy was regarded as the one amenable to systematic elaboration. It thus allowed the building of a scientific approach to the study of at least one aspect of human interaction with the world, namely the production and distribution of material wealth. This approach inaugurated the tradition of political economy, later to be transformed into neoclassical economics and, still later, into rational choice theory.

While political economy was based on a highly abstract, but for the same reasons an extremely powerful, assumption of human rationality, the other conclusion from the individualist foundational principle was possibly even more reductionist but much more cautious. Avoiding any substantive assumptions whatsoever about the driving forces in human beings, the statistical approach, often under the label of political arithmetic, resorted to the collection of numerical information about human behaviour. The space for substantive presuppositions was radically evacuated in this thinking, but the methodological confidence in mathematics seemed to have increased in inverse proportion (Brian 1994; Desrosières 1993). This approach would later lead into quantitative-empirical research and behaviourism.

Up to this point, I have interpreted the seventeenth-century religious wars and the eighteenth-century revolutionary upheavals as events of social disruption that made observers inclined to adopt a rationalist-individualist position. The objective of this withdrawal from richer social theories was to identify the point from which order could be rethought, in the first instance, and then reconstructed. At the same time, the establishment of the European state system, in the treaty of Westphalia, and the creation of the French Republic, in the course of the Revolution, were obviously also moments of the founding or refounding of social configurations. In the case of the French Revolution, a certain rationalist individualism indeed informed republican political language. Overall, however, European consciousness saw other, substantive resources with which to refound social order as still being sufficiently available after these events, and thus rationalist individualism did not achieve an overall breakthrough in social and political thought. However, from a later European point of view, this was much less the case for the creation of the American republic, the master-case for the founding of a polity in the West.

Of Europe and America

During the early twentieth century, in particular between the two wars, a European image of America developed in which an individualist-rationalist modernity was seen to have been established in America and, owing to some of its features, had expanded from there to transform Europe in a similar way. I shall briefly summarise the main features of this view. 'America' is what we may call *presentist*, that is, without history and tradition. It was a country without tradition, 'where no medieval ruins bar the way, where history begins with the elements of modern bourgeois society', as Friedrich Engels (1958: 354) already pointed out in 1887. It was even 'the specific country of ahistory', as Alfred Weber, Max Weber's brother, remarked in 1925, in stronger tones (Weber 1925: 80). America is also *individualist*, that is, there are no ties between human beings except for those that they themselves create. And it is *rationalist*, that is, it knows no norms and values except the increase of instrumental mastery, the striving to use efficiently whatever is at hand in order to achieve one's purposes. Again Tönnies (1922: 357), here using Max Weber's concept of rationality, succinctly expressed his view on American public opinion as 'the essential expression of the spirit of a nation': it is '"rationalistic" . . . in the sense of a reason which prefers to be occupied with the means for external purposes'. Or, in D.H. Lawrence's (1962: 28) words, the American 'is free to be always deliberate, always calculated, rapid, swift, and single in practical execution as a machine'. And, finally, America is what we may call *immanentist*, that is, it rejects the notion of any common higher purpose, anything that transcends individual lives to give them orientation and direction. In other words and in sum, this view saw the ideal society of rational choice theorists as already established on earth.

There are very strong reasons to doubt whether this image provides a proper representation of American social life, but this is not the question that I want to raise here. It is for two other reasons that this image of America is important in the context of a discussion of rational choice theorising. First, it provides the major, and historically early, example of a use of such theorising to describe an existing social configuration; and it does so in comparison to another one, namely by way of the – largely implicit, but sometimes explicit – comparison of Europe and America that informs these writings. Since in doing so it also suggests that the 'other' society provides Europeans with a view of their own future, a *hypothesis* about the *direction of history* can be derived from it. More precisely, it suggests that the history of humanity lead to the emergence of a social order inhabited and sustained by rational individuals. To be sure, most of the European traffickers in this view also criticised and rejected this perspective. Second, we can nevertheless infer a *normative* perspective, namely a *metaphysics* of the rational individual, by inverse reasoning, i.e. by identifying precisely what the Europeans were rejecting. I shall briefly discuss these two features before drawing conclusions about the particular force of their combination.

The European image of America resonates strongly with a specific mode of theorising, and specifically of theorising modernity. This theorising is *modernist*, rather than modern, because it builds on the double notion of autonomy and rationality, which are key characteristics of modernity, but it also turns this notion into an unquestioned and unquestionable assumption for theorising the social world. Such thinking pervades many areas of intellectual life, and possibly its strongest version is rational choice theory in social thought. At its core, such theorising proceeds by a double intellectual move, as discussed earlier. It first withdraws from the treacherous wealth of sensations that come from the socio-historical world to establish what it holds to be those very few indubitable assumptions from which theorising can safely proceed. Subsequently, it reconstructs an entire world from those very few assumptions. Its proponents tend to think that the first move decontaminates understanding, any arbitrary and contingent aspects being removed. The second move is held to create a pure image of the world, with scientific and/or philosophical validity, from which yet further conclusions, including practical ones, can be drawn.[27]

This description of theoretical steps fits a certain view of American history, namely as one of self-foundation *ex nihilo*. The European writings that convey this image of American rationalist individualism certainly contain no thorough sociological interpretation of this American specificity. However, there are fragments of such an interpretation, and they point to the effects of large-scale migration and of the creation of a society by emigrants and exiles. The experience of emigration and exile is one of distancing from that which was known and familiar, from all that which appeared as given and natural. Such distancing – even when it was imposed – can liberate the mind to think of the world in different terms. Emigration and exile as forms of distancing therefore lend themselves to a formal discourse in social theory and political philosophy, one that aims at avoiding or eliminating any contextual and particularistic information.

In the light of such distancing, the experience of going away is sometimes seen to change the character of the social bond with other people, at least at the level of the entire society or polity. Raymond Williams once observed that the exile will usually 'remain an exile, unable to go back to the society that he has rejected or that has rejected him, yet equally unable to form important relationships with the society to which he has gone'. Williams' remark suggests that there is something irrecoverable, once one leaves one's place of origin. The social bond cannot be recreated in the same way in which it existed before; the same density of social relations and density of meaning in the world around oneself can no longer be achieved. Sometimes emigration has even been related to a radical loss of the ability to give meaning. The liberating effect that distancing may have turns into the inevitability of negation and, normatively speaking, into cynicism. Having no roots, no history, no tradition of its own, one of the protagonists in *The plumed serpent* (Lawrence 1987: 77–8) holds that America is incapable of any creation. Its very emergence in an extended process of migration is indicative of some degree of exhaustion of the creative power of humankind.

In such characterizations, we re-encounter the two steps of rationalist theorising, albeit in a different form. In the process of migration, it is alleged, all substantive ties in social life are shattered and human beings are left without any important moral orientations. This is the first step. Then from the loss of all these fetters grows the hubris of wanting to re-erect a world without any such substantive bases. Rather than referring to a territorially locatable society, 'America' stands here for a specific – a 'modern' – way of living, which is traced to something like a generalised migratory experience. The – liberating – willingness to throw off the burden of history goes hand in hand with the impossibility of relating positively to a society with 'thick' social bonds. The experience of migration and exile that sociologically is taken to account for the specificity of 'America' can then be related to the tendencies towards rationalisation and of individualisation, as postulated in social theory from Marx and Weber onwards.

The historical hypothesis contained in such views thus focuses on a decreasing historical depth of social life due to the recomposition of societies, and on the overburdening of singular human beings with the task of not only reconstructing their lives but also reconstituting the guiding frameworks for the social world of which they have become a part. As a result, those beings are seen to be left on their own, without substantive ties to others, and with reason as the only resource they could reliably draw upon, given that other resources presuppose that they are to some degree shared or recognised by others. In the course of 'modern' human history, it is seen as inevitable that a 'flattening' of the temporal depths of social life and a 'weakening' of the social bonds occur. In the most general terms, these are considered to be effects of the dynamics of modernity, although precise interpretations vary considerably in terms of their socio-historical explanations.

Looking at the history of social theory, we find here a theme which unites its critical tradition from the eighteenth century onwards, in particular in that strand which runs from German idealism to the Frankfurt School.

Obviously, in critical theorising, these tendencies are both diagnosed and opposed. It is precisely the task of critical theory to identify the conditions under which they came about or the forces that brought them about, with a view to challenging them. Rational choice theory basically provides for an inversion of that perspective. If it had a historical dimension (which most often it has not), it could broadly accept a Marxian-Weberian narrative of individualisation and rationalisation, but rather than deploring this development, it would celebrate this course of human history as the progress of reason.[28] At the same time, it takes licence – again implicitly – to derive a general theory of human action and social life from this supposed historical tendency. However, this brief analysis of images of America has shown that such reasoning starts out from a quite exceptional situation, namely the founding of a society by – for a variety of reasons – 'disembedded' people.

Of words and worlds

The diagnosis of an increasing rationalisation and individualisation of the social world is a workable hypothesis for sociological inquiry, even though a complex and difficult one. It would have to be tested by research in comparative-historical sociology.[29] In contrast, the presupposition that it is possible to analyse human social life as if its basic units were rational individuals is a statement of basic social ontology, or of 'social metaphysics' (Boltanski and Thévenot 1991). It would have to be judged in terms of its adequacy, necessity and consequences.

Starting out from the latter, the observations at the beginning of this chapter were meant to demonstrate that the application of rational choice reasoning leads to an impoverishment of social theory. A wide variety of registers of social and political philosophy is reduced to the application of instrumental rationality by individual human beings. Sometimes this step is justified in terms of an increase in the consistency of theoretical elaboration. However, the differentiation within the field of rational choice theorising between doves and hawks shows that such consistency has indeed not been achieved. Crucial questions have always remained open to a variety of different answers.

If the consequences cannot be considered as unequivocally desirable, then the case for rational choice theory would have to be made in terms of its empirical adequacy. If the world were populated by rational choosers, it would certainly have to be described and analysed in terms of rational choice theory. An analysis of existing discourses about moral-political evaluation, along the lines of the comparative cultural metaphysics hinted at above, would show that this is far from being the common way in which human beings justify their actions. In addition, comparative analyses of disputes and controversies in social and political life also reveal the variety of forms of justification that are actually applied (Lamont and Thévenot 2000).

This leads us to the case for the necessity of the rational choice approach. The brief historical analysis of 'contexts of discovery' resulted in the observation that rational choice theory is a state of emergency thinking. It applies either in situations of violent strife within a given social order, or in situations of founding an order without common ground. The two kinds of situations are indeed not entirely distinct. Hobbes transformed an analysis of conflict into a hypothetical rationale for the founding of an order. And the French Revolution was the attempt at founding an order that turned into violent strife. The problem being addressed is the lack of common cultural resources – or in the terminology used throughout this chapter, of a common register of moral-political evaluation – to deal with a socio-political situation. Individualist rationality is then proposed as some kind of bottom line on which everybody can agree – or at least would be willing to agree to end a dispute.[30]

It is in this sense that rational choice theory provides the default mode of social theorising – and it has a value and a place among the modes of social theorising on this very ground. However, the social world is neither in a state of permanent crisis and strife nor in a condition of continuous change of such dimensions that everything is always uncertain and in question. In most situations most of the time, much more than such a very limited repertoire of evaluation is available to human beings in order for them to successfully 'go on'. Only a social theory that remains sensitive to the richness of those repertoires will be able to understand social life.

There is even more at stake than 'mere' understanding. The adoption of a rational choice perspective in situations in which richer repertoires are indeed available is not just a matter of description or analysis. It is an alteration of the situation, in the sense described above. By means of redescription, it aims at turning that situation into one in which individual human beings make means–ends decisions on the basis of a conscious preference ordering. In other words, it suggests reading a situation as one of deep crisis, distrust and lack of common resources, in which a default mode then would need to be mobilised, when in fact there may be no such crisis at all and common resources may be abundantly available. If successful in persuading the actors themselves of such an interpretation, the rational choice approach would provide the ground for its own application. But the price to be paid would be the loss of those common resources.

The rational choice approach is the bird which social theorists will always have in hand. But out there in the social world there are many other animals, and social theory should not stop striving to grasp them, unless forced by necessity.

7
ACTION AND INSTITUTION

Often, collectivism is seen as the only consistent alternative to individualism. In sociology, Durkheim is the classical proponent of this view. Growing out of this tradition, recent French work has shown that one can start out from the actions of singular human beings without presupposing individuals and instrumental rationality. Furthermore, and unlike the interactionist mode of thinking, this approach has also focused on the emergence and maintenance of social institutions. But let us start out from the Durkheimian view:

> Collective ways of acting or thinking have a reality outside the individuals who, at every moment of time, conform to it. These ways of acting and thinking exist in their own right. The individual finds them completely formed, and he cannot evade or change them . . . Of course, the individual plays a role in their genesis. But in order that there may be a social fact, several individuals, at the very least, must have contributed their action; and in this joint activity is the origin of a new fact. Since this joint activity takes place outside each of us . . . its necessary effect is to fix, to institute outside us, certain ways of acting and certain judgements which do not depend on each particular will taken separately. It has been pointed out that the word 'institution' well expresses this special mode of reality . . . One can indeed . . . designate as 'institutions' all the beliefs and all the modes of conduct instituted by the collectivity. (Durkheim 1938: lvi)

This excerpt from Emile Durkheim's preface to the second edition of his *Rules of sociological method* may be said to offer – in a highly condensed form – the view of the 'old social sciences' in France, as formulated by the founder of the so-called French school of sociology and continued as the mainstream of sociological thought until at least the early works of Pierre Bourdieu (1968). This is a view which draws a sharp distinction between the social and, as one should later say, structural, on the one hand, and the individual and coincidental, on the other. Being dubbed a 'philosophy without subject' (Bourdieu and Passeron 1967), it also gives analytical priority to the former over the latter – a view which was widely adopted in the sociological tradition outside France as well.

Since the late 1980s, sociologists, economists, political philosophers and historians in France have developed a new research perspective, sometimes called a 'new configuration in the social sciences' as well as a 'theoretical breakthrough' (*EspacesTemps* 1992: 5; Dodier 1991: 427).[31] In the following I shall try to sketch, in three steps, the main theoretical lines of these works and shall argue that they allow, in particular, a different view on that social phenomenon which Durkheim called 'collective modes of thought and action', or in short 'institutions'. First, I shall aim at identifying the direction of criticism of more conventional science which these works entail. The rebuilding of social thought after this critique then, second, proceeds via a rethinking of the concept of human action and reconsiders finally, third, the theoretically highly loaded notion of institution as well as the related issue of the stability and coherence of social practices. The 'genesis' of such institutions is in the focus of this perspective, as a process in which – according to Durkheim, too – the individual played a role, but which, at least in this regard, was of little interest as a 'social fact' in the old view.[32] A concluding section will try to show where these 'new social sciences' come from, in terms of French intellectual traditions, and where they might most fruitfully go.

Praxis and history: dissolving theoretical presuppositions

After the derailment of a train a controversy is likely to emerge over the responsibility for the occurrence between the train conductor, the heads of the stations involved, the legal representatives of the railway company and of injured passengers as well as possibly many others (Chateauraynaud 1991a). When the French daily *Le Monde* receives a letter to the editor in which a reader wishes to denounce the inacceptability of a certain behaviour or event, then the editors will weigh the story as to its meriting public attention (Boltanski 1990). When, on 4 January 1914, Henry Ford announced an extraordinary increase of the regular wage to $5 per day, he inadvertently started a chain of action of wide temporal and spatial extensions the outcome of which was described as a new social formation by some observers, occasionally called Fordism (Boyer and Orléan 1991). When in 1896 the French *Office de travail* defined the term 'unemployed' and began to use it in its statistics, a categorial reordering of economic life commenced in the course of which the rate of unemployment was to become a key indicator for the state of national economies some decades later (Salais et al. 1986; Zimmermann 2000).

Controversies over the evaluation of occurrences on the one hand, and historical transformations of social categories and conventions on the other, are typical objects of inquiry in the 'new French social sciences'. Luc Boltanski (1990: 25) has even used the label 'sociology of disputes' for this approach, though this term may be unduly restraining the range of issues tackled. Investigations from which the examples used above are drawn are, among others, a comprehensive study of *fautes professionnelles*, work accidents, professional misbehaviour and the like (Chateauraynaud 1991a); analyses of *dénonciations*, accusations of illegitimate social behaviour (Boltanski 1990: part III); and a great number of investigations of controversies in the firm (Salais and Thévenot 1986; Boltanski and Thévenot 1986; *Revue économique* 1989).

Such disputes (so-called *causes* or *affaires*) are situations in which the actors involved produce an explicit evaluation, a judgement, making visible the criteria of justification that they use. Luc Boltanski and Laurent Thévenot also speak of tests or examinations (*situations d'épreuve*), in which the competences and means available to the actors are brought openly into play. In terms of research strategy, thus, the emphasis on disputes is motivated by the assumption that such controversies, and the social transformations that they may entail, make the resources and competences particularly visible which are at hand to human beings to master social situations.

At the same time, a methodological maxim states that as few categories as possible should enter the analysis that have not been introduced by the human beings themselves when dealing with such situations (Chateauraynaud 1991a: 25; Boltanski 1990: 57). This maxim of 'scarcity of presuppositions' (Dodier 1991: 437–40; Boltanski 1990: 23) is based on a pronounced scepticism with regard to structuralist and functionalist sociology as well as to neoclassical economics and rational choice and their highly presupposition-rich conceptualisations. The new approach turns away from the 'social metaphysics' of these disciplines, as Boltanski and Thévenot (1991: 42), for instance, formulate. The dissolution of many of the presuppositions of the predominant approaches can then be considered the *first* step in the theoretical programme of the 'pragmatic turn' in French social science, as these developments have also been called (*EspacesTemps* 1992: 5; Bénatouïl 1999).

What is called for here is simple and appears almost self-evident. Current descriptions of the state of social theory assume most often a fundamental opposition of two possible perspectives, under a variety of different names: individualism and atomism may be opposed to collectivism and holism; and utilitarianism to normativism, or – using the labels of the disciplines – economic to sociological approaches (for critical views see, for example, Etzioni 1988: 6–7; Taylor 1989a: 159; Joas 1992a: 216). 'Our approach,' however, Boltanski and Thévenot (1991: 43) write, 'aspires to make the elements of similarity visible, below the apparent irreducibility of the methodological opposition between explanations of "individual" conduct and explanations of "collective" behaviour.'

Both variants of such opposed theories are based on nothing other than a certain kind of 'rules of agreement' each (through the exchange of goods on the market or through collective identity). But none of them is capable of dealing with the relation between these two forms of accord. Boltanski, Thévenot and Robert Salais do not primarily accuse – as many other critics of disciplinary theorising do – the constructions of utilitarianism or normativism, of the optimising market or the socially integrated society, as being overly formalised abstractions, un-related to the social world. To them, the very existence of such constructions in social theory is sufficient evidence for a social reality worthy to be analysed (Boltanski and Thévenot 1991: 33). These constructions, however, do not exist as 'positive scientific laws'; they should rather be regarded as 'common principles of a superior order'. In a formalised way, such principles are found in political philosophy. They can be detected equally well, however, in justifications given for everyday activities. The fault of disciplinary social science is exactly the identical transformation of such principles of political philosophy into social laws of a scientific nature (Boltanski and Thévenot 1991: 43–7). Thus, the task is to dissolve the disciplinary codifications and to recommence the analysis of social action, in conceptually more open terms, with regard to the forms of achieving agreement and coordination. Whether the two forms of justification occupy an important space in social reality can be discussed after such an analytical reconsideration only.[33]

Ce qu'agir veut dire: reformulating the theory of action

Focusing, thus, on the analysis of past and present social practices in situational controversies and historical transformations, the *second* step in the French theoretical programme is an attempt at reconstructing the notion of human action. No further efforts are made to isolate individual actions analytically and to ask for the intentions and rationalities in them, on the one hand, or for the accepted norms and applied rules, on the other. In the centre of interest, instead, we find the situation in its temporality, the individual's uncertainty about the identification of the situation and the interpretive effort that is required to determine, together with others, the situation as a shared and common one (Quéré 1993: 49–52; Thévenot 1990: 39–44). I may add that Hans Joas' recent criticism of teleological interpretations of the intentionality of action emphasizes in a quite similar way the 'constitutive, not merely contingent situativity of human action' (1992a: 235).

Once such a starting-point is accepted, a number of well-known issues of sociological theory are in need of reformulation. The new works share with more conventional approaches the view that social action requires some form of communication and understanding between human beings; this issue is called the 'exigence for agreement' (*exigence de l'accord*, Boltanski and Thévenot 1991: 43) or 'exigence for coordination' (*exigence de coordination*, Thévenot 1990). These terms may sound vaguely reminiscent of a time-honoured issue of social and political thought, namely the explanation of social order, from Hobbes to Parsons and beyond. However, this requirement is phrased here in quite different terms than the classical sociological problem was. The classical question presupposed the existence of such an order, or at least the tendency of social relations to achieve and maintain such order – without ever satisfactorily clarifying the empirical conditions for its existence. The authors to be discussed here, in contrast, turn the production of agreement and coordination itself into the key issue. I would like to emphasise three consequences of such a revision.

First, the reformulation of the question demands that one specifies under which conditions and on which issues an exigence for agreement exactly exists. Many situations have not actually to be dealt with in common between human beings, or at least not in a comprehensive sense (Boltanski and Thévenot 1991: 51). Between walkers in a park on Sundays, for instance, there may indeed be some shared understanding of the commonality of their situation, albeit a very limited one. Different and again very specific and typically limited efforts at coordination are required between buyers and sellers of a commodity, between citizens in political decision-making, or between parents over the raising of a child. 'Society', then, is not an encompassing social order, rather multiply produced agreements – as well as persistent disputes – of highly varying extensions, durability and substance (see ch. 9).

Second, it is emphasised that reaching such agreements may not simply be conceived as the application of – pre-existing and unequivocal – rules. In contrast, 'social labour' (*travail social*, Boltanski 1982; Quéré 1992: 45–6) is constantly demanded to interpret situations, to mutually adapt interpretations, and to determine modes of agreement in common. 'The work of transformation, performed by the agents to deal with the situation, lies between the event and the form through which the objects and relations that have emerged in the event are made coherent – i.e. what classical sociology has termed structure' (Chateauraynaud 1991a: 25). The capability of the agents, the competences they bring into the situation – '*ce dont les gens sont capables*; what people are capable to do' – turns then into one of the key questions of social science, a question to which more conventional approaches have considered the answer as given.[34]

Third, thus, the result of a process of reaching an agreement cannot be derived from the nature of the controversy or from the social positions of the people involved. What is to be expected, in contrast, is a plurality of criteria to determine the situation and a process of selecting the appropriate criteria that is itself part of the reaching of an agreement. As a result, a plurality of possible 'worlds' emerges, as some authors formulate (Dodier 1991; Salais and Storper 1992; 1993). Throughout its history, the very concept of a social science has strongly relied on the possibility of identifying the social determinants of human action. Even the more recent debates on the relation between human agency and social structure are often – though not always – cast in terms of corridors of action that provide limited openness within broader frames of structural determination. Without denying the existence of constraints to action, this approach, however, rejects the analytical confrontation of the willing subject to something objectively given (and sociologically fully intelligible), which is external to her/him. Instead, the 'structure' is seen as itself being determined in the process of interaction. Therefore, determinism and evolutionism become unthinkable.

If we stopped our discussion of these 'new approaches' at this point, readers could well be reminded of symbolic interactionism and, possibly, of ethnomethodology. This would mean, at the same time, that the limits of such approaches are evoked, not least their inability to move beyond so-called micro-sociological perspectives (Dodier 1991: 440–1; also Joas 1992a: 215–16; 1992b: 56, 60). It could easily be objected that social interaction looks multifarious only as long as the more extended and more solid constraints of human action by stable institutional forms are not systematically brought into view. The specificities of the individual case are retained only under the condition of not even searching for the potentially generalisable features.[35] A theory which radically emphasises the 'permanent negotiation of social order' – as Chateauraynaud (1991a: 413) writes on ethnomethodology – will hardly be capable of developing a concept of institution. And if, despite such objections, the French researchers insisted on concluding from their findings on identifiable social plurality, they would surely suffer the verdict of analytical voluntarism – and their works would lack originality.

Boltanski himself (1990: 86) has used the term 'relativism' to characterise this kind of social thought. There is a link to postmodernism, however, only if the latter is regarded as a criticism of presuppositions of rationality rather than as the inverse commitment to an equally general as well as ahistorical and asociological presupposition of contingency – as appears to be assumed by Richard Rorty (1989). These theoretical conceptions are no *a priori* assumptions in the same sense in which rationality or normguidedness of human action have been presuppositions of more conventional approaches. The variability of exigences for coordination, the interpretive activity of the people involved as well as the plurality of results are empirically researchable. Such research may then result in identifying social conventions that have a wide spatiotemporal extension and may thus fit a standard definition of 'institution'. Indeed, the new French social sciences do inquire specifically into the emergence of such conventions, and the problématiques of institutions can be regarded as the key common question of these scholars – although under the condition of a reconceptualisation. That is why I consider the reconstruction of a notion of institution as the *third* step in their theoretical programme.

Travail de rapprochement: the genesis of institutions

Let us look, as an example, at the 'invention of unemployment' to which Robert Salais, Bénédicte Zimmermann and others have devoted some long-term historical analyses. They show how, since the closing decades of the last century, the term 'unemployed' gradually emerged and became related to a new conception of the normality of wage labour. Under such a conception, unemployment – like sickness and old age, but also like strikes – was seen as a deviation from such normality which needed to be made intelligible and to be handled politically. Trade unions, employers, local and national administration waged long struggles over the legal, economic and political definition of 'unemployment' as well as over its demarcation from other kinds of interruptions of the wage–labour relation. The interpretation of the phenomenon and its conceptual fixation were always tied to its definition as a social problem and to the conclusions that various concepts would entail as to the handling of the problem. Most importantly, various conclusions were drawn as to the responsibility for unemployment – which could reside, for instance, with the unemployed, the former employer, the state or the anonymous workings of the economy – and as to the definition of the caring social group of which the unemployed was a member – which could be the company, the local commune, the national state or the profession.

A definition was agreed upon nationwide and this definition was made part of political strategies in the nation-state during the 1920s and 1930s in Germany and France; with modifications, analogous achievements were reached in other industrial countries. The Keynesian full employment convention was the result of this historical accord, a convention which is today being challenged under the impact of globalisation and flexibilisation, to put it crudely and briefly, undermining the viability of the nation as a defined economic field of action (Salais et al. 1986; Zimmermann 2000).

These works on wage conventions and unemployment should be regarded as an analysis of the historical transformation of an institution.[36] They show how the relation between employers and workers is disputed and renegotiated, how new actors and arguments are drawn into the dispute, until this relation is nationally framed by new conventions. By the 1960s, the ubiquity of the wage relation, the government commitment to full employment, and the distribution of unemploy-ment benefits to the remaining deviant cases had become a set of accepted rules and norms. Many economists and sociologists of the time have spent their intellectual energy trying to show for which rational, functional or socio-structural reasons these norms and rules had to come into existence. In the 'new French' view, however, institutions are not perceived as systems of rules, norms or roles that emerge because of common social determinants and fix and homogenise human behaviour.

Generally and legitimately, the notion of institution has been linked to the explanation of regularities and similarities in human social life. A critical rethinking of this concept must not deny that some kinds of regularities and similarities do indeed exist. Thévenot (1990: 57) agrees that terms such as rules or norms could be justifiable under certain empirical circumstances: 'Such an explanatory approach may provide a quite good approximation for limited spaces of action in which the permanence of a universe of objects and routines guarantees stability and similarity of conduct.'[37] To acknowledge such a limited validity, however, means nothing less than claiming the inadequacy of such a conceptualisation of institutions for 'a more general theory of action'.

A basic theoretical terminology must be able to account for two different types of situations likewise. In social life, there are such 'moments in which the activities of persons hold together, [people] adapt to each other and achieve agreement over an order of things, moments that tend to allow for notions of objective constraint, social norm, equilibrium, successful communication, fulfilment of the speech act and the like'. But there are also those 'moments in which unrest dominates the scene and reveals disputes over what is at stake, moments of uncertainty, of more or less critical doubt' (Thévenot 1990: 57–8).

To put the difference schematically: conventional social science regards the former case as the normality towards which social situations always tend to move, for reasons variously conceived in different approaches and disciplines. Deviations from this case may then be treated as something singular or particular, of no sociological import. The 'new social sciences', however, consider the latter case as the conceptually more open, and that is more general, one. To move from a situation of this latter type to one of the former kind requires the above-mentioned 'social labour' or 'labour of *rapprochement*', the success of which is never certain. 'We look for an access-point to human action,' writes Thévenot on this research programme, 'which does justice to the uncertainty over the possibility of co-ordination' (1993: 276; see also Hoarau 1992: 17–19).

That is why situations are distinguished according to their specific 'exigences of coordination'. The identification of a situation and the persons and objects involved in it leads to the determination of exigences of coordination that vary between 'a *familiar gesture*, which refers to nothing but personal conveniences, a *communicable judgement*, which presupposes some appreciation of what is adequate assuming an understanding of commonality, though one which is but little controlled, and [finally] a *generalisable judgement*, which requires collective conventions that can be subjected to common examination as well as revision' (Thévenot 1993: 287, my emphasis).

Accordingly, there are varying modes 'of closing the process of qualifying [an event], reaching from personal convenience to collective conventions', which differ not least in spatiotemporal extension and in the kind and the extent of labour of *rapprochement* that they entail.[38] By drawing such analogies between situations of different kinds, it is possible to move analytically from studies of interactions to those of transformations of greater (i.e. spatiotemporally more extended or more general) orders of action – brought about, namely, in the course of *causes* which include many people by means of producing equivalences. Such a widely extended work of interpretation and *rapprochement* is what more conventional macro-sociology used to term 'a structural crisis' (Thévenot 1993: 280–1).

The concept of institution is thus being relieved of some of the theoretical burdens it used to carry. It will continue to be used for naming those social practices that show a certain regularity and stability through time and space. The continuous existence of such practices, however, requires a steady construction of common-alities, a 'making equal' of persons and objects whose 'equality' or 'equivalence' is neither natural nor self-evident.

The empirical interest of the French authors in statistical procedures and processes of classification results from such considerations. In somewhat economistic terms, Thévenot called such labour of making equal 'investment in form'. It is being pursued to establish, often only temporarily and involving many efforts, a stable relation between persons and/or things, thus reducing the uncertainty about how to identify a situation. Taylor's 'scientific work organ-isation', for instance, can then be characterised as the 'immobilisation of a reproducible relation' (Thévenot 1985a: 26). Owing to such reflections, that branch of the 'new French social sciences' which is particularly interested in allocative practices has also become known as the 'economics of conventions'. The term 'convention' is introduced to subvert the atomism and utilitarianism of neoclassical economic theorising. 'Conventions are practices, routines, agreements, and their associated informal or institutional forms which bind acts together through mutual expectations . . . Coordination between economic agents takes place within a context of pervasive uncertainty with respect to the actions and expectations of others. Conventions emerge as responses to such uncertainty' (Salais and Storper 1992: 171; see further Salais and Thévenot 1986; *Revue économique* 1989; for an overview see Kramarz 1991). In a sort of critical linkage to, and modification of, neoclassical economics, market exchange is then analysed as being based on conventions the most basic of which would be one that makes it possible to regard goods as equivalent (such as a certain number of sparrows to a dove, to return to the example in Chapter 6).

The work of 'making equal' is a prerequisite for collective action to emerge. Those engaging in collective action will envisage a certain commonality with others at least with regard to what is relevant for their common activities. There is a close linkage between 'addition (rendering equivalent) and coalition (action)', as Alain Desrosières (1991: 200; 1993) emphasises, who titles his analysis of the relation between social sciences, statistics and the state programmatically as 'How to make things which hold together'. Orders have to be created by assembling diverse elements to groups of equals. This work will have to be continuously repeated, and never can doubts about the adequacy of the assembly be entirely eliminated. Such a social scientific perspective will have to 'renounce any conception that regards the unity and cohesion of a group as the product of a substantive similarity between its members and an objectively shared interest'. Attention will instead be directed towards 'the immense historical labour that is necessary to unite disparate beings around the same system of representation, to constitute the reality of such a heterogeneous ensemble, to inscribe it into devices [*dispositifs*] by an intensive effort of objectification and to endow it with a common interest' (Boltanski 1990: 70).

Or, in other words, such a perspective rejects the 'two restrictive definitions . . . which presuppose the safeguarding of order and refuse to deal with the doubt: (a) a unanimity or similarity of behaviour subject to common material constraints or well mastered by shared ideas (beliefs, representations); (b) a diversity of actions integrated through systematic articulation (division of functions, of roles) . . . These approaches share the reduction of coordination to the maintenance of an order' (Thévenot 1993: 276).[39]

However, at the very least, the labour of coordination during historical transformations of institutions cannot be reduced to the continuity of a safeguarded order. Thus, Luc Boltanski (1990: 25) describes his research on the formation of the *cadres* as a social group as the attempt to understand the development of a *cause* into an institution, as 'work at the construction of "collective persons"' (Thévenot 1990: 59). Or Alain Desrosières relates cognitive transformations in the social sciences and in statistics to the formation of the political institutions of the welfare state, a state developing generalizable, collective rules for treating individuals.

In as far as institutions of a certain coherence have been erected over social spaces (which, it needs to be emphasised, is not necessarily the case), notions such as normality or even rationality may again become usable, without though involving a return to the sociological concepts of rule and norm in their classic senses. 'The requirements for coherence of a judgment orient towards some idea of normality' (Thévenot 1993: 287–8). However, 'it is necessary to include into the notion of normality the ability to deal with uncertainty about the future, and rationality has to be conceived as the coherence of an adjustment, avoiding the separation of objective means from an end that is enclosed in representations and beliefs' (Thévenot 1990: 57).

Agir dans plusieurs mondes: forms and conditions of coherence

At this point, one of the classical questions returns, albeit in different form. It is obviously not intended to claim that there will necessarily be a unique optimum result of *rapprochement*, sometimes an implicit notion of classical social science. Nor is there reason to assume, however, that arbitrary forms of generalisation could emerge from the work of *rapprochement*. This leads to the need for specifying conditions for 'coherence or congruence' (Thévenot 1985a: 64). Such coherence, too, is first of all an empirical phenomenon. The degree of existing coherence refers to the social spaces in which assumptions and expectations are valid, to the degree to which boundaries of validity are relatively well defined with regard to space, time and persons. 'Different kinds of conventions' can be distinguished according to such coherence, and to their 'rigidity' in particular (Thévenot 1985b: V; 1985a: 54, 63–4).

The value of a mere such good description should not be underestimated. Complete applicability of institutional rules is often too easily assumed for too broadly conceived social spaces, such as the laws of a nation-state, the law of competition on the world market, or the rules of academic recognition, and their determining effect on action is then taken for granted. More fine-grained analyses – of practices of production, for instance – reveal a multiplicity of conventions with their specific forms of coherence each, which cannot simply be declared to form niches under a reigning paradigm of industrial mass production (Salais and Storper 1993).

On the basis of such a thick inventory of the diversity of practices, moreover, the forms and conditions of coherence have been systematically analysed, i.e. the range of viable possibilities to shape uncertainty and to create a kind of normality has been searched for (for a comparative overview of three models, including Jürgen Habermas' theory of the public sphere, see Chateaureynaud 1991a: 415ff). Boltanski and Thévenot's *De la justification* is devoted to the tentative determination of the available set of interpretive possibilities of justification of one's actions, i.e. the possible figures of argument that could be deployed in a controversy with the objective of closing the dispute (on the legitimacy of such work of reduction, see Boltanski 1990: 87–8).

Again, the starting-point of the analysis is the concrete controversy, a *cause*. A controversy is about the mobilisation of resources and competences with a view to achieving an *ajustement* or *rapprochement* (Thévenot 1990: 58). Generally, each situation will show specific modes of mobilisation; no situation is completely predetermined. To arrive at an agreement, however, the persons in controversy have to refer to something beyond themselves, to resources that they have in common and that exist and reach beyond the situation and its specificities (Boltanski 1990: 74). Exactly because of their capacity to reach beyond a situation, two kinds of such resources are emphasised: things, material objects, on the one hand, and orders of justification, sets of interpretive possibilities for grounding a reasoning, on the other (on the 'relations between reasons and things', see Boltanski and Thévenot 1991: 30).

Linking up especially to the works of Bruno Latour, the analysis of forms in which objects are mobilised in controversies will lead to a reformulation of the sociology of object relations (or, in more current jargon, of technology), an issue I will not deal with in detail here (see Chateauraynaud 1991b for a critical presentation). Two aspects seem to be particularly important: the limitation of the possibilities for interpretation through material prestructuring is accompanied by the extension of the spaces of interpretation beyond the immediate situation. This extension is reached through the introduction of objects as 'spokespersons' (Latour) for a specific interpretation, which thus may be extended over enlarged spaces and/or times. In such a perspective, Gérard Noiriel (1992: 155–80), for instance, has analysed the identity card as an object that is used to make adherence to an order of classification visible and, by this means, serves to strengthen this classificatory order itself, containing the idea of national identity, among others.

The other major means of extension, of 'generalisation' of a situation, is the recourse to a criterion of justification whose validity reaches beyond any particular occurrence.[40] Boltanski and Thévenot have tried to identify, on the basis of their empirical studies, a limited set of forms of justification with claims to universality. Going back to classical texts of political philosophy, they distinguish six *cités* – orders of judgements each governed unequivocally by a single dominant principle. These are the orders of the market, inspiration, the public sphere, the domestic order, the civic order, and industry.[41] Boltanski and Thévenot demonstrate the existence of these orders of justification in contemporary social reality by going through manuals in current usage, meant to guide behaviour. A look at a guide for public relations work in a company, thus, may illustrate the recourse to the *cité* of the public sphere.

As real-life situations are characterised by ambiguity with regard to their belonging to any single *cité*, the interpretive work of the persons involved will crucially consist precisely in determining this issue of belonging to a specific realm of validity claims. Denouncing a political scandal, for instance, such as accusing somebody of transferring public resources to a friend, means voicing the suspicion that justifications valid in the domestic *cité* have illegitimately been applied in the civic *cité*. An action that would have been considered not merely justified but even morally demanded in the former, namely supporting a member by personal intervention, is unacceptable in the latter. The identification of the situation determines the applicability of criteria; to create a consensus on the character of the situation means closing the controversy.

Now, social institutions should not be regarded as resulting from the codification of such or other criteria, rather they display 'simultaneous presence of hetero-geneous resources'.[42] To make this point of distinction from other sociologies, such as theories of differentiation, unmistakable, Boltanski and Thévenot selected all texts that serve as evidence for the actual existence of these *cités* from one single social space, namely a business enterprise. All six orders of justification coexist in a company, i.e. an organisation that others would count as belonging clearly to the economic 'sphere' or 'subsystem' of society. That is why situations tend to be ambiguous and in strong need of interpretation, and efforts have to be recurrently invested to achieve compromises over the validity of orders of justification. Such plurality of worlds creates at the same time the permanent uncertainty over expectations and actions of others and the possibility to escape the inevitability of a dictated judgement by making recourse to criteria from some other *cité*.[43]

De la justification is an attempt at conceptual synthesis with regard to the variety, stability and coherence of social configurations. Beyond that, however, it also demands, though cautiously, to reconsider some key issues in normative political philosophy and in social theory – notwithstanding the authors' insistence that it is neither a theory of justice nor a theory of society.

The two main liberal positions in political theory, if I am forgiven for simplifying, argue that criteria of justice are to be derived either from an 'original position' (John Rawls) or from the social location of the issue, its occurrence in one of a plurality of spheres (Michael Walzer). Boltanski and Thévenot, however, first look at how human beings actually evaluate their own behaviour and that of others; they develop, one might say, an anthropology of justification. They observe that criteria are used which can indeed be traced back to traditions of political philosophy. They do not find, though, one superior set of criteria or even moderately well demarcable spheres in which a single consistent set of criteria reigns. Instead, inconsistent compromises are established situationwise, and are even set on a more permanent basis, that is, they are institutionalised. Doubting the possibility of any formal theory of justice, they seem to demand, finding themselves closer to Walzer than to Rawls,[44] that political theory needs to be better sociologically informed – and that normative concerns be reintegrated into sociological theory.

In terms of social theory this means that Boltanski and Thévenot, using terms such as *cité* and *grandeur*, take a marked distance – even though they do so rather implicitly – from the key concepts Pierre Bourdieu developed for his social theory, such as *champs* and *capital* (Ernct 1992: 37). In a later work, *L'amour et la justice comme compétences* (1990), Boltanski points towards a further extension of the emerging grammar of regimes of justification. If the forms of justice described by the *cités* refer to peaceful ways of determining equivalences, then there are also other regimes, which are not peaceful – such as violence – or are not based on explicated forms of equivalence – such as love. These considerations allow one to develop a double distinction – between regimes of dispute and those of peace, and between regimes with a mode of rendering equivalent and those without – from which four basic forms of interaction emerge: justice, violence, appropriateness (*justesse*) and love (1990: 110–11). These basic terms do not merely refer to the existence of other human beings within an objectively defined social space (in a 'field' or a 'structure'), but point to the processes in which spaces of common validity of universal criteria are first of all being socially determined, that is, the situative mutual recognition of the other is turned into an open – sociological and historical – question.[45]

Theoretical trajectories and perspectives

Some doubts with regard to the originality of these 'new French social sciences' may not yet have been completely dissolved by my brief sketch. Regarding the above-mentioned linkages to American, and partly also German, sociological approaches, theories of justice and social philosophies, could it not be the case that we witness here merely some sort of overdue internationalisation of French social thought? While I will argue that there is a significant contribution by this network of researchers to rethinking the social sciences more generally, to understand what exactly this contribution could be it may indeed be useful to first consider the way it has come within French intellectual traditions.

In the realms of sociology and anthropology, Pierre Bourdieu had already started reformulating structuralist thought by opening it up to perspectives of a theory of action. Boltanski, Thévenot, Desrosières and the late Michael Pollak refer to this work, but they radicalise Bourdieu's more reluctant rejection of determinism and rationalism. In some other authors, notably Louis Quéré, an analogous relation can be detected to Alain Touraine's sociology of social movements, a relation of linkage and further elaboration. In the realm of economics, the regulation school around Michel Aglietta and Robert Boyer had reopened the strong French tradition of institutionalism towards historical analysis; it remained caught, though, in systemic reasoning inspired by neo-Marxism. Salais, Thévenot and others build on these works and modify the approach by breaking entirely with evolutionism and emphasising the simultaneous plurality of 'worlds of production'.

The maxim of 'scarcity of presuppositions' that I mentioned above is known from the sociology of scientific knowledge under the denomination 'symmetrical treatment' and is then linked to the Edinburgh 'strong programme'. Michel Callon and Bruno Latour, whose works go also under the label of the 'new social sciences', pursue a similar kind of sociology of scientific knowledge in France (Dodier 1991: 442; Boltanski and Thévenot 1991: 21; Chateauraynaud 1991b; Bénatouïl 1999). If the key intention here is the reopening of access points to the social world that had been closed in some of the disciplinary constructions, some other authors try to achieve this objective by reappropriating hermeneutics and phenomenology, often in their French variants through the works of Paul Ricoeur und Maurice Merleau-Ponty (see Dosse 1995 as an overview).

I have tried to describe the theoretical movement as an opening; and I think such a move is important for two reasons, a more purely theoretical one and a historical one. Theoretically, as I tried to argue extensively in the first section of this chapter, the French approach widens the space of reasoning within the human sciences. It rejects the foundational character of theoretical constructions such as rationalism or collectivism without denying them their validity as existing modes of human reasoning. Thus, it is able to relate such assumptions, hitherto mostly seen as mutually incompatible, to each other on the basis of a broader social ontology.[46] To some extent, the same is true for the cleavage between normative and analytical types of scholarly argumentation. By insisting on the normative character of observable human behaviour, such as in expressed justifications, they reintegrate the two types and open the way for rethinking the relations between sociology, economics and political philosophy, disciplines which are divided not least along those lines.

The historical importance of this opening is related to the suspicion that the theoretical consolidation, not to say petrification, of twentieth-century social sciences went along with a relative stabilisation of major social conventions (Wagner 1990). The 'new French social sciences' provide elements of a thick description of our societies which, if developed into an empirically rich, historical sociology of social configurations, could help to understand this process and, maybe, make it amenable in what today appears as a current major social restructuring uprooting those conventions.[47]

Boltanski and Thévenot (1991: 347–56) allude to this possibility when they place the core problématiques in Durkheim's diagnosis of his time, at the turn of the nineteenth century – the creation of organic solidarity by means of intermediary social institutions between individuals and society – in the context of the transformation of a social configuration based on a compromise between the justificatory orders of the market and the citizen, i.e. nineteenth-century liberalism, to one based on a different compromise, namely between criteria from the industrial, civic and domestic orders. This latter configuration is mostly known as industrial society, or advanced capitalist democracies, dominating the first two-thirds of the twentieth century in the West. And it does not appear as a coincidence – or, at least, it should not be treated as such – that a great number of the available French studies deal with those transformations of economic and social conventions – unemployment, professional classifications, work organisation, wage conventions – that have been created around the turn of the nineteenth century and have achieved a high degree of coherence from about the 1930s onwards – and are being challenged now. If one attempted to exploit the findings of these works in parallel ways and started complementary projects in a systematic way, then the research programme of the 'new social sciences' could grow into a conceptually sound historical sociology of modernity which takes the idea seriously that social institutions are created by human beings but which remains capable of recognising the specific historical limits and boundaries, as well as opportunities and enablements, which they entail (see Wagner 1999a for further debate; and Boltanski and Chiapello 1999, Lamont and Thévenot 2000 for the further results of this research programme).

8
CULTURE
(with Heidrun Friese)

In the view of the social sciences of some two or three decades ago, social life was seen to happen in structures or systems, and human beings were defined, if not even determined, by their roles and interests which could be derived from their position in the social order. True, there were differences between approaches that used these concepts for a critique of contemporary society and others that adopted a more affirmative position, often both a positive and a positivistic one. However, what distinguished the former from the latter was that they identified contradictions of interests and roles rather than assuming harmonious interrelations – not much more. More recently though, such language has fallen out of fashion. Social life now appears to be ordered by meanings and beliefs; human beings live together in cultures, and they recognize the similarity or strangeness of the other not by their class locations but by their identities (for similar observations see Lamont 1992: 179–80; Lash 1994: 214–15; Griswold 1994: xiii; Smelser 1997: ch. 3).

Conventionally, one may think of two reasons for the shift to have occurred, and for the likelihood of it staying with us for a while. The first reason is intellectual progress. Could it be that scholars in the social sciences have ultimately realised how human beings really group together, and have overcome earlier misconceptions? The other reason is major social change. Maybe our societies were structurally ordered and were tied together by roles and interests until very recently, but have now changed towards a predominance of cultural relations and the grouping of individuals according to identities. Very bluntly, we may see here just a reflection of a change in the most visible social conflicts. Class struggle seems to have given way to national and ethnic strife; concern for equality appears to have been replaced or superseded by the assertion of the right to diversity.

It should not be entirely ruled out that the one or the other or a combination of the two explanations is indeed valid. Before any such conclusion can be reached, however, it seems to us that some rethinking of both the structural and the cultural language has to be undertaken. It is disturbing, to put it mildly, that this intellectual shift has occurred without an appropriately explicit debate about its merits. No elaborated arguments have been made to support either of the two above-mentioned reasons for the change. Should we see ourselves in the midst of a change of paradigm or of research programme, as Thomas Kuhn or Imre Lakatos described, when an established theorising without being refuted is just gradually abandoned, because it no longer produces interesting findings and because a younger generation flocks away from it to other perspectives? While all this may well be the case, the least one could do is to reflect about the causes and consequences of intellectual shifts while they go on, and not leave this to historians of science. We will here just make one modest attempt.

Our main ambition is to discern some presuppositions of common modes of conceptualisation and to show what effects those presuppositions may have on the analysis. Far from being able to offer better foundations for social theory, we will argue for the need for a theorising that is reflexive of its presuppositions even while working with them (see Friese 1997; Wagner 1994). Reflexivity is the attempt to take a step back from current practices (Bauman 1991: 272); as such, it gives a different perspective but no higher-order knowledge, and reflexive criticism should also be applied to the outcomes of the reflexive endeavour itself.

Modernity and contingency

Any direct comparison of the structural and the cultural language is limited by the fact that it cannot recognise elements which both constructions have in common.[48] That is why we intend to direct attention to a third approach, to which both structural and cultural theorising stand in a problematic relation. The recent intellectual shift did not occur as smoothly as we suggested above. At a closer look, an interim period can be identified, broadly the 1980s, in which structural analysis had already lost its power of persuasion but cultural analysis had not yet emerged as the successful contender for the succession.

There were some years of pervasive doubt as to whether the social world could at all be described in terms of a limited number of stable features. To some observers, increasingly labelled postmodernists, it appeared to be of very limited intelligibility; to others, it just did not show the solidity and stability required to give a strong representation of it. In 1982, for instance, Marshall Berman recalled the time-honoured view that modernity dissolves all stable linkages between human beings, that it introduces a social dynamics that will leave nothing untouched. 'All that is solid melts into air', as Marx and Engels had said in the *Communist manifesto*. Social life will thus become ever more contingent as modernity unfolds. And towards the end of the 1980s, Richard Rorty (1989) published what is probably the most comprehensive and consistent eulogy of such a view, his triple praise of the contingency of all human life, of language, community and selfhood. The assertion of principled contingency of the social world provides the third position, from which structural and cultural theorising can be compared and commented upon. In its radical version, it is a position from which social analysis can probably not itself be pursued, but it is one which enables the reflexive considerations we deem necessary (for a related discussion see Derrida 1978: 292–3).

In a long-term perspective, the argument on increasing contingency may be considered one, if not the guiding theme of much social theorising – and even more so of the political philosophy of individualist liberalism. In the stock of the tradition of social theory,[49] we find the idea of a dissolution of 'community' and its transformation into 'society'. 'Society' gives much more room to individuation and individuality, though these individuals may be characterised by their roles and interests which are specific to their location in the social order. Somewhat later we find that modernisation theory relaxes its idea of role-boundedness of human beings and ends on the theorem of individualisation. Finally, poststructuralist theorising, despite its self-image as a critic of the mainstream of social theory, can also be read as the latter's radical continuation assuming that the individual is ultimately dissolved, fragmented and dispersed. One way of reading modern social theory is to see it as being basically concerned with the increase of contingency in modernity.

However, this is only one side of the matter. If this observation were absolutely valid, social theory would seem to have chosen a very peculiar task. What is commonly considered as 'social' about human life tends to be weakened with increases of contingency, at least so it may appear. Social theory would then have selected a vanishing phenomenon as its object of consideration.[50] If truly all that is solid melts into air, social theory will be among the victims.

Indeed, after the bourgeois revolution that was supposed to melt everything into air, it was not least social theory, including Marxian theorising, that was centrally concerned with identifying what was solid or could be made solid. Its rise was associated with concern about the incalculable effects of the bourgeois revolution. If there were no features in human life that imposed order somehow from the outside – via physical or biological determination, or via a religious or otherwise eternally conceived authority – and if human beings were to self-determine their individual and collective actions, to identify how they would do so became a question of key importance. The modes of human sociability, or in other words the form and nature of the ties between human beings, thus stood in the centre of interest in emergent social theorising (Heilbron et al. 1998).

Conceptualising social ties

There is no way of writing about social theory without already using socio-theoretical terms. Our own brief sketch of the history of social theory given above was based on at least two such terms, human beings and relations between human beings. A recognisable objective of this description was to be as unspecific as possible – to make only few presuppositions, in other words – about the latter; this question will occupy us during the remainder of this chapter. To be so unspecific with regard to one key term, however, and to yet write in a comprehensible language, we had to be adamant with regard to the other key term. It is indeed here presupposed that the bodily existing human being, though not a foundation in an ontological or methodological sense, is a phenomenon of some key interest to social theory, a phenomenon around which theorising may sensibly go on.

To assume that human beings in their bodily existence are a highly relevant unit in social analysis does not presuppose that they are prototypical bourgeois-humanist subjects. The 'hypostatisation of the individual in the conception of the subject as the main form of social reality marks one extreme' of social theorising, as Marlis Buchmann (1989: 75) writes, the 'dismissal of the subject as pure fiction . . . the other. Both ways of looking at the individual are one-sided interpretations of social reality, insofar as they reify one element in the development of advanced industrial society and neglect the other.' Thus, neither the much-debated 'end of the individual' or 'end of the subject' nor the dominance of the rational and autonomous individual that is hailed in economic and rationalist approaches enters as an assumption into the argument. Both are possible, though extreme, findings at the end of the analysis. But it is even difficult to imagine that the absolute predominance of the one or the other extreme conception would result from any specific socio-cultural analysis. Rather, they mark the space over which the human condition may be traced.

This view on human beings in social theory generates, or implies, the second key term we needed in our introduction as well as the way we dealt with it. If it is not postulated that human beings are either autonomous or totally submerged, then they have relations to other human beings, linkages whose form and nature we do not know beforehand. This may be called the assumption of sociality. It emerged very early in what became known as social theory, and much of this theorising has been occupied ever since with determining more specifically what the nature of this sociality is (see Heilbron 1995: 72–7).

Most of such social theory made fairly strong assumptions about the relations between human beings, but these assumptions were also fairly diverse, even contradictory. Many of the recurrent controversies in the social sciences – such as between individualism and collectivism, between determinism and voluntarism or, indeed, between structural and cultural analysis – can be discussed in terms of different assumptions about these relations. In our attempt to review the shift from a predominantly structural social analysis to a predominantly cultural one in the light of the contingency theorem, three assumptions about social relations are particularly important: assumptions about their form, their impact and their stability.

The form of social relations tells us something about the way groupings of human beings form and what holds them together; the notion of impact of social relations is meant to indicate whether they determine human action; and the notion of stability refers to their persistence over time. If strong responses to all three issues are given, if human beings form stable collectivities with common modes of interaction which persistently determine their individual actions, then human social life shows very little contingency. We shall discuss the sustainability of these assumptions in turn.

The form of social relations: boundedness and coherence

Two of the major modes of relating human beings to each other that were conceptualised in social theory were the structural or cultural linkages mentioned above. In the sociological tradition, the term 'social structure' refers relations of social characteristics – as diverse as age, wealth and income, election behaviour – to each other within and across categories.[51] Such relations are analysable but they may well be unknown to the persons themselves (e.g. the impact of somebody's position in a demographic structure on professional opportunities may be unknown to the person concerned). However, even if they may be partially unknown, positions in a social structure shape the interests of persons, or the roles they will assume, who are thus tied together by structural characteristics (group or class interests). The problematic relation between the structure which 'objectively' shapes interests and the views on their interests which the persons themselves hold has been a standard topic of such structural sociology (neo-Marxist or otherwise).

The term 'culture', in contrast, refers to commonly held beliefs, norms, values and ways of doing things. In some sense, at least, people thus always know cultural traits of their lives, though they possibly may not explicate them unless asked, or they may be unaware of the range of people with whom they share them.[52] In many cases, however, cultural analysts argue, they have some view and sense of the community they are a member of, this sense being called collective identity. This identity, then, this sharing of beliefs and practices constitutes a social tie in a cultural perspective.[53]

If there was then a recent shift in hegemony from the structural to the cultural mode of reasoning, it does not necessarily entail much, since there are important similarities between them. Structure as well as culture can be seen as objective entities existing regardless of the consciousness and the volition of their member human beings. Both would then also be regarded as macro-phenomena with firm boundaries and, often, their specific modes of maintaining coherence or, as the more common term was, integration.

During the recent resurgence of cultural theorising, however, a number of different perspectives were developed. We shall have to distinguish between two quite different guiding threads, which intermingle in the new fashion of cultural analysis. On the one hand, cultural analysis emerged as a response to the deficiencies of structural reasoning. Such analysis would try to take the contingencies and uncertainties of social life better into account than structural theorising did. Doubts had risen as to the existence and objectivity of the supposed 'structures'. A broad movement of rethinking set in which argued not least for reflexivity in sociology, for instance in the works of Anthony Giddens and Pierre Bourdieu. Social constructivism in areas such as gender and science studies, a turn to 'micro-histories' in the historical sciences, and increased emphasis on the openness of language leading to a plurality of modes of representing the social world, are other parts of this movement. Though the conclusions drawn from such reconsiderations vary between and even within any of those approaches, most of them attach considerable importance to the meanings human beings give to their practices (that is why they may be labelled 'cultural' in a broad sense), and they all have in common to see social linkages as much less clearly established and unequivocally identifiable than most earlier thinking did. In this sense, some might want to see these theoretical openings as paving the way for the theorem of contingency.

On the other hand, cultural analysis was also revived as a means to counter the supposed weaknesses of the contingency perspective. Even though it may not be social structures, something solid remained in the social world that did not melt into air, namely ties of cultural belonging. Though remaining in the continuity of traditional views on culture, this thinking has been considerably modified, too. In contrast to structural theory, which assumes that people within a given macro-phenomenon are different, since they have (groupwise) different locations therein, cultural analysis keeps maintaining, despite some sophisticated arguments on cultural complexity (Hannerz 1992), that people are rather alike in a given culture (and differ from members of other cultures). Given obvious limits to empirically sustain such a view for current nations, for instance, the possibility of several cultures on a given territory, of subcultures and countercultures, has been introduced. Or, inversely, it has been emphasised that cultures may extend over large spaces without covering them completely (as national cultures were supposed to do). Obvious examples are Jewish culture, or the 'culture of science', but those cultures that were the traditional objects of anthropology, like the Samoan culture, have also been analysed as 'multi-local cultures' in such a perspective, thus trying to emphasise the double feature of spatial extension through migration and maintenance of ties of belonging (Sahlins 2000).

Despite this relaxation of earlier assumptions, however, many of these analyses remain confined to some of the limiting connotations of the term 'culture'. As James Clifford (1988: 232) puts it:

> Culture, even without a capital C, strains toward aesthetic form and autonomy . . . The inclusive twentieth-century culture category . . . , this culture with a small c orders phenomena in ways that privilege the coherent, balanced, and 'authentic' aspects of shared life. Since the mid nineteenth century, ideas of culture have gathered up those elements that seem to give continuity and depth to collective existence, seeing it whole rather than disputed, torn, intertextual, or syncretic. (see also Archer, 1988: xv; and now Eagleton 2000)

Some cultural analysts may want to argue that, while the criticism may still be valid for much of the work done in this field, there is no need to retain such a view of culture as a whole. The analysis of 'cultural practices' may replace that of 'cultures'. If there are varieties of differently conceived linkages between human beings, there is no reason why they should lead to a bounded, coherent collectivity.[54] Such a conclusion, though, would hit a core element of cultural analysis and introduce a degree of indeterminacy, which endangers the whole enterprise. The presupposition of boundedness and coherence is dear to many theorists not least because it provides an important link to political theory.

In general, political theorising demands criteria for determining the extension of the polity as well as the depth of political regulation, i.e. the identification of entities of representation both for the constitution of a polity and within a polity. Liberal-individualist political theory does not provide such criteria; it depends on social and/or cultural analysis in this respect. Our suspicion is that the second intellectual shift we described above, from postmodernism to cultural theory, is supported not mainly by empirical insights, but rather by a desire to end what came to be seen as a political indecisiveness produced by postmodernism.[55]

Nothing is wrong, in principle, with trying to move beyond indecisiveness. However, one needs to look very carefully where one is going and what kind of situation one is in. The result of a normative assessment of the current move depends very much on what cultures and identities are in focus (ranging from feminist to nationalist and elsewhere), and how these cultures and identities are conceptualised. We will not deal with these issues here,[56] since we think some analytical questions need to be openly confronted first.

To avoid misunderstandings, it may be useful to explicitly state at this point that it is not our intention to deny that many of the recent analyses have brought important insights.[57] Neither do we want to claim, in conceptual terms, that the notions of structural and cultural linkages between human beings should be entirely abandoned. What we try to argue instead is that there have been serious conceptual flaws in the ways such phenomena have been dealt with in conventional social analysis, and that these flaws have not completely been overcome in more recent debates. Though a significant movement of reconceptualisation has started, in particular in the first kind of above-mentioned approaches, it is now important that it be carried further rather than partially withdrawn, as is the tendency in some works of the second kind. In the remainder of this chapter we shall try to sketch what such carrying further might entail.

The impact of social relations: determination and interpretation

Structural and cultural theory used to share rather strong assumptions about social linkages, at least before these more recent debates. They both tended to assume – in quite analogous ways – that there are predominant types of linkages and that these linkages basically determine the size and shape of the collectivity that is relevant to individual human beings as well as to the individuals' behaviour. The simple guiding assumption was that people who find themselves in similar positions to others, in structural analysis, or who think alike, in cultural analysis, will tend to act alike and/or see themselves as part of a group. This conclusion is arrived at by coupling a term denoting a collectivity of human beings somehow linked to each other (related to each other, or belonging together), described as a macro-phenomenon (structure or culture respectively), to a sister term denoting basic orientations of human beings which provide the linkage between members of this collectivity (interest or identity respectively).

A key question here is obviously the mode of coupling the orientations of human beings to the collectivity they are (supposed to be) a part of. In traditional versions of structural and cultural reasoning this coupling was an assumption. One may even hold that it is an essential part of the sociological mode of explanation (see ch. 9). By interrogating the impact of social relations, we try to loosen the conceptual link and open the issue to analysis.[58] In this sense, high-impact social relations shape decisively – the conventional term was 'determine' – the orientations and actions of human beings; low-impact relations do not. The task of sociological research then is to identify whether relations have a low or high impact.

There are two related but quite different issues at stake here. At first, it may seem that a presupposition has been transformed into an empirical question, which then generates its own research programme. Cultural analysis is opened to the identification of a possible multiplicity, and even inconsistency, of values and beliefs a person may hold and of overlapping boundaries of 'cultural communities' with regard to different beliefs, including – as mentioned above – the possibility that cultures may not be territorially based, or that cultural practices might not cohere. If such research concludes on diversity, plurality and inconsistency of values and beliefs that individuals and groups hold, as it often does nowadays, the idea of a direct relation between culture and action is strongly challenged. However, beyond challenging the earlier presupposition, very little can be added to an understanding of human action on this road alone.[59]

The relation between beliefs and action is not a mere matter of holding some action-relevant belief, but of actualising it in a given situation. The situated interpretation decides which of a number of cultural resources a person has at her disposal are activated to deal with an exigency to act. Principally, no resource is unequivocally destined to serve in a given situation; and every situation is in need of interpretation. Structural-functionalist sociology has made a modest attempt to take the multiplicity of situations and interpretations into account by introducing the idea of 'multiple role-sets', but it has ended in the same dead end as class analysis, because it was unwilling to relinquish the strong relation between social status and role. Or in other words, it could not envisage a conceptual openness as to which interpretations apply to which situations but has maintained a pre-established conception of this linkage. In contrast, this issue has been more fruitfully addressed in the interactionist tradition of sociology. Rarely, however, have the conclusions for sociological reasoning at large been fully spelt out.

Taken seriously, the conclusions from these reflections demand the renunciation of 'any conception that regards the unity and cohesion of a group as the product of a substantive similarity between its members and of an objectively shared interest' (Boltanski 1990: 70). The presupposition that 'a unanimity or similarity of behavior' results from people being 'subject to common material constraints or well mastered by shared ideas (beliefs, representations)' (Thévenot 1993: 276) entails a restrictive definition of action that is incapable of dealing with either doubt and uncertainty or creativity in human interaction (see ch. 7).

This is not to say that functional exigencies or common history could not play a role in shaping a society. Indeed, the 'historical labour' which went into, say, the creation of a national compulsory unemployment insurance in Germany, is an effort a group of people have embarked upon in common to deal effectively with a situation defined as problematic. That the struggle was long and the issue contested does not preclude that the new rules create an order of representation that is likely to be accepted by people society-wide (in the specific case, this actually did not immediately happen). A situation of dispute and uncertainty can be transformed into one of greater consent and certainty that may reign over a significant historical period (Zimmermann 2000). However, as the current questioning of both the viability and the justifiability of compulsory insurance shows, the rules of an institution only reign if they are constantly re-enacted. There are no unequivocally superior solutions to social problems; and common history itself does not explain anything.

The stability of social relations: reality and possibility

Having already questioned the link between common history and common practice as a foregone conclusion of much of cultural analysis in the preceding section, we shall now point to an important implication of this presupposition, which will enable us to get a third requirement for reconceptualisation in social theory into focus.

For the purpose of the argument only, we will imagine an empirical 'case' in which our earlier two requirements are fulfilled. This would be a context in which, at the time of analysis, members of a given collectivity tend to converge in their statements about their beliefs as well as in their interpretations of a situation and in their ways to deal with a situation. In such a case, may one say that there is a shared representation of the social world, and may cultural analysis justifiably want to provide a mirror image of this world? Even for such a very special case, such terminology and such ambitions are problematic, because 'representation requires a suppression of time; mirroring necessitates a standing still' (Game 1991: 21).

As long as one assumes that the social world is truly solid, ontologically solid, the suppression of time may appear unproblematic. And for a long time it was almost a founding assumption of (at least, important variants of) social science that a substantive social ontology is both needed and possible. More recently, however, the problematic character of this claim went no longer unnoticed, and attempts were made to introduce temporality into social theory. Pierre Bourdieu (1979) turned the temporal aspect of social life into a cornerstone of his critique of structuralism. Margaret Archer (1988) introduced agency together with temporality into cultural theorising precisely by making a distinction between cultural practices, in her terms socio-cultural interaction, and a coherent cultural order, the cultural system. And, to complete this short series of examples, Michèle Lamont (1992: 183) criticised the assumption of a 'stable set of actors' over time even in Bourdieu's analyses.

Despite the considerable merits of such works, there are further, yet hardly noticed implications that go with the need for an empirically more open understanding of the stability of social relations. Basically, the more recent analyses argue that cultural practices may differ between two points in time with regard to all their key characteristics: the size and composition of the cultural community, the substance of the beliefs and values, the importance of those beliefs and values for actions. Some analyses, like Archer's, specifically underline that it is, or at least may be, the agential capacities of the people that bring these changes over time about.

Saying this, however, appears to imply that the notion of culture, and analogously that of structure, no longer performs the theoretical task it was created for in the first place. Culture and structure were introduced, as we argued above, to allow a focus on the coherence and stability of human social behaviour. Once these certainty-providing phenomena were identified, they permitted a conclusion on expectations as to the future behaviour of human beings. If cultural practices are now seen as potentially variable over time in all the above-mentioned respects, then such conclusions are no longer possible. We seem to be back to the theory of contingency, and to the insight into the impossibility of social theory.

To avoid such a conclusion – and there are good grounds to avoid it – it is necessary to further rework the idea of temporality of human action. To do this, we will for a moment revert to the conventional assumption of cultural theorising that common history may explain the existence and the stability of collectively shared orders of beliefs. One of the problems with this statement is that, strictly speaking, there is no 'common history' but always a multitude of experiences which all differ from each other. The evocation of 'common history', as for instance in nationalism, is an operation that is always performed in the respective present. It is a specific representation of the past, reworking it with a view to creating commonalities. As such, it may indeed 'work', it may create the idea of belonging among human beings in the present. But it is not the past, as 'common history', that produces this effect, but the present interaction between those who propose to see the past as shared and those who are convinced by this reasoning and accept it for their own orientation in the social world.

Such a view might be taken to downplay the importance of history for social analysis. Indeed, we were admonished for producing a typically postmodernist 'ideology of the present'. However, this seems to be a strong misreading of both postmodernism (whatever that may exactly be) and of our proposal. From Nietzsche to Derrida (if that is a postmodernist lineage), the questioning of the status of the present and reflections about the interpretive appropriation of history have been key concerns. And our own intention is precisely to open social analysis to a more adequate understanding of temporality and historicity (see Friese 2001b as well as Wagner 2001: ch. 4 for more detail).

Currently, many works still fall into the trap of either resorting to atemporal snapshots of the social world or using history to explain the present in a deterministic way. In the former case, so-called empirical evidence, say, the views respondents voice in interviews is synchronically analysed as present facts without any consideration of their historical construction and their possibly limited durability. This is true theoretical presentism, and a rather modernist invention at that. In the latter, the analyst, working in the present, selectively appropriates the past to explain this present. Given that the identification of continuities between past and present is a methodological *a priori* in this approach, it becomes impossible to say whether the coherence of the analysis is an effect of the selection or indeed the result of causally effective linkages between past and present actions (de Certeau 1988; Friese 1994; 1996).

There are certainly no methodological highways that bypass the epistemological obstacles on the way to dealing with historicity more adequately. The only viable conceptualisation, however, is to see the relevance of 'history' for present actions as a combination of 'traces' of past action in the present, such as a building whose physical structure will both enable and constrain present action, and of the appropriation of the 'past' in the minds of present beings, its endowment with action-relevant meaning. Cultural practices may leave imprints, such as inscriptions in the body of the pugilist from training and fighting, as emphasised by Loïc Wacquant. But any 'culture' is also a representation of the past in the present, whose relevance for present action is subject to appropriation and interpretation by present human beings.

It is not least in the situated interpretation of their own past experiences that human beings create a 'gap between past and future' (Arendt, 1961: 3), which enables them to make a distinction between reality and possibility which neither presentist empiricism nor structural or cultural determinism can grasp. The present world is neither just there nor predetermined in the past; it is the creation out of a plurality of possibilities which existed at the moment before.

Contingency and solidity of the social world

Nothing of what we said, thus, amounts to adopting a version of the theorem of contingency. However, reflecting on the possibility of utmost contingency of human action allows us to identify principled shortcomings of more conventional social theorising, both in its structural and its cultural varieties. The widespread adoption of the cultural approach in current social analysis risks being not much more than a change of fashion. Despite the relaxation of some of the strong assumptions of cultural analysis, the danger is that the problematic analogies between structural and cultural theorising will reassert themselves against the more reflexive tone in some recent contributions.

Thinking about contingency, then, should not lead one to abandon the attempts, characteristic of social theory, to understand linkages between human beings. Rather, it is a means to emphasise the issues of form, impact and stability of such linkages as permanently open questions of social theory and research, including the question of their very intelligibility or, at least, describability in terms of a social science.

One does not have to assume that there are no stable linkages at all, that everything is contingent and in flux, a position often associated with sociological postmodernism. But rather than rushing to replace one kind of terminological hegemony by another, one should seriously conceptualise the kind of social linkages that may be stable, extended and creative of collectivities as compared with others that tend to remain fluid, narrowly confined and changing between persons.

The intellectual shifts we described at the outset, from structural theorising through the emphasis on contingency to cultural theorising, entailed a double move. First, all that was solid seemed to melt into air. Then, that situation appeared unsustainable, both analytically and politically; too much of what was solid had melted into air. We continue to think that not all that is portrayed as solid in social theory and research has ever been so. And that we should devote more attention to ask what solidity might mean in the social world.

9
SOCIETY

An entity called 'society' became an object of scientific study during the nineteenth century. Its emergence, or its discovery, gave rise to what was then seen as new sciences, variously called 'social science', 'sociology' (a term coined by Auguste Comte) or directly 'science of society' (or in German *Gesellschaftswissenschaft*). While the study of the gregariousness of human life can be traced to almost any point in intellectual history, there is nevertheless some validity to the claim of novelty on the part of these sciences, a validity that hinges to a considerable extent on the existence of the new object 'society'. Whether there was such an object at all or whether it was of such novelty that a new science was required for its analysis, however, was contested from the beginnings and has remained so up to the present day. The purpose of this chapter is not to exhaustively review these debates – an objective which could not possibly be achieved in the space of one chapter. Rather, I shall try to identify some basic problématiques which were at the roots of the coming into being of 'society', and shall attempt to demonstrate how such problématiques shaped the form of this object of inquiry. My attempt will focus on the middle of the nineteenth century, the time when 'society' had its strongest presence as an object and when debates about it had acquired considerable momentum. Moving from there briefly backwards to the late eighteenth century, and then forwards through the twentieth century to the present, will allow, even though only cursorily, to relate the question of the existence of 'society' to historical transformations of social configurations in the West.

The coming into being of 'society'

Rupture and continuity

From an etymological point of view, the term 'social' – and its correlates in other European languages – refers to the connectedness of a human being to others. We could say that it enables us to talk about situations in which human beings create relations to each other. In this sense, we can regard as 'social sciences' all those theories that reflect upon why and how human beings link up to each other, such as conceptualisations of passions and interests, of individualism and collectivism, of rational, expressive and other orientations of action toward others; Immanuel Kant's thoughts on the 'unsocial sociability' of human beings; and many other theorems originating in the seventeenth and eighteenth centuries. However, a very specific way of talking about connections between human beings was introduced into those discourses with the term 'society'; and it is significant that the term 'social sciences' emerged only in the eighteenth century for those modes of thinking that were rather referred to as 'moral and political sciences' or as 'state sciences' up to then.

From the mid eighteenth century onwards, the term 'society' came to be used in the moral and political sciences, in particular within French and Scottish debates, and it acquired the place of the denomination for the key object of socio-political life there. Originally, in combinations such as 'political society' and 'civil society', it referred to nothing else but the state, but from a point of view of contract theory, namely as the aggregation of human beings that have come together for a purpose. But in some late-eighteenth-century theories, 'civil society' came to be seen as a phenomenon that was different from the state – but different from the individual households as well. And it is here that the story of 'society' as a scientific object starts.

Up to then, in everyday language, 'society' used to refer to phenomena that existed in the interstices between the private and the public. In France up to the beginning of the eighteenth century, the term 'society' denoted 'small social units that belonged neither to the realm of "the state" nor to that of the family or house-hold' (Heilbron 1995: 87). These units were basically either social circles or legally defined associations, i.e. specifically human aggregations for a purpose. Such usage of the term continues today, as in 'high society' or in 'German Society for Sociology', alongside the sociological meaning.

The introduction of the term into the moral and political sciences – and the change in the semantic position that accompanied it – can, on the one hand, be seen as a reflection of the growth and multiplication of these 'small units'. Rather than an arbitrary array of phenomena whose only commonality was to be part of neither the state nor any particular household, 'society' may have gained in importance and coherence such that it could no longer be ignored in moral and political philosophy.[60] The broadening of the meaning of 'society' is then a response to an observable change in the structure of social relations, i.e. in the ways the lives of human beings are connected to each other.[61]

On the other hand, the specific new position of this term reveals its initial dependence on another discourse – a discourse, indeed, against which the talk about 'society' was directed. The new object 'society' inherited the status of being neither state nor household. The new language thus affirmed that a moral-political entity consisted essentially of (a multitude of) households and a (single) state. It merely added a third category of phenomena; and by the way it did so, it also posited that this third category had a single member rather than a multitude, though the oneness of society was of a different nature than the one of the state.[62]

The new threefold division of the moral-political order has therefore to be understood against the background of the earlier twofold division. The latter stemmed, to stretch the point a bit, from some basic continuity from the Aristotelian conception of the *polis* and the *oikos* through to the political philosophy of liberalism which made a fundamental distinction between the individuals and the state. The 'classical liberals' of the seventeenth and eighteenth centuries continued to assume that the free and responsibly acting 'individual' citizens were owners of property which included women, children and servants, i.e. that they were heads of households rather than single human beings. Their relation to the members of their property was one of mastery; it was at the same time private and of little interest to political thought. Between the citizens, however, Aristotelian or liberal, there was nothing but action and speech, essential freedom. This perspective, thus, gave a very clear-cut view of the structure of the moral-political order in relation to the ways human beings connect with each other: needs determined the private linkages in the house, but the public linkages between men were free. Admittedly, the image I give here comes close to a caricature, but it is important to recognise that the sociological discourse maintained an, often implicit, reference to this earlier view on the background of which it was modelled. To assess the relation of rupture and continuity in this intellectual transformation, we need to take a look at the historical context.

The case for society's existence

Even though the coming into being of 'society' can be traced to the mid eighteenth century, the historical event which accelerated the intellectual transformation was the French – and to some extent also the American – Revolution (for an overview see Riedel 1975a; 1975b). The issue of a new structure of the social world was of crucial importance after the old order had been torn down and claims were made that a new one could be consciously built. The social sciences as the scientific study of that new 'society' owe their forms and contents to a large extent to the transformation of political issues related to what one may call the onset of political modernity. However, rather than providing the radical rupture which it had announced, the Revolution proved to usher in a rather gradual, and not at all linear, transformation of political and social life. 'Society' had a slow coming into being, and it was only by the middle of the nineteenth century that some observers could call 'the invention of the social' an accomplished fact, particularly for France, whereas others, notably Germans, remained doubtful whether any important change had occurred at all.[63]

During this half-century, German observers had made persistent efforts to assess the importance of the events west of the Rhine and to decide whether and how far one would or should have to follow their neighbour's example in the German lands. In the 1850s, when the dust from revolutions and wars had settled, but France seemed to remain somewhat unstable, 'state scientists' Robert von Mohl (1851) and Heinrich von Treitschke (1927 [1859]) led a debate about the need for a recasting of the political sciences due to the transformations of the social world. The existence of 'society' as a scientific object was at the heart of their dispute, which, somewhat off the centre of events, is particularly elucidating for our purposes. It provides something like an anchor halfway down the stream. The (international) debate about the new object 'society', and about the need for social sciences to analyse it, is fully developed at this point, and these two authors attempt a systematic assessment from a somewhat distant point of observation.

Mohl opened the debate in 1851, stating that 'for about fifty years' – the reference to the French Revolution is evident – 'something entirely new' has come into being, the 'particular being' of society (1851: 6). Consequently, the political sciences, hitherto only occupied with the 'individual' and the 'entirety', should recognise that there is 'between the two, and well distinct from either, a whole, wide area, which similarly has laws which accordingly demand research and ordering'. The task was to look at the forms through which 'human beings unite, not through the state and its commands, but by way of an accord of their immediate needs, through single but sufficiently powerful interests'. These forms vary between peoples, but they 'do not fail to appear in any bounded number of humans, i.e. in any people' (1851: 12–13). A few years later, Treitschke followed through all of Mohl's argument and concluded that 'it has not been proven that society was a particular element of human conviviality' (1927: 58–9); there was no need to abandon or even complement the state sciences.

Mohl had tried to make a very general argument which took all the theorising on society into account that had been offered during the preceding fifty or so years. To evaluate claims as to the existence of the new phenomenon 'society', it was important to determine its nature and the change in the structure of social relations that it allegedly entailed. By the time of Mohl's writing, one main line of debate on these new kinds of connections between human beings described them as being of a commercial character. Need and work had left the sphere of the household to which they used to be confined and had been exposed to public light. Markets and the division of social labour became the basis of 'society' in the tradition of political economy from Adam Smith onwards. The argument was taken up and – twice – modified by Hegel in his integration of the division of labour into civil society in the *Elements of a philosophy of right* and by Marx in his critique of Hegel's conception. By implication, this move of needs-related activities into the public sphere entailed that the latter consisted no longer purely of speech and action alone.

A second line of debate focused on associations as the basis of society and regarded those associations, at least partly, as a response to the effects of the commercialisation of life. Along those lines, Lorenz von Stein, for instance, reported in Germany about the 'social movements' in France that announced a major change in the social order. Alexis de Tocqueville studied associative life as the basis of a democratic polity in America. And Marx, later, again gave a central place to the 'working class', as a newly formed social phenomenon, in his social theory and philosophy of history.

All these approaches have one feature in common about which Mohl is very explicit. They all claim that major elements of the social world cannot, or can no longer, be grasped through the mere distinction between polity and household or, in the modern liberal form, between polity and individual. In this sense, these 'sociologists' perform a break with an earlier representation of the moral-political order on grounds, as they claim, of a transformed empirical reality. Doing so, however, they used the earlier representation as a resource with which to model the new one; i.e. they added one key element to an existing discourse rather than develop an entirely new representation. This choice, I shall argue, was motivated by the fact that these authors retained the interest in theorising the form and feasibility of moral-political order that had informed both Greek and classical liberal thought. 'Society' was investigated because of the change in political reasoning its existence might require, not because, say, the production of pins or the associative life in America was found inherently interesting. The discovery/invention of 'society' in early sociology was also an event in political philosophy, and sociology then can be regarded as a transformed, empirical version of political philosophy.[64]

As such, the introduction of 'society' into the moral and political sciences created a very specific linkage of empirical-historical observation and normative-conceptual investment. Such linkages are rather common in the social sciences. In this case, it can even be considered as constitutive for the sociological debate on 'society', as I will try to demonstrate. At the same time, however, it creates a basic tension between two perspectives on the 'object'. The main thrust of the remainder of the chapter will be to discuss how these two aspects have historically been constructed and have been related to each other (or, at times, conflated) in various ways.

Characteristics of 'society'

Mohl's writings have particular significance in this context. Though he shares the background in 'state sciences' with other authors, he refuses to subordinate the 'sciences of society' (*Gesellschafts-Wissenschaften*) that he calls for to the exigencies of political theory. The phenomena of his 'society' are not ontologised. They are many and manifold, and they emerge from crystallisations of more fluid interactions. 'How many and what kind of interests are sufficiently big, persistent and general enough to turn into the core of such a crystallisation can neither be determined on general grounds nor on the basis of experience' (Mohl 1851: 50). He does not open any path towards relating them directly to political issues, unlike Hegel with his 'civil society' or Marx with his 'class'. At the same time, his conceptual investigation, which combines programmatic ambition with scepticism as to strong assertions, explores all the three discursive possibilities which the introduction of 'society' between the polity and the individual entailed, namely the counterposition of society to the polity (the state), the relation of society to the individual, and the argument that 'society' could have causal effects.

Society and the state

Mohl denies that societal phenomena are necessarily related to the state: 'With regard to their extensions, [they] do not at all orient themselves towards political boundaries' (1851: 44). This proposition may at first sight look innocent and fairly unproblematic. Unless reasons or mechanisms are given, it should not appear as evident why the phenomena belonging to 'society' should acquire polity-wide extension. Indeed, straightforward observation should show that that was rather unlikely to occur. Most relations between human beings in the Western Europe of about 1850 were within a local community, such as many family relations. Some others, like production for a world market as described in classical political economy, acquired extensions beyond state boundaries, at great effort given available technologies of production and transport. In between the two, there certainly were social phenomena that could best be characterised as state-wide, but nothing in them endowed them with special importance from the point of view of a 'science of society'. Any arbitrarily chosen multiple set of social relations should normally be expected to show an incoherent variety of extensions. The question then imposes itself, however, why Mohl should emphasise this fairly obvious fact.

In fact, though, it was this statement that made explicit that Mohl was arguing against a long tradition of 'state sciences' in Germany and even against some of the newer social philosophies that had been proposed during the preceding half-century. He broke with the assumption that the emerging social structures of 'society' would show a coherence and boundedness in a specific way, namely as being coextensive with the boundaries of existing polities.[65] Such assumption, translated into the terms used here, means that chains of linkages extend from any given member of a 'society' so that the web of all these chains forms a bounded whole which is of a certain stability and that the extension of this web coincides with that of the polity. The predominance of this – very strong – assumption in much of the debate on 'society' as well as, indeed, the very emergence of 'society' has to be explained by the intention to analyse historical transformations with a view to issues of political philosophy and as a contribution to political problem-solving.

Mohl, in contrast, took the autonomy of societal phenomena much more seriously. In a forceful criticism of German state-oriented sciences and philosophies, he tried to show that such phenomena were only included into consideration there if they could be subordinated to requirements for political order, their autonomous existence being denied. Treitschke, his great opponent, misunderstood the move Mohl made and showed himself to be part of the state-oriented German intellectual tradition when he claimed, after discussing all the empirical phenomena Mohl introduced, that there was no independent existence of society. In his view, all these relations and organisms had constitutive links to the state, the latter indeed being 'organised society', society under the aspect of its organisation (Treitschke 1927: 73, 68).

It should be granted, though, that Treitschke could have been empirically right where he conceptually erred. In the German states in the mid nineteenth century, very few social phenomena could indeed be understood without taking their relations to the state into account. That this should remain so, that order needed to be safeguarded through state-led organisation, was Treitschke's normative stand. With this emphasis on exigencies for order, he, the anti-sociologist, was closer to an important stream of the sociological tradition than Mohl who tried to argue for sociology in Germany in an intellectally and politically hostile environment.

Without following Treitschke's political preferences, his intervention demands the careful assessment of possible grounds for tying the shape of 'society' to a polity to which it belongs and for underlining its coherent and bounded nature rather than allowing for a more undetermined plural and open-ended being. Among the reasonings which were brought forward during the nineteenth century, we can roughly distinguish a politico-historical, a cultural, a biological and a statistical argument.

In politico-historical terms, as has often been observed, sociology tended to conflate the idea of the nation-state with 'society'; sociology's society was indeed 'national society' (see recently Smelser 1997). But why such an assumption was made is not entirely incomprehensible. The French Revolution posited the nation as the container of the liberal polity, and under its influence other such national projects of societal organisation emerged in Europe. Thus, even if there is nothing inherent in 'society' that focuses practices so as to create coherence and bounded-ness, such focusing could be a historical attempt pursued by nation-building elites. One could envisage historical actors trying to extend 'smaller' practices to the national dimension, such as abolishing communal sick relief in favour of a compulsory national health insurance, and cutting off (or at least monitoring) those 'longer' linkages that stretched across its boundaries, such as by protectionist measures reducing cross-border trade. Once regarded this way, it can indeed be shown that significant such attempts were being made during the period of social policy innovations and increasingly aggressive nationalism towards the end of the nineteenth century, with the state being a main organiser of these national social practices (Zimmermann et al. 1999). If this is the case, however, the autonomy of 'society', and its justification as a fundamental and not merely historical concept, are very much in question – as indeed Heinrich von Treitschke pointed out, though with his particular normative agenda in mind.

In cultural terms, it is possible to argue that the existence of 'society' is insufficiently explained by recourse to connections between human beings through social practices. For such connections to come into being and to develop, there must be other, foundational principles for a collectivity, such as shared values and norms and commonality of language. This argument featured prominently in German romanticism, and it was in part consciously developed against an Enlightenment conception of individual human beings getting together on reason-able grounds. But it also inaugurated a tradition of social thought that emphasised pre-individual sociality of humans and attempted to locate this sociality in observ-able and analysable social phenomena (see ch. 8). An understanding of society as 'collective representations' can be found in Durkheim's early *Rules of sociological method* (see ch. 7). In his later writings, it appears to gain dominance over the more material concept of societal integration through the division of social labour. Weber, too, is more ready to give conceptual status to 'culture', as shared meanings, than to society, as coherent practices. A full elaboration of a social science that reflects on language as the starting-point for conceptualising the shared – and thus social – nature of human practices was then offered by Peter Winch in his Wittgensteinian *Idea of a social science* of 1958. Such thinking, thus, retreated from the full-fledged concept of coherent and bounded social practices across all – or at least major – realms of human action to a more limited range of phenomena that could more justifiably, but also more strongly, be considered as shared, bounded and coherent.

A similar form of argument, though based on a different justification, can be found in affirmations of the existence of 'society' that used biological terms. Throughout the nineteenth century (and up to the present), it was contested whether the sciences of human social life operated exactly like the natural sciences, whether they were similarly scientific but devoted themselves to a distinct part of reality that demanded different concepts, or whether they had to develop a different 'scientificity' owing to the essentially different nature of the social world as compared with the natural one (Heilbron in press). The former two of these conceptions allowed the drawing on concepts borrowed from the natural sciences, and many social theorists of the nineteenth century likened 'society' to an organism. An organism consists not of individuals but of parts which together form a functional whole. Coherence and boundedness of an organism are not an issue of empirical observation, but are the goal of 'society' for which its parts are functionally predisposed and constantly mobilised. Versions of such thinking, though mostly without explicit reference to biology, have persisted in functionalism and systems theory. These forms of theorising fail, however, to provide underpinnings for the strong claim that, and how, 'society' is capable of self-organisation, a claim which goes much beyond that made for its mere existence prior to individuals in cultural thinking.

Finally, there was also an argument for the existence of 'society' that appeared to operate without strong presuppositions but on the basis of empirical techniques alone. Statistical and demographic research were said to reveal some solid and lawlike features in the characteristics and movements of a population and thus to underpin the idea of the existence of 'society'. However, these kinds of research produced the unity and coherence as much as they revealed it, in their operations performed on units assumed as given, normally by administrative boundaries. Statistics, as its name indicates, is historically the state science *par excellence* – and not a science of 'society', though its results were often taken to give a proof of the latter's existence (Desrosières 1993, Porter 1986; 1995).

Mohl is sober enough not to accept any of these arguments in their strong versions. Observation-minded as he was, he rejected the biological one. To adhere straightforwardly to the cultural argument, he was too strongly rooted in the liberal tradition, which emphasised individual autonomy. However, this did not make him a classical liberal for whom there was nothing between the individual and the state. He could not follow any longer the politico-historical argument, because post-revolutionary events had made social life much more complex than this one would allow. And while he indeed turned the extension of societal phenomena into an issue of empirical investigation, he did not accept that statistical research had shown any unitary nature of the social body.

Society and the individual

If the debate on the relation between society and the state was shaped by concerns of political philosophy at least as much as by the empirical-analytical interest in knowing the 'particular being' of society, the attempts to conceptualise the relation of society to individuals were not free from socio-philosophical assumptions either. The very counterposition of state and society made sense, in the traditional way, only if society was somehow on the side of the individuals. In Hegel's philosophy of right, for instance, civil society was the realm of the particular, where subjectivity was expressed and where interests governed action. Similarly, the economy, the relatively independent realm as it was portrayed in political economy, was a part of society, and distinct from the state, exactly because individuals expressed their particularity there.

If this was the emerging conception in the late eighteenth and the early nineteenth centuries, it was to lose its persuasiveness later. Romanticism was an early reaction, as discussed above, but one which was often – not generally rightly – regarded as looking backwards to a harmonious pre-revolutionary order. Mohl's writings mark again a transitional point in the sense that, after him, society came to be seen as a *sui generis* reality which, while being composed of, or 'crystallised' from, social relations, was more than the individuals themselves. If the romantic view of 'society' presupposed, so to say, pre-individual connections between human beings that constituted this entity, it was the 'modern' connections through the division of social labour or through individual will that brought society into existence in much of later sociology. This was the case in Emile Durkheim's early works and in Ferdinand Tönnies' writings on 'community' and 'society', for instance, which inaugurated a distinction between a traditional and a modern sense of belonging and of social unity. This viewpoint could receive a strong theoretically anti-individualist bent, then counterposing sociology as the study of collective phenomena to economics devoted to individuals and their rationalities. The earlier social philosophy had then split into two parts, diametrically opposed as to their ontological foundations.

Society and causality

Such a society then, third, was an entity that could have causal effects on individuals' actions. What a human being thought and did was determined by her or his position in a society, in a social structure. Actions and events could thus be explained, and under conditions of good knowledge even predicted. Mohl's text offers fine examples of how the argument for the relevance of societal phenomena can be linked, by some force of reasoning, to a form of social determinism, even though a cautious one in his case.

In his lengthy identification of non-state, non-individual phenomena, Mohl described, for instance, aristocracy as a 'widely diffused, lasting condition, which entails, for its adherents, a similar feeling, willing and acting'. On the clergy, he notes similarly that it is 'a community of thought, of interest, and consequently of willing and acting' (1851: 36). To find yourself in a certain lasting social situation has an impact on your volition and action; this is how Mohl puts what has become known as the sociological mode of reasoning and explanation. Even though the social-deterministic form of reasoning and explanation has always remained contested among sociologists, and even though it has been held in a variety of – weaker and stronger – versions, it certainly is a defining characteristic of the sociological tradition. Its viability depends on the possibility of claiming the existence of causally efficacious social entities such as 'society' (Hacking 1990; Manent 1994).

Mohl himself moved from those observations of his to a general argument that both justified sociology and demonstrated its necessity. The societal phenomena he identified can be said to be, first, persistent; second, of major importance because of underlying interests; and third, of more general diffusion (1851: 41–3). If that is the case, a science is needed to order these phenomena and identify the laws of their existence. 'As soon as it has been stated that society is a specific human relation, the possibility of a special scientific perception of it has been proven' (1851: 52).

Mohl's advocacy of social science is a combination of firmness with regard to its necessity and caution with regard to its foundations and rules. Society exists, it has impacts, but it is autonomous, not coherent, not bounded, has no unequivocal relation either to the individuals of which it is composed or to the state. For a long time, this view remained unpersuasive, in Germany where the 'state' continued to predominate intellectually over 'society' until far into the twentieth century,[66] as well as in France where the inverse was the case but society, in the Durkheimian tradition, was turned into a higher entity endowed with metaphysical faculties. Or in other words, after about a century of sociological debate, nothing else appeared to have been arrived at than the unfortunate dilemma of having to choose between, on the one hand, denying the relevance of those 'societal' phenomena that exist between the individual and the polity and conceptualising the polity basically in the same way as before; and, on the other, claiming their overarching importance and subordinating the political problématique to the respective structure of 'society'. Such a situation was unsatisfactory, both in intellectual and in political terms. The debate on 'society' was to continue (for an overview see Frisby and Sayer 1986).

Persistence of 'society' as an object

From the preceding discussion we could provisionally conclude that, at the time of the broadening of its meaning in the eighteenth century, 'society' was an intellectual construction that served some needs of political philosophy – in confirmation of liberal political theory or as a counter-argument against it, depending on the author. But that did not necessarily mean that it was completely devoid of empirical content; in contrast, it is possible to show, at least, that it had some empirical underpinnings (Medick 1973: 23–4). To say that there was an increasing number of phenomena in the social world which could be adequately subsumed neither under the category of the individual nor under that of the polity, appeared perfectly plausible. However, there were few empirical reasons to assume that the life of this 'society' should show a strong degree of boundedness and even coherence, the most important one being the existence of a nation-state apparatus that effectively focused social practices (along the lines of the politico-historical and the statistical argument presented above). No social theory, however, provided for inherent mechanisms why the commercial exchanges, the associative life, the division of labour should hold together in the absence of such an apparatus which did not itself emerge from societal exchanges. At the beginning of the twentieth century, a line of reasoning emerged which attempted to relax such strong theorising on 'society' without abandoning the entire project of a social science, broadly in the Mohlian tradition.

Interim doubts

This proposal was to regard 'society' no longer as an entity but in terms of – spatially and temporally open-ended – processes and relations. Max Weber directed his methodological considerations against what he perceived as a predominant inclination to analyse alleged collective phenomena with concepts which were not solidly founded. In the German intellectual context and in his reworking of the methodology of the so-called Historical School, this admonishment rather focused on terms like 'people' or 'spirit of the people', but by implication 'society' was affected by the same verdict. His own historical sociology started out from human action and its meanings and employed processual concepts instead, of which 'rationalisation' is certainly the best known. Such concepts are not unproblematic either, in particular because of their evolutionist leanings, but Weber thus succeeds in avoiding any undue ontologisation of social phenomena without becoming incapacitated to analyse the social world at all. His *Protestant ethic*, regardless of the validity of the particular argument, carefully – even if, as one may want to argue, ultimately not successfully – tries to maintain the objective of sociological explanation without succumbing to simple determinisms.

Georg Simmel, a contemporary of Weber, accepted the problématique or, as he called it, the 'riddle' of society as indeed the fundamental 'problem of sociology'. To solve the riddle, however, meant grounding sociology not on 'society' as a 'unified being' but rather on the ways human beings relate to each other, their forms of sociation – his terminological means to turn 'society' into a relation rather than an entity – and interaction. The concept of the mutual constitution, in interaction, of self and other as well as of the totality in which interactions take place foreshadows the sociological perspectives that would later become known as symbolic interactionism and social constructionism.

'Society' as the key object of sociological study

Mentioning Weber and Simmel brings us to the turn to the twentieth century and, thus, to the so-called classical period of sociology, which proved to be in many respects formative of the institutionalised discipline (see ch. 1). In striking contrast to Weber's and Simmel's reasoning, Emile Durkheim then developed the strongest notion of society as an object that ever existed hitherto, a notion that through its adaptation by Talcott Parsons had a lasting impact on one major current of sociological theorising during the twentieth century. Durkheim offered a representation of society in which the elements of the social order were defined according to their position in the division of social labour and their relations regarded as interlocking in the form of 'organic solidarity'. Parsons modernised the vocabulary by introducing the concepts of 'social system' and 'system integration', and he enlarged it through elaborate ideas on role systems and mechanisms of functional adaptation.

Parsons and his associates had a strong influence on sociological theorising between the 1940s and the early 1970s, first in the US, later in Europe and Latin America as well. At various points, they advertised their approach in key statements about the social sciences, such as the two international encyclopaedias which appeared in 1934 and 1968 respectively.[67] In both cases, the presentation centres on the postulation of 'society' as the key object of sociological study, and each time the key problems that were discerned in my earlier analysis resurface – despite the intentions of the contributors to these works to conceal them.

In the entries on 'society' and on 'sociology' in the 1934 *Encyclopaedia of the social sciences*, Talcott Parsons and Robert MacIver respectively give their work a far-reaching genealogy by reading 'society' back into earlier, pre-1750 writings in political philosophy. They go back to Plato and Aristotle, whose language did not yet have an 'actual equivalent of the English word society' (Parsons 1934: 225) and whose 'thought on society never takes specific sociological form' (MacIver 1934: 233), to gradually move towards the period when society is finally 'thought of as an independent focus of theoretic interest and of scientific study' (MacIver 1934: 235), and 'as possessing in some sense independent reality' (Parsons 1934: 229).

This strategy has the reputational advantage of both endowing sociology with an object of eternal duration and demonstrating that the very emergence of sociology marked intellectual progress, namely the discovery of this object. However, it underestimates the importance of changes in social practices that go along with terminological shifts. If there was neither 'word' nor 'thought' in the proper form, maybe 'society' did not really exist before sociology?[68] In the ancient Greek view as well as in much of later political thought, there was no 'social' world; and its postulation was not just a discovery but transformed key issues of political philosophy (Arendt 1958). Parsons and MacIver disregard the alternative justification of the emerging 'social' sciences, namely to regard them as new sciences for a new phenomenon. As I tried to show, however, this is how they were indeed offered by some of their proponents. But the historicisation of the object would threaten its ontological status, and it would open the breach for those kinds of questionings Mohl and others were struggling with but which Parsons and his colleagues hoped to bypass.

After he has established the existence of 'society', MacIver (1934: 244) goes on to emphasise that it was exactly its being seen as 'distinct from the state' that made society the object of a new discipline, sociology. The separation of the social from the political realm is also hailed as an achievement by Parsons in the same volume. However, that separation was mostly conceived in the terms of socio-philosophical presuppositions which did not give 'society' the potentially autonomous existence that Mohl thought was required. It signalled that human social life had its particularities and subjectivities which were to some extent independent of the laws of the state. But such sociology did not really think of social relations developing independently of state exigencies; the concern about the 'social contract', now sociologised as the need for 'integration', remained predominant. As Talcott Parsons (1934: 230–1) put it, 'without a system common to the members of a community social order itself cannot be accounted for'.[69]

Again, however, it is difficult to historically confirm any such view of 'society'. And, as argued above, other sociologists such as Weber and Simmel well knew about the flaws in such a conceptualisation. If 'society' was nevertheless (re-) emphasised in an increasing part of the sociological discourse during the early decades of the twentieth century, the basic reason lies in the perception that social practices did in fact not cohere or remain within a bounded order, and that this situation was seen as politically problematic. By that time sociology had somewhat successfully presented itself as a scientific approach to contemporary society and its problems. Trying to show how a new coherence could emerge after the turmoils of industrialisation, workers' struggles, urbanisation, in short 'the social question', was at least as much a political action as a sociological proposition. To some extent, sociologists participated in constructing 'imagined communities' (Benedict Anderson) for solving problems of social coherence and boundedness. It is to their merit that many of them, and in particular those whom we have come to call 'classical' sociologists, have kept using much more sober terms than many of their contemporaries who tried to provide foundational readings for a new community (see ch. 10).

The concept of the social system then provided a kind of anti-foundational foundation for social coherence and integration. It is the hitherto last incarnation of 'society' that attempts to maintain the double orientation towards both the exigencies of political philosophy and the empirical analysis of the structure of social relations. However, the tensions in the conceptual construction could not be overlooked. If they could not be resolved, they had to be glossed over. The entry on 'society' in the *International encyclopedia of the social sciences*, published in 1968 at the likely historical apex of the cultural importance of sociology, can serve to confirm this suspicion.

Through the voice of Leon Mayhew, then one of Parsons' doctoral students, this authoritative source defines society as 'a relatively independent or self-sufficient population characterised by internal organisation, territoriality, cultural distinctiveness, and sexual recruitment' (1968: 577).[70] This definition sounds highly empirical, but it is also loaded with presuppositions. It gives no fewer than four, at first glance unrelated, criteria which need to be fulfilled at the same time, and it turns them into strong criteria by demanding that the resulting phenomena should be 'independent and self-sufficient'. A naive reader might readily arrive at the conclusion that 'society' must be a rare occurrence in the social world. Without good reasons to the contrary being given, should one not assume that cultural practices and patterns of sexual partner choice may have different spatial dimensions, and that both could well be unrelated to other aspects of social organisation – the boundaries of the polity, for instance? Why, first of all, should we think that human beings dwell in 'independent and self-sufficient' groupings rather than have a variety of links to different other groups, and possibly not form any identifiable collectivity whole at all? In line with the tradition outlined above, our sociologist might answer that it turns out they do, as a matter of fact, and that this is not least the discovery of sociology. However, Leon Mayhew is well aware of the complexity of the issue. He takes a number of steps to qualify his assertion.

First of all, he alleviates the burden of the criterion of self-sufficiency. It should not be understood as a situation of isolation and autarchy, but rather one of 'controlled relations with an environment' (1968: 584). People do interact across the boundaries of societies, but societies can control these boundary crossings. A different type of complication is evidently created here, since societies are now being endowed with agential capacities rather reminiscent of a state agency such as a customs office. However, the strong, and hardly tenable, point on self-sufficiency is abandoned.

Once this avenue is opened, more sceptical thoughts can no longer be avoided. Indeed, the different kinds of human practices could have different spatial and demographic extensions. Only when such spaces overlap, 'when a relatively broad range of such systems cohere around a common population, we may speak of a society' (1968: 583). Such rethinking may even go as far as demanding an alternative approach: 'The emergence of a bounded, unified social system is no longer assumed but becomes an object of inquiry' (1968: 584), the consequence being that 'the concept of a society with exclusive boundaries may be obsolete' (1968: 583). Sociologists could analyse the extensions of modes of internal organisation, cultural practices and sexual recruitment as well as of other social practices and could then try to characterise specific configurations that might emerge from such an analysis. The existence of society, as defined above, would become a purely empirical issue.

However, the reflection does not stop here. Mayhew assumes that there are other, apparently non-empirical reasons for sticking to the idea of society.[71] 'Social theorists have found in "society" a convenient foundation for relating their specific problems to a larger context' (1968: 578). Since the author does not provide any further detail, this phrase remains enigmatic, to say the least. What are the specific problems of the social theorist? And why should it be useful to relate them to a larger context (instead of, as the alternative may be, solving them)? What implicitly happens here is that the author acknowledges the most important issue of 'society' as a sociological object to be unresolved. The very specific linkage of empirical-historical observation and normative-conceptual problématique that was invested into this object created tensions that kept breaking up.

The passing away of 'society'?

Since the late 1960s, the time when Mayhew wrote, the acknowledgement of this tension has become more widespread within sociological debates, and the insight that the idea of 'society' as an object may need to be given up has gained ground (see e.g. Touraine 1965; and later Mann 1986: ch. 1). The normative-political problématique is still with us. There are again good reasons to assume that the structures of social linkages do not cohere and show no strongly overlapping boundaries. And again, there is much talk about the need for new coherence, now often straightforwardly under the title of 'community' – as well as renewed debates about the nation as the allegedly natural container of shared practices. In contrast, hardly anybody outside systems theory seems any longer convinced that 'system integration' – or any other concept for 'society' – could be sufficient to deal with the time-honoured political problématique of relating the strivings of a multitude of individuals to the requirements of sustaining a polity. Significantly, sociologists are not even the key participants in these debates (though some schools are present); they are rather led by political philosophers.

In this most recent development we may find indications that sociological analysis of the structure of social linkages might ultimately fully separate from the politico-philosophical concern about the sustainability of the polity. The tension in the concept of 'society' would then be abolished and, as a consequence, it appears very likely that the concept could no longer be sustained; the interest in it would subside. If this were the case, one would have to conclude that it was only the ambivalent relation of sociology to political philosophy which upheld the idea of 'society' as an existing object. By way of conclusion, I shall try to review the findings of my brief history of the concept in the light of the current possibility of such an immanent passing away.

The need for some new language

In the preceding observations I have tried to identify the places which 'society' occupies in the various discursive formations which make the claim of the existence of this object. Without being explicit about it, I have gradually introduced a language for speaking about 'society' that is not itself dependent on any specific one of those discourses under study. Thus, I tried to characterise the broadest possible space of a sociology, i.e. to offer a conceptualisation which allows for the possibility for 'society' to exist but does not presuppose its existence. The purpose of this construction was to show how historically existing approaches to sociology have moved in a broader, common space and which relative position they have taken with regard to each other in this space.

When the terms 'social' and 'society' were appropriated as key concepts of the emerging 'social sciences', they were simultaneously considered as a rather general and as a very specific way of talking about connections between human beings. With regard to the nature of these connections, i.e. to forms of 'sociability', there was probably not even much novelty in so-called early social science after the mid eighteenth century (as Hont 1993 argues). However, by some important participants in the debate, the new term 'society' was meant to denote a structure of such connections, i.e. the variety of their extensions in relation to substantive contents, which did not exist before a certain time, or which could not well be described by earlier languages (or both).

Key importance was given to the extension of the chains of connections due to the development of commerce, and to some extent also due to the freedom of expression and the constitution of a 'public sphere',[72] as well as to the newly relevant boundary of these extended chains provided by the nation-based constitutional polity. These were, in various combinations, the decisive elements of the novel structure of connections that came to be called 'society'. However, though some novelty was without doubt brought by the effects of the industrial and democratic revolutions, one may well remain very sceptical as to whether the structure of social connections was in any way decisively transformed before, at least, the middle of the nineteenth century, so as to call for an entirely new language. It was at that point that an open-minded observer such as Mohl could make an effort at a summary account of empirical phenomena of a 'societal' nature.

Mohl himself provided what we could call a justification for a 'weak' concept of society. To him, it sufficed that a number of durable and important phenomena existed which could be analysed neither from the viewpoint of methodological individualism nor as derivative of the polity. In the German lands, he had difficulty in getting even this 'weak' position heard. Elsewhere, a much 'stronger' reasoning on society was offered. Social theorists tended to have specific views on how these phenomena formed chains of linkages and how their coherence – or, for critical theorists, their self-contradictory nature – was brought about. This is to say they had substantive theories on the solidity of society or its historical direction that made many more presuppositions than any empirical analysis of chains and webs of connections could ever confirm. From our present, historical point of view, some of the elements of such substantive theories of 'society' can be assessed with a view to identifying which of them are probably to be maintained and which have to be discarded.

The disappearance of 'society' as an object

First, it seems difficult to reject the most general proposition that there are relevant phenomena between the house (the individual, the private sphere) and the polity (the state, the public sphere). The only question that may be raised is whether their conceptualisation as being between these two phenomena does not accept too much of a specific discourse, namely political theory, so as to limit the analysis of 'society'. This suspicion finds confirmation in some of the further issues to raise.

Second, in some discourses on society, this object came to take the place which 'polity' held in political philosophy. One could not say that it was synonymous with polity, since the whole discursive structure was transformed, but it served as the term for signifying the integration of a multitude of diverse 'parts' (which could be, but did not have to be, 'individuals') into a 'whole'. Organicist theories of society as a body are the most obvious example, even translating the metaphor of the 'body politic' into a new discourse. But Durkheim's 'organic solidarity' and Parsons' 'system integration' equally subject 'society' to an analogous operation. If one wants to do justice to the repeated postulate of the 'autonomy' of society from the state, such reasoning risks a severe conflation of issues.

Third, a weaker version of the preceding assumption is the idea that society is an effectively bounded whole, whether well integrated with the polity or disruptive of it. Reference is then often made to some special, often explicitly non-state aspect of relations within the polity. But there is something artificial about this conceptualisation. If 'societal' relations, such as 'cultural' or 'economic' ones, remain 'within' the boundaries of a polity, then they are most often not truly of a 'non-state' character, but indeed are manipulated or even controlled by, for instance, state educational institutions or customs regulation. Otherwise they would most likely not remain confined to state boundaries. And the shift from social practices to meanings and language is, in principle, open to the same criticism as are stronger notions of society. Why should cultures and languages be more prone to boundedness and coherence than other social practices? And is not the impression of their being 'systems' of orderly interrelated elements nothing given once and for all but rather a result of the historical labour of making them closed and coherent, with the nation-state being again, at least in Europe, one important source of such efforts?

Fourth, the idea of nationwide extension of such phenomena as we found it in encyclopaedia definitions of society indeed leads to a further variation of this kind of assumption. My analysis did not identify any theoretical ground for such an assumption. Instead, the historical development of sociology happened to coincide with a period of conscious attempts to 'nationalise' social practices. Rather than the firm foundation of a science of society, the sociology of 'national society' is itself a historical phenomenon. Such historical coincidence may then to some extent explain the longevity of the two before-mentioned assumptions, since this is how nation-state, national society and the latter's relative cultural-linguistic homogeneity were indeed linked.

Fifth, and of a different order, is the use of 'society' as a means to demarcate a sociological way of thinking from an individualistic one, as prevalent in economics and psychology. Much of the sociological criticism of ontological individualism is well justified, but its force does not really depend on holding the inverse proposition of ontological holism such as in the postulate of 'society'. A sociology can well be based on a concept of sociability or social relations that allows for the open-ended nature of the chains of connections created through such relations.

Sixth, if the objective of sociological analysis were defined as the investigation of social relations, in the above sense, then some of the fundamental debates in the history of sociology could be recast. Instead of asking whether 'society' was a historically emerging phenomenon or a fundamental condition of human life, changes in the extension of effective connections between human beings would have to be analysed. Furthermore, such an analysis would have to distinguish whether such connections are material, such as in a new division of social labour, or rather discursive, such as in a redefinition of membership communities in 'collective representations', society as an 'object of consciousness, of volition, of thought' (Mohl 1851: 6; see ch. 8 in this book).

Finally, furthermore, no such identification of a particular 'structure of society' would allow one to draw immediate conclusions as to whether the position in the structure determines the thought and action of an individual. The position may be seen as firm, stable and socially defining, but it may also be seen as unimportant, transient, a momentary fact. The sociological tradition tended to regard the social and socially determined nature of human life as one of its most important insights. Without entirely doing away with it, we should rather consider it as the question sociology contributed to social and political thought, not as the answer to all questions.

Some inescapability of 'society' as a concept

At the beginning of the twenty-first century, the suspicion is widespread that 'society' is a concept difficult to uphold, not least for reasons of its decreasing empirical reference due to the internationalisation even if not always globalisation of practices, on the one hand, and alleged individualisation, on the other.

Predictions of its passing away will almost certainly come true if the concept of 'society' is meant to carry several or even all of the strong assumptions it was historically endowed with. However, none of the alternatives to the sociological mode of reasoning which are currently in vogue, and certainly not rationalist individualism, will be able to deal with what could more prudently be called the representation of the state of social relations (I owe this way of putting the issue to discussions with Luc Boltanski).

'Society' was a conceptual tool to represent the state of social relations in a particular temporal and cognitive space. In its strong versions, it was never fully convincing. However, it addressed a key issue of social thought, namely a transformation in the political problem of unity in liberal theory, in a way that tried to take certain changes in social relations into account. Tensions between these two aspects of the term, a politico-conceptual necessity and an empirical phenomenon, could never be overcome. But between the early nineteenth and the late twentieth century – the coming into being and the possible passing away of 'society' – no superior solution to an inescapable issue could be offered. 'Society' will not entirely disappear until this has happened.

If 'society' is currently out of fashion without being superseded by a more appropriate concept, this means that a political sociology that conflated issues in conceptual shortcuts has been replaced by a return to a sociologically ill-informed political philosophy, on the one hand, and a sociology that is blind to political issues, on the other. It is difficult to say whether such development is a liberation or a loss. It seems evident, however, that some new relation of sociology to political philosophy will have to be built that addresses the inescapable issues of politics without imposing constraints on social analysis.

10
POLITY

Sociology, at least major parts of what goes under that name, has been an attempt to understand the viability of a polity by means other than those offered by political philosophy, including importantly means of empirical analysis (see ch. 9; and Wagner 2000: ch. 2). The problem has been defined, I shall argue, as that of the relation between social identities, social practices and modes of collective rule-setting. Sociology has mostly insisted on some need for – as well as tendency towards – a neat coherence of identities, practices and rules in a society. *Coherence*, in this sense, means that there is a collectivity of human beings, forming a 'society' by virtue of the fact that they share common understandings about what is important in their lives (identities), that they mostly interact with each other inside this collectivity (practices), and that they have ways to determine how they regulate their lives in common (rules of the polity).[73] However, it has been notoriously difficult to argue under which – empirical – conditions such coherence can be said to exist, why and to which degree it is needed, as well as how it would actually be brought about and maintained. To lay the groundwork for the search for an adequate understanding of this issue, I shall first try to exemplify what is meant by identities, practices and rules of the polity.

Self-identity I take to be the understanding somebody has of her or his own life, the orientations one gives to one's life. Mostly, self-identities are composed of a number of elements, such as being caring mother to children, loyal employee to a company and good citizen of a nation. And, as this example shows, its elements may have different width, referring to others or groups of others at smaller or greater distance from oneself. Under modern conditions, it is often argued, self-identity is closely linked to the idea of self-realisation. Again, self-realisation may be conceived in quite different ways. In romantic terms, it could mean the discovery of an inner self and the attempt to live up to that inner self's exigencies. In more profane terms, it can be read as giving priority to one's own goals at the possible neglect of 'higher' values (for two different ways of putting the issue, see Taylor 1989b; Rorty 1989: ch. 2). In the latter variant, self-identity appears as highly individualistic, referring to the possibility of a choice of identity and of being responsible for that choice to oneself only. However, it is important to recognise that every process of identity formation is a social process. Even a highly individualistic concept of self-identity relates to, and is to a certain extent dependent on, an individualistic culture in which it can be realised.

By *social identities*, specifically, I refer to the effective rooting of individual identities in social contexts of others. To see oneself as part of a larger group may be the crucial element of one's self-identity. The classical examples are national identities and class identities. Thus, natives of German parents on German soil may feel part of a greater group of 'Germans' to whom they consider themselves tied by historical fate even though they will not actually meet most of them ever during their lives. Or, workers may have felt united with other workers anywhere in the world by defining their social situation as a common one and seeing themselves as engaged in the same struggle. More recently, gender and 'non-national' ethnic identities have explicit foci in the formation of social groups, such as in the women's movement and among African-Americans and Hispano-Americans in the US.

By *social practices* I mean to refer to the activities people pursue and, importantly, to the effective links such activities provide to others – by sharing a residential location and meeting each other frequently, by exchanging goods, or by communicating with each other and exchanging information. Some of such practices are direct, involving face-to-face interaction. However, people are also linked to each other indirectly through widely extended chains of interaction. The global circulation of goods through what has become known as the world market, or the wide transmission of information by electronic means, are among the currently widely debated of those chains of interaction. We may note already here that social practices may be related to social identities: think of environmentalists buying organically grown foods, of workers reading journals of the workers' movement, or of socially and ethnically homogeneous neighbourhoods where you mostly meet others to whom you feel some affinity. However, very often they are not: many of the human activities in contemporary societies – buying food in supermarkets, salaried work for a big company – have rather thin links to the self-conception of those who pursue them.

Finally, by *modes of collective rule-setting* I mean what is conventionally called politics, namely communication and deliberation over rules that apply to a collectivity of human beings with a view to regulating what they have in common. Key issues in the determination of such modes are the extension of the group to which they apply; the rules for participation in their deliberation; and the definition of the realm of practices collective rules may legitimately cover. Liberal politics used to claim that it has neat solutions for all these issues: the nation-state setting the natural boundary of the polity; universal adult suffrage in regularly recurring elections of representatives being the major rule of participation; and the distinction of the private and the public sphere limiting the legitimacy of political intervention to the latter. However, as some of the preceding examples show, these solutions may be not all that neat. In world market exchanges, for instance, social practices may exceed the boundaries of the nation-state in politically relevant ways. Migration has changed the composition of many nation-states so that sizeable minorities are often excluded from participation rights. Or, bringing gender identities to the political agenda violates the public–private distinction as it was commonly understood.

It is here that we approach the question of coherence of identities, practices and rules of the polity. A common way of putting the argument is as follows: a nation-state is a viable polity only if most, or the most important, social practices link the people inside its boundaries to each other, and if these people share a sense of their being part of one collectivity. In more generic sociological terms, one would speak of 'society' instead of the nation-state. However, owing to the historical coincidence of the emergence of sociology and the strength of the nation-state, both terms tend to be conflated in sociological reasoning. And, in some variants, the idea of a need for coherence is replaced by the analytical argument on an inclination towards coherence. By this move, though, the emphasis is merely shifted to the question of how such coherence should come about.

Let us briefly trace this argument through social thought. First, by way of delimitation, it is important to note that the question is meaningful only within a conceptual space whose boundaries are marked by two extreme political possibilities: regimes which are based exclusively on some external reasoning or force rather than consent, or cooperative orders of free individuals which do not rely on political force that does not arise from consent. The former conception assumes either some natural interlocking of the polity with identities and practices or a complete suppression of 'deviant' identities and practices. The latter, based on the assumption of an automatic production of a harmonious coherence of identities, practices and the rules of the polity, is the basic conception of a self-sustained individualist liberalism. Whereas some may regard this view as describing a desirable state, most observers of nineteenth- and twentieth-century societies did not consider it to have been achieved by any actual society, and many regarded it as illusory and unreachable. The ideal remains, however, as a key to the self-understanding of Western societies, to what one might call, following Castoriadis (1990), the imaginary signification of modernity.

In the case of these two possibilities, the problem of this chapter does not arise. For other societies, the question of the relation of identities, practices and modes of collective rule-setting is a highly general formulation of the object of political sociology. At the same time it describes an inescapable key political problématique of modernity, and, as such, one of the most time-honoured problems of social thought. In the beginnings of political modernity, Adam Smith, Auguste Comte and Georg Wilhelm Friedrich Hegel, among others, dealt with it each on their own terms, offering self-interest and market, science and the state respectively as means to reconcile tensions in these relations (or rather, to evaporate them conceptually). Talcott Parsons, a towering figure of modernist sociology, called it the problem of social order, ascribed it to Hobbes, and later formulated it in terms of the integration of the cultural, the economic and the political 'systems'. Zygmunt Bauman (1992: 53) has spoken of a new relation of 'individual life-world, social cohesiveness and systemic capacity for reproduction' as the key to understanding postmodernity, that is, our own time.

The issue, then, has an impressive genealogy. The different historical terms in which it has been cast indicate divergences in the ways in which social relations are perceived in intellectual discourse as well as, to some extent, how they are actually lived. My own exercise of reconceptualisation, in this chapter, will proceed by comparing two different ways of conceiving this relation, each of which occurred at a different point in the social history of modernity. The first dates from the period broadly around the turn to this century, 1890 to 1920; and the second period is the present, which may be said to have begun at some time between 1968 and 1973 (see ch. 5; and Wagner 1994). Both periods were critical periods of sociological thought, critical in the double sense that they were highly fruitful and that in each period the sociological project came to the verge of collapse (see ch. 1). Both were also periods of major transformations of a social formation, or 'crises of modernity'; the intellectual reorientations were ways to critically reflect on, and actively deal with, these transformations.

Classical sociology and the politics of the first crisis of modernity

In political terms, classical sociology needs to be understood against the background of the discursive hegemony of liberalism. During most of the nineteenth century, the century after the democratic revolutions in the United States and in France, liberalism and liberal theorising had been at centre-stage of intellectual debates on politics. Even the adversaries of liberalism saw themselves in relation to it – as progressives who went beyond liberalism, or conservatives who resisted it. At the end of that century, however, intellectuals were generally well aware of the failure of liberal theory, in politics as well as in economic matters, either to understand the changes in societal practices or to provide criteria for their regulation. In those *fin-de-siècle* debates, the position of the classical sociologists was marked by the fact that they agreed that societal developments had superseded classical liberalism, but insisted that revisions had to be made within that political tradition (Seidman 1983: 278). What was it that had brought about this shift in politico-intellectual climate, and how did the sociologists fare in the process of rethinking?

Mostly, liberal theory is known for its claim to have resolved the questions of political expression, economic interest and scientific validity. In principle, democracy, efficiency and truth were to be achieved by leaving them to open contestation and competition. However, a closer look reveals that most early-nineteenth-century liberals did not actually advocate a fully inclusive liberal society. Restrictions based on criteria such as gender, race, culture or social standing persisted. The ideas of liberalism were restricted to male household and property owners who alone were reasonable and responsive enough to be free. All others, most notably women, workers and 'savages', needed to be taken care of and/or excluded from free activities. One might say that the guiding representation of society was of a dual nature: 'domestic' relations prevailed between women and men as well as between workers and entrepreneurs, whereas 'market' relations were dominant between free citizens (see Boltanski and Thévenot 1991). This representation showed a certain coherence, as long as the practices of women and workers remained confined to the house and the factory respectively, and as long as they regarded these as the right places to be. Even if one may accept, with many qualifications, that such was broadly the case early in the nineteenth century, much of the social history of the second half of that century can be analysed as the erosion and active destruction of that coherence.

This is not the place to repeat accounts of the dislocation of large parts of the population, of the growth of industry and the industrial cities, of the struggles for the extension of the suffrage, of the phrasing of the social question or the labour question, or of the formation and rising strength of the workers' movement, its parties and social theories. Suffice it to say that these processes, reordering social practices and disembedding individuals from the social contexts in which they had grown up, uprooted social identities and created widespread uncertainty about individual life chances – about the place in society of those who were disembedded, and among the elites about the order and stability of society as a whole. Classical liberalism proved absolutely unable to deal with these questions and a rather radical reconceptualisation of society was at stake.

Reform movements during the latter half of the nineteenth century tried to re-establish some solidity and certainty into the social fabric. Many reformers came from the bourgeois elites, and their idea was not least to safeguard order; they often drew on the idea of the nation as a collective of people who shared a common history and had developed a collective social identity. But an equally important element was the self-constitution of the working class as a collective body capable of defining and representing its own interests. Socialism, trade unions and labour parties spring from this attempt at developing organised responses to social change on the part of a new collective, the working class. Besides their political and economic objectives, the movement also created a new social identity as an industrial worker, an identity at struggle for a full place in society or in the combined forces of the future of humankind.

In very broad outlines, this was the political context of those writings that we know as classical sociology. Their authors saw the contemporary situation as one in which a major political restructuring was occurring without a clear objective or guiding vision. They turned this into their major theme. Theories of 'organic solidarity' and the relation of religion and morality as in Durkheim, of forms of legitimate domination and 'charisma' in Weber, of the political class and the 'circulation of elites' in Pareto were the products of such attempts at reconceiving somehow orderly relations between extended social practices, uprooted social identities, and polities in need of adaptation. I shall return to the type of these responses below, but before doing so, I shall sketch how political thinking in sociology went on.

A key feature of the sociological tradition, well worth remembering, is its discontinuity. From the turn of the century onwards and especially during the inter-war years, the classical sociological reappraisals of the liberal tradition lost their persuasiveness. In the larger crisis of the liberal utopia, both the intelligibility of society by the classical sociological means and the manageability of social order by drawing conclusions from such means were increasingly doubted (see ch. 5). The disillusion was far more profound in Europe than in the US. In Europe, sociological discourse fell to pieces. One piece, its considerations on a theory of action, was taken up by highly voluntarist philosophies of action, often referred to as 'philosophy of the deed'. Another piece, what was later to be called empirical social research, developed a practical orientation towards the use of such infor-mation on people's opinions and behaviour, and was often on the fringes of or outside academia. Both parts of the broken discourse flourished under the fascist regimes. Philosophies of action underpinned the idea of a strong man and his will and power to rejuvenate the nation. Empirical social research was often specifically organised to acquire strategically useful knowledge about the state of the population. But both pieces flourished separately. Taken together they might have formed an empirically supported social theory of collective action that could have been inscribed into a normative theory of democracy.

At least elements of such latter discourse existed in the US. If the political philosophy of John Dewey is linked to the social theory of George Herbert Mead and the empirical sociology of the Chicago School (Joas 1993), we have a body of theoretical and empirical knowledge which emphasizes the human ability to create and recreate one's own life individually and collectively. These thinkers did not fall into voluntarism, much less irrationalism, but instead studied empirically the enabling and constraining conditions under which such creative action occurred. One might say that such reasoning tried to offer ideational and empirical tools for people to construct coherent identities, practices and polities on their own.[74]

But pragmatism did not become the dominant discourse of American society. Its broader social and political theory remained undeveloped and even its continuation within sociology, as symbolic interactionism, provided no strong theoretical impetus after the Second World War, but rather moved to the periphery of the discipline (Joas 1992b; Manicas 1987: 214, 275). The shift of hegemony in American sociology was from the Chicago School in the 1920s and 1930s, to the Columbia School in the following decades, to social policy research in the 1960s. Neither continental European nor North American academics and intellectuals were successful in interpreting social transformations in such a way as to enable individuals to interactively reconstruct a meaningful set of social relations. In contrast, one might say that political sociology after the Second World War moved to prefabricate a well-ordered representation of society for people to accept readymade.

The organisation of modernity and the consolidation of sociology

The 'modernisation' of the social sciences went a third way, which bypassed the problems of either classical European or pragmatist sociology of linking identities to practices and political orders. In the US, Talcott Parsons tried to reappropriate the classical European heritage by showing that there were elements in those works of a social theory that could deal with entire social formations while at the same time being able to account for the rationales of human action. Parsons gradually developed these selectively appropriated ideas into a theory of modern societies as systems which became differentiated into functionally related subsystems whose combined workings would safeguard system integration.

System integration is nothing but the term for a coherent and stable relation of identities, practices and collective rules. The theory of modernisation works with a foundational distinction between two coherent forms of society, traditional and modern; and the transition from the one to the other is a coherence-seeking movement called development. Once this process is started, it entails modernisation. It is only at the stage of 'modern society' that a new coherence is reached.

Some works inside the modernisation paradigm have shown how such coherence is achieved. It did not escape these observers that the imaginary signification of modernity as such, linked as it is to liberty and autonomy, was neither coherent nor a source of stability. An example relevant for understanding modes of collective rule-setting from the modernisation perspective is provided by Gabriel Almond and Sidney Verba (1963) in their seminal study of civic culture as a political ideal of modernity. Dissociating themselves from an activist, participatory ideal of the citizen, the authors emphasised that a certain degree of passivity and lack of involvement, which is typical of so-called civic culture, is functionally necessary to secure democratic processes. They ignored the liberal principle of political inclusion and its history of violation; for them 'moderated' change, even if 'moderation' necessitated restrictions to participation, was a legitimate objective. As they saw the modern state, participation in collective rule-setting was a privilege to be granted only to those whose orientations have adapted to the modern polity. This thinning out of the liberal ideal of inclusion and participation is reinterpreted as a sign of progress toward political modernity.

The core of this theory was not the liberal ideology of the open society, but the idea that a 'fit' between societal requirements and individual strivings was characteristic for the modern order. Starting out from the assumption of the need for a basic overall coherence of society, it identified related substructures or subsystems in it, each of which would have its own logics or mode of operation, and which together could secure overall coherence. The activities of individuals were tied into these social phenomena via behaviour-guiding norms and the learning of these norms or, in some variants, via structural constraints. These theories emphasised the organised, relatively closed nature of overall social relations but tended to see this as an achievement rather than a restriction.

With hindsight, one may understand such reasoning against its historical background. After the Second World War, an unprecedented growth of production and consumption, i.e. a strong dynamic in certain social practices, occurred parallel to relative tranquillity and stability of authoritative practices, while at the same time only limited formal restrictions were imposed to free political expression, especially compared with other times and places. The core problématique was to explain the coexistence of these features as a specific social configuration. This extraordinary conjuncture of dynamics, stability and nominal liberty was treated not only as 'normal' but as the end state of all social change. Modernisation was defined as the process leading to this end.

The representation of society in these discourses was not completely flawed. Modernisation theory did make valid observations about some basic features of the advanced industrial societies of the 1950s and 1960s. I will call this 'organised modernity' (see in more detail Wagner 1994). The general features of organised modernity are these: social practices were organised so that they moderately cohered on the level of national society and formed interlinking sets of institutional rules. A discursive image of these interlinking practices emphasised their coherence and long-term stability, and associated them with a solid developmental perspective. Such completion of modernity, in the sense that its imaginary significations reached the end of their effectiveness as an ideal, did occur historically, even if the order did not prove to be stable over the long run. What has largely been neglected in discussions of this order was that it had been constructed through intense struggles in the relatively recent past, and that its closure was not as complete as some post Second World War theorists thought.

In the period between the First and the Second World Wars, the perceived instabilities of the post-liberal regimes motivated proposals for societal organ-isation, which relied on the definition of a, mostly national, collective body and on the mobilisation of the members of such a collective body under the leadership of the state. The programmes and practices of these political experiments of the period all restricted the notion of individual liberty in the name of some collectivity, though of course to highly varying degrees. In these political experiments, liberal practices, based on the free communication and association of a multitude of individual agents with a view to determining the degree and actual substance of collective arrangements in society, gave way to organised practices. Those practices relied on the aggregation of groups of individuals according to some social criterion before communication and decision-making about collective arrangements were made in and between the organisations whose leaders were speaking and acting on behalf of, i.e. representing, their allegedly homogeneous memberships. The setting of boundaries and the social production of certainties is generally privileged against the liberal assertion of the unlimited autonomy of everybody to create and recreate oneself and one's social context.

The second crisis of modernity and the renewed debate on sociology

The 'achievement' of organised modernity was that it transformed the dis-embedding and uncertainties of the late nineteenth century into a new coherence of practices and orientations. Nation, class and state were the main conceptual and institutional ingredients to this achievement, which provided the substance for the building of collective identities and the setting of boundaries. They were materials that were all at hand, historically, to those who participated in building organised modernity. But they obviously did not cohere naturally. It took half a century of political struggle and of unprecedented violence and oppression to form a social configuration that seemed not only to satisfy major parts of its membership but also to develop a dynamic of its own. This dynamic was what came to be called the 'long prosperity', the 'thirty glorious years', or the 'golden age of capitalism'.

If the building of organised modernity can be understood in terms of the conventionalisation of social practices within set boundaries, many recent changes can be seen as the erosion of boundaries and as processes of deconventionalisation. With very few exceptions, current analyses of the organisation of sets of social practices stress the breaking up of established rules. In some cases, a terminology is chosen that leads to positive associations, such as flexibilisation and pluralisation. In others, when the emphasis is on disorganisation, instability or fragmentation, negative connotations prevail. We learn about the disorganisation of capitalism, the decline of the nation-state, the crisis of political representation and the like.

This second crisis of modernity reoriented the modes of intellectual representation of society, too. The questioning of the order of practices extended to a questioning of their imaginary representation, and ultimately to doubts over the very possibility of representation. Because the achievements of organised modernity were bought at the price of setting strict boundaries and conventions, the critique of organised modernity was directed at the constraining effects of those boundaries and conventions. Intellectually, the recognition of the social construction of conventions was the major tool of such critique. It is made visible that strong grounds are lacking for rules that are nevertheless universally applied and enforced within a polity.[75] Thus, during the past two decades, much critical intellectual energy has been devoted to attempts at deconventionalisation (some may call this deconstruction) and recreation of ambivalence in a social order that was regarded as over-conventionalised and closed to any freedom of action beyond pre-established channels.

Sociological critics started by questioning the accounts of a well-ordered society that had dominated the discipline. Efforts at reopening the analysis of social relations focused on notions of action and interpretation as well as historicity, as discussed in the preceding chapters. Such concepts reintroduced the potential for identifying forms of plurality and diversity in social relations that could not be accounted for in the language of structure and integration. The sociological critics also reapproached the activities of the sociologists to those of 'ordinary' human beings. Both were capable, in principle, of reflexively monitoring their own activities and those of others. Sociology was increasingly seen as a reflexive enterprise, itself part of the society to the analysis of which it was devoted. The destruction of the boundary between sociological and lay discourse allowed the questioning of the very possibility of a science of society.

We may begin to draw the analogy between the era of classical sociology and our own – in the following way. The preceding turn of the century witnessed the emergence of classical sociology as a reasoning on society that was much more open, and less reliant on strong preconceptualisations, than earlier evolutionist, organicist and/or determinist social thought. Analogously, from the late 1960s onwards, comprehensive structural-functionalist or structuralist models of society lost their persuasiveness. In both situations, then, rather closed representations of the social world were profoundly questioned, and in both cases, the alternatives that were proposed were of broadly similar kinds (on the notion of closure, see Eisenstadt and Curelaru 1976: 102–4, 245–73, 347–50).[76]

Very schematically, I shall distinguish four such kinds of response. First, much of Durkheim's work can be regarded as the modified continuation of the project of a positive science of society, building on earlier views and trying to strengthen them at places where they had been found deficient, without altering their basic outlook and ambition. A similar attitude can be found today in theories of 'neo-modernisation', but also in those of 'reflexive modernisation'. All other responses view the 'crisis' as touching the foundations of prior social science more deeply.

A second view, which we may term formalisation, acknowledges a basic difficulty in conceptualising social phenomena, but also offers a clear-cut solution. If nothing else is certain, then the isolated human individual, without assuming specific social ties, has to be taken as the sole methodological (if not also ontological) basis. Everything else will have to be derived from this starting-point. In the first crisis of social representation, this perspective was developed by authors of the marginalist revolution, which led to what we call today neoclassical economics. In current debates, the extension of rational choice theorising far beyond the discipline of economics reflects a similar standpoint (see ch. 6). While this approach sticks strongly to the possibility of a science of social phenomena, it offers a very asocial version of such a science.

Third, if one shares the scepticism of rational choice theorists about the validity of other sociological concepts, but is also inclined to strongly reject the economistic idea of the autonomous subject, one will easily tend to the abdication of the entire project of 'sociological theory'. Historical approaches which emphasise the particular, or philosophical ones which focus on the general, may become more dominant, leaving between them, so to say, the space for a social science empty. The dissolution of the sociological discourse in Europe between the two great wars came close to such an abdication. Its present form goes most often under the name of postmodernism, a form of thinking that emphasises diversity and singularity, on the one hand, and resists all universal statements, on the other, except the one that no well-founded universal statements are possible.

The fourth response, which I would like to call reconsideration, straddles all three others. What I have in mind here is a form of thinking that takes all objections to social science seriously, but concludes with the possibility, though a very precarious one, of maintaining the project, even if under considerably changed assumptions. Most importantly, in the context of my argument, this approach reverses the question of the relation of identities, practices and polities by rejecting any idea of a preconceived need of, or tendency toward, coherence. It is on this point in particular – and on epistemological and methodological thoughts that are related to it – that this response differs from the response I have called modified continuation. The remainder of this chapter will try to understand what 'reconsideration' would mean today by continuing to focus on this problem of political sociology.

Social identity and political community between 'globalisation' and 'individualisation'

Drawing an analogy between the problématique of classical sociologists and the current one, as I have tried to do, was possible in part because the former lived through, and tried to make sense of, a major social transformation that can be compared, in some respects, to the one we are going through. Weber and Durkheim faced societies whose members had broadly accepted, or could no longer escape, a basically liberal imaginary signification. By their time, it was obvious to them and many others that the restrictions that had been applied to the liberties – and which had radically divided each of these societies into 'two nations' of included and excluded – could no longer be upheld. It seemed clear that these restricted liberal orders would have to be transformed to ones with fully inclusive social rules. How that would occur, however, was very much an open question. Many doubted that it could occur without immense social costs. The sociologists intended, among other things, to contribute to the viability of such an inevitable social transformation.

Classical social science intended to diagnose emerging phenomena such as the increasing individualisation that appeared to result from the dissolution of *Gemeinschaft*, the formation of 'society' as a larger order based on different rules, and the construction of bureaucratic apparatuses in the big industrial enterprises, state administration and the mass parties. Some observers recognised in such new institutions and rules the potential for a new coherence – though others, notably Weber, remained sceptical. But the intermediate historical outcome of the transformation then under way – through political struggles and disasters – was 'successful': an organised modernity that effectively focused 'modernised' social practices was built. Focusing involved a double movement. On the one hand, theoretically global, open-ended practices were reduced to national, bounded ones. On the other hand, the potentially infinite plurality and diversity of people on a territory were ordered and bound by a relatively coherent set of conventions for action. The order of organised modernity was one which was fully inclusive within nation-state societies, the extension of equal suffrage to all adult people and the recognition of gender equality in the law being the most indicative examples. At the same time, however, possibilities for participation were channelled into the prestructured paths of mass parties and welfare bureaucracies, and the boundaries to the 'outside', to people of other nation-states, were much more firmly controlled than before.

By drawing on institutional and cultural means that were available in the nineteenth century, the actual structure and extension of social practices (what came to be called society) were made to overlap strongly with the rules for collective deliberation (in the polity, defined as the nation-state) and many of the socially important means of individual orientation (social identities). With hindsight, the creation of imagined communities, such as nation and class, can be identified as a means by which the political problématique was temporarily fixed. For much of the twentieth century, national and class communities – being English or French, a worker or a *cadre* – appeared not as creations and imaginations but as the natural locations of human beings in a post-traditional society.

The last two or so decades can be read as the breaking up – or active dismantling – of this three-layered coherence. Analyses of our time again stress processes of dissolution and of individualisation. Theorists of dissolution argue that 'the world market . . . has erased the territorial inscriptions of the productive structures . . . The occidentalisation of the world is a broad movement of uniformisation of the imaginary involving the loss of cultural identities' (Latouche 1985: 39–40). Theorists of individualisation claim that all stable social orientations, such as class, culture and family, are breaking up and leaving individual human beings in much greater uncertainty and at greater risk when shaping their lives. If these two observations are joined together, then a second-crisis-of-modernity equivalent of the theory of the mass society emerges. Theorists of the latter had argued that the bureaucratic nation-state is the grand individualiser and destroyer of social structures and collective identities, that it isolates human beings and makes them dependent on its own, anonymous and machine-like organisation. Currently, the same is said to occur on a global scale: the nation-state then appears as an almost homely, 'intermediary' institution and container for authentic cultural expression. Such ideas are found both in those theories of postmodernity that have an air of the tragic, since they see these developments as losses and as inevitable (see Lyotard 1985a: 63–4), and by conservatives who try to maintain or reconstruct bounded institutions based on substantive notions of culture. Significantly, a normatively opposed interpretation of the same observations is also possible, in which the trends toward globalisation would be seen as enhancing enablements, as widening and easing the human capability to reach out widely in space and time. Individualisation may be regarded as a liberation from social constraints which have limited and channelled the ways in which human beings could draw on the historically available enablements. These views can be found in continuations of the modernist perspective in social thought, in neomodernisation theory, but they are also found in those strands of postmodernism that hail the new liberations.

Where, though, do these opposed assessments of globalisation and individualisation leave us with regard to the current condition of modernity – and the sociological possibility at understanding it? Let me begin an assessment with the issue of social identities. The concept of the nation as a strong basis for social, namely cultural-linguistic, identity rested on an idea of the historical depth of community, of bonds and commonalities created over long periods. Such a concept tends to 'naturalise' boundaries and distinctions with 'others' outside the historical community and to limit cross-boundary exchange. The concept of class was less 'deep' than that of nation, and not least for that reason its identity-constituting potential was more short-lived. However, it is probably generally valid to say, in spite of some resurgence of nationalism, that the hold of these quasi-natural identities has been loosening over the past quarter of a century in the West. From the 1960s onwards, the cultural revolution against organised modernity emphasised the normative unacceptability of such limitations and undermined the persuasiveness of the idea of any 'natural' community. What we have witnessed since then is not individualisation but rather the creation of communities on other substantive grounds, chosen by the acting human beings themselves, and possibly more fluid and open to reconsideration than the classically modern, national and class, communities.

How then are such modes of identity formation related to the current organisation of social practices? The quasi-naturalness of social identities during organised modernity stemmed from the overlap of social identities with coherent sets of practices and polity boundaries. Under such conditions, there may be very little choice of social identity, even if awareness prevails that identities are not ascribed but 'only' socially determined. But this overlap was not natural, it had been produced by cultural policies emphasising national identity and by controlling and restricting cross-boundary travel of people, goods and ideas (see e.g. Noiriel 1992). At the end of organised modernity this overlap is much less pronounced, and the formation of social identities is freed from such predetermination. Today there is a strong dissonance between social identities and social practices, each of which are highly diverse and variable.

What impact then does such a situation have for conceptions of the polity? Political agency during organised modernity resided in practices and identities focused on the sovereign nation-state and its idea of representation, both of which are now strongly challenged. Thus, modern politics faces a radical dilemma. On the one hand, the very idea of political deliberation depends on concepts of boundaries, membership and representation (Walzer 1983). On the other hand, the social practices to which politics refers may become increasingly 'atopic' (Gilbert and Guillaume 1985: 92), that is, not confinable to any space, so that no possible definable membership group could be found for deliberation, far less any community with a significant degree of shared values and, thus, a substantive basis for common deliberation.

The split between the organisation of social practices, boundaries of polities and modes of identity formation a century ago led sociologists to argue strongly for the need for the emergence of a new, coherent social order. They were not particularly successful in their predictions of what form it would take. The division of social labour did not produce 'organic solidarity', contra Durkheim; contra Weber, the legitimacy of existing forms of domination remained in doubt in European societies during the first half of the twentieth century. But sociologists contributed to identifying the political problématique of the time as well as the social and cognitive resources that were available to bridge the splits between identities, practices and polities.

In the current situation, it appears as if those splits are even wider and the social and cognitive resources to bridge them scarcer than in the earlier situation. Any attempt to forge a new coherence on the model of the late-nineteenth-century European nation-states could hardly be other than very restrictive, if not repressive, with regard to the pursuit of social practices and the expression of identities. In the face of multiculturalism, and violent racism and nationalism, the dissolution of class structures and the emergence of new social barriers, and homogenising globalisation and heterogenising tribalisation, I think, one can formulate the basic task of a political sociology today as the analysis of the current relation of social identities, social practices and polity boundaries. The objective would be, on the one hand, to understand the degree and form of overlap or cleavage, but, on the other, also to rethink the very idea of the need for coherence.

Earlier sociology and political thought have rarely been able to work without some assumptions on tendencies toward coherence, through mechanisms of adjustment of values and norms, or on the need for coherence, to be enforced and safeguarded by supra-individual entities as guardians of the common, like the state, 'society' writ large, or a universalist discourse on morality. In their own time of social transformation, the classical sociologists took significant steps in opening up this issue. But mostly, they have not been able, or have not dared, to free their thinking radically of such presuppositions. That is where the limits of their political sociology can be found.

The existence of a certain overlap between social identities, political boundaries and social practices may be a precondition for (re-) establishing political agency, but the extent and its possible current forms need to be assessed sociologically by looking at the actual 'relations of association' between human beings and the degree of social and moral contingency of their communities.[77] Relations of association have to be analysed with regard to the extensions and permeations of practices which human beings share with others and therefore should want to regulate in community, and assessed with regard to the conditions for such a potential political community to emerge, that is the possibility of proceeding with common deliberation in such a form that political rules meet the other social practices at their level of extension, reach and impact.

To start out from the actual relations of association and their – potential or real – plurality, diversity and even incompatibility, means to radically loosen both the analytical and normative presuppositions common in social thought. Such a sociology renews its ties to political theory. It recognises the fallacies of self-sustained individualist liberalism and accepts the notion that rules and boundaries of polities are related to identities and practices. It does not preconceive, however, what the mode of such a relation would or should be. Sociologically, this question is left to empirical, strongly interpretive analysis; politically, it is left to the open deliberation of the people who enact these rules.

I have tried to describe the task of current sociological reconsideration in terms that made it comparable to earlier efforts, and translatable into their languages. This analogising should not conceal that I see this task as a radical one indeed. Accepting diversity of practices and identities brings back an idea of politics as open, creative human action; the sociology that goes along with such a politics will be quite different from most of either classical or modernist sociology.

11
MODERNITY

Halfway through the fourth volume of his monumental tetralogy on the past two centuries of world history, historian Eric Hobsbawm unexpectedly uses an extraordinary phrase when he characterises the period of 1945 to 1990 as 'the greatest and most dramatic, rapid and universal social transformation in human history' (1994: 288). Historians are usually quite reluctant to come out with such grand propositions. That is one reason why the assertion comes as a surprise.

The second reason for surprise is more strictly sociological. Even though no extended period of world history is without some important changes, the second half of the twentieth century could be considered one of unusual stability. In global terms, the most significant institutional transformation was certainly decolon-isation. But if the focus is on Western societies, all that seemed to happen was gradual change without major ruptures or unpredicted events. In striking contrast to the first half of the century, in which there were wars and revolutions of global dimensions and the establishment of novel socio-political configurations, notably socialism and fascism, the second half can be described in terms of the institutional consolidation of liberal-democratic market societies.

Sociology and modernity

Assertions of Hobsbawm's kind are always contestable. How do we measure the magnitude of social change? Neither historians nor sociologists have an overall convincing answer to that question. But there is a conceptual question in the background of such assertion that needs an answer – or at least a reflective discus-sion. Sociologists have long tended to theorise contemporary Western societies as 'modern societies'. One can even take it to be the founding assumption of sociology that there was a rupture with earlier modes of social organisation by which societies were put on an entirely different footing. The Reformation and the scientific, industrial and democratic revolutions are the major points of reference, and even though the precise dating is debatable, at the very least the sum of all those transformation put modern society firmly into place. Importantly, this thinking went with the additional assumption – which often remained implicit, but was sometimes spelt out – that there could be no further major social transformation. When 'modern society' was established, a superior form of social organisation was reached that contained all it needed to adapt successfully to changing circum-stances. If Hobsbawm was right about the second post-war period, then something was wrong with the sociological view of modern society.

What are the issues that are at stake? Assuming we accept his diagnosis of a recent major social transformation, there are several possibilities of interpretation.

First, one can see this transformation as a rather comprehensive one that touches more or less all societies. This generates two further conceptual options. Either one can see this change as a major adaptation of modern society to new circumstances. Or one can see it as the end of modern society and its transformation into something else. We shall see that indeed both options have been embraced. Second, there is the possibility that this transformation does not occur everywhere, or not everywhere in the same way. Such an interpretation would cast doubt on the general applicability of the concept 'modern society'. Third, and radicalising this idea, this transformation – which after all was unexpected by sociologists – may call for a reconsideration of the very way sociology approached the study of contemporary societies. Was the 'modernity' of modern society ever understood?

Initially, our latter suspicions are confirmed by some peculiar developments in terminology. At some point some quarter of a century ago, the sociology of entire contemporary societal configurations – sometimes somewhat infelicitously called 'macro-sociology' or also 'political sociology' – lost its vocabulary. Around the end of the 1960s, it disposed of – as far as this can go in a pluralistic discipline like sociology – a coherent set of concepts, centred around terms like 'industrial society' (Clark Kerr and others) or 'modern society' (Talcott Parsons and others). In this framework 'modernisation' and 'development' were the terms for social change, which was thought to be as predictable as the structure of society was analysable. From the 1970s onwards, however, in the light of observed changes that had not been foreseen, sociologists became inclined to add prefixes like 'post-' or qualifying attributes like 'late' to their key concepts, thus implicitly giving up on all theoretical coherence. For a certain time during the 1980s, the diffusion of the term 'postmodernity', even more radically, signalled a momentous transformation by suggesting that the very core of Western self-understanding, namely being 'modern' – which, etymologically speaking, means nothing but being up to the exigencies of one's time – was in question. And even worse (for sociology), the term carried with it the implication that the very intelligibility of the social world was cast into doubt.

Sociologists' response to this challenge was the introduction of the term 'modernity' into their vocabulary. In this chapter, I will try to show that what is at stake in this enigmatic terminological shift is the very possibility to analyse entire societal configurations and their historical transformations. To provide a bit more of a background, I shall first sketch in some more detail the intellectual developments over the past three decades. Then I shall discuss the questions introduced above, namely: was there a major social transformation? If so, to what new societal configuration(s) has it led? And what do these considerations entail for our understanding of 'modernity' and 'modern society'?

From 'modern society' through 'postmodernity' to 'modernity': a short intellectual history

Sociology in general, and also the sociology of entire societal configurations at issue here, had its heyday during the 1950s and 1960s. Its knowledge was in broad demand, and the writings of its proponents exuded an enormous air of confidence and an exceptional degree of epistemic certainty about having firmly grasped that which held the social world together (Wagner 2001: ch. 1; and chs 3 and 4 in this book). The strength and coherence of this conceptual grip on the contemporary social world can easily be read from textbooks of the time. The greatest testimony to this period is probably the *International encyclopedia of the social sciences* of 1968, edited by David Sills, but prepared under the guiding influence of Talcott Parsons.

In this view, the US and some West European societies had reached the stage of 'advanced industrial society' or 'modern society'. Other societies still had to undergo 'modernisation' and 'development', leading up to where the more advanced societies already were. Major upheavals or ruptures were not envisaged, and all societies had basically embarked on the same historical path. The power of this interpretation, as exemplified in Parsons' work, stemmed not least from the fact that it managed to combine a broad empirical-historical observation on institutional stability in the West with two explanatory elements, which in their combination appeared unbeatable. As elaborated – somewhat too affirmatively – by Jeffrey Alexander (1978), Parsons started out from the voluntarism of human freedom, which historically led to the differentiation of social institutions. In a second step, he aimed at showing that those differentiated institutions would functionally interrelate to form an overall social system that was superior to others in all respects. He thus produced a sociologised version of the Enlightenment view that human affairs were self-regulating once freedom and reason were permitted to have their way.

Although not everybody agreed with this affirmative view, the major alternative approach or critical view painted a picture with similarly clear contours. From the 1940s to the 1960s, critical theory in the tradition of the Frankfurt School held that the reign of instrumental reason had succeeded in containing all social change in 'administered society' (Theodor W. Adorno) or 'one-dimensional society' (Herbert Marcuse). And Marxist social theory, which revived during the 1960s and 1970s, saw 'capitalism' or 'late capitalism' (Ernest Mandel, Claus Offe, Nicos Poulantzas and others) as neither harmonious nor stable, but contradiction-ridden. Mostly, however, these critical theorists argued that if capitalism could not control those contradictions, some form of socialism would evolve.

As stable as this double – *affirmative* and *critical* – image of contemporary Western societies still appeared by the mid 1960s, objections to it began to accumulate. I will just mention three important ones. First, historical sociologists were able to demonstrate that theorists of modern society had neglected historical information or downplayed its significance to an utterly unacceptable degree to arrive at their story of smooth and linear development. As Reinhard Bendix (1967: 312) put it: 'Seldom has social change been interpreted in so managerial a fashion, while all contingencies of action are treated as mere historical variations which cannot alter the "logic of industrialism".'

Second, events in Western societies themselves led to doubts about the inherent and unshakeable solidity of those social orders. On the one hand, '1968' became and remained a symbol for the possibility of major unrest to emerge almost without any warning. The protest movements of the 1960s certainly did not achieve the major political revolution some of their protagonists were hoping for. But the significant cultural transformations of the ensuing decades – most prominently a new understanding of selfhood, sometimes called 'new individualism' – are often traced to this period. On the other hand, the similarly unexpected economic crisis of the early 1970s led to a questioning of the sustainability of the post-war economic model. Standardised mass production was accompanied by growing mass consumption patterns and a mode of government regulation of the economy that mechanically protected capitalist expansion by fiscal and monetary policies. This model seemed to allow for projections of stable economic growth that stretched far into the future. As of 1975, those projections were no longer even worth the paper on which they were printed. It is not only that crises and recessions recurred; economists and economic sociologists also detected increasing signs of the transformation of the economy away from mass production towards 'flexible specialisation' and away from nationally controllable economic flows towards 'globalisation'.

Third, the observation of those and other, more gradual developments, such as the changing composition of the workforce, started to demand revisions of the prevailing sociological image of society. The first major response came to be known as the idea of a transition from 'industrial society' to 'post-industrial society'. This transition was characterised by a shift from industry to the service sector as the major employer and to scientific-technical knowledge as the major productive force. Although this new theory of post-industrial society initially tried to match its predecessor in terms of explanatory tools and precision, it never achieved the same coherence. Some of its proponents, such as Alain Touraine (1969), even made it a key point that post-industrial society is perpetually changed by the activity of social movements. Sociological analysis had to change in tandem with social change, in his view.

The power of these various objections to the predominant sociological way of representing contemporary society was brought together in a short report 'on knowledge', commissioned by the University Council of Québec, that did not initially appear destined to become a classic (Lyotard 1984a [1979]). The philosopher Jean-François Lyotard started the report, which he chose to give the title *The postmodern condition*, much like the kind of diagnosis of post-industrialism that was quite common by the late 1970s. As he went on, however, the radical nature of his analysis became clear. He criticised both affirmative and critical ways of conceptualising the 'social bond' as 'no longer relevant' (1984a: 14). Alternatively, he proposed to restart the analysis of social relations as based on language games and without any presuppositions about societies as functionally coherent or inherently contradictory entities. Later, he added that this view indeed questioned the possibility of subsuming the multiple events of human history under one single meta-narrative. Similarly, he argued, the translatability from one language game to another in social life could no longer be presupposed; rather, it had to be made a topic of investigation itself (Lyotard 1985b).

Among sociologists and social theorists, this proposal has largely been considered as unacceptable. The critique of epistemology and of ontology that it presupposed was seen to make any analysis of entire social configurations impossible. If postmodernity meant the questioning of any possibility of providing a valid representation of the social world, then a postmodern sociology would be a contradiction in terms. Trying to domesticate the proposal somewhat, it has also been suggested that Lyotard is essentially diagnosing a major transformation of Western societies and is seeing this transformation as much more profound than it is analysed in the theory of post-industrial society. That is why the term 'postmodernity' is necessary, and a sociology of postmodernity – unlike post-modern sociology – then becomes a feasible project (see e.g. Bauman 1992: 111). The problem with this interpretation is that it far too easily divides the debate between one position that holds that sociology can basically just carry on and another one that holds that everything is anyway in vain.

Sociological diagnosis suffered from such a divide during the 1980s and 1990s. As a field, sociology has lost much of its appeal to those who take the so-called postmodern challenge seriously; they have just moved to other genres of inquiry. And within sociology, partly as a consequence of this withdrawal, the consolidation and application of established methods and concepts have regained priority over the questioning of the mode of investigation and interpretation in the face of an often recalcitrant and unpredictably changing social world. Against this background, I intend to demonstrate that there are other ways out of this situation. In particular, I want to show that some strands of the sociological debate about 'modernity' have tried to live up to the full impact of the so-called postmodern critique without abandoning the attempt to analyse contemporary societal configurations. My presentation will proceed along the lines of the issues at stake in this recent debate. By and large it will move from the more easily treatable issues towards the more difficult and risky ones. I shall start by coming back to Hobsbawm's question: has there been a major transformation in Western societies during the second half of the twentieth century, or can sociology work on the assumption of some basic continuity? And if there was a transformation, where have Western societies gone from there?

Continuity or rupture?

Looking again at Hobsbawm's assertion, we find that he gives little attention to institutional restructuring but looks at phenomena that formerly were termed 'socio-structural' and 'attitudinal'. That is why it is possible to diagnose a major transformation during the period in question despite the great stability of institutions. At the same time, this asymmetry helps us to understand why a more institutionally oriented sociology was rather reluctant to acknowledge major change – beyond its theoretical predilection to rule out the possibility of such change. This observation, however, still leaves open the question as to how one can diagnose a major social transformation – such diagnosis is always also a theoretical act – without any major institutional change. Surveying sociological literature that compares the closing decades of the twentieth century with the years following the end of the Second World War, one finds that recent emphasis is placed on the changing ways in which human beings relate to institutions. Those changes are considered to be more important than the constancy of institutional form.

In substance, such comparison shows that the 'modern society' of the 1950s was characterised by a high standardisation, even institutionalisation, of the life course, not least due to state regulation in conjunction with economic rationalisation. This order, however, has tended to break up in more recent years, when stages in the life course were destandardised and biographical perspectives emerged more strongly. During the 1970s and 1980s, those 'highly standardised life trajectories have been "shattered" by structural and cultural developments in all major social institutions'. And such 'transformation of the life course regime' can be connected to the emergence of 'the formation of a highly individualistic, transient, and fluid identity', which is increasingly observed in Western societies (Buchmann 1989: 187–8).

Elsewhere I described this and related changes as the breaking up of a highly institutionalised social arrangement, namely 'organised modernity' (Wagner 1994; and chs 5 and 10 in this book). The institutions of organised modernity were formed as a response to the crises of capitalism at the end of the nineteenth century with industrialisation, urbanisation and 'the social question'. They were erected such that the increased demand for participation could be granted, in terms of both universalised political rights and broadened access to consumption. At the same time, such participation was channelled and, indeed, organised in such a way that the viability of the social order was not put into question. It was basically this social arrangement that Talcott Parsons and others described as 'modern society' and mistook for a more general and universal model than it actually was. Their concern about (accomplished) functionality tended to overemphasise the consistency of the well-ordered set of 'modern' institutions and saw human beings as living their autonomy within that institutional framework. 'Modernisation' was then predominantly conceived as the building of functionally differentiated institutions and the securing of a consensus about compliance with rules.

The changes since the 1960s can then broadly be interpreted as a weakening of the grip of those institutions on human beings, or, vice versa, of a liberation of human beings from the institutionally suggested standards of behaviour. More, however, needs to be said about the nature of the transformation and its impact on the overall societal arrangement. Much of current sociological observation converges on this weakening of the institutional grip on human beings, a process called 'individualisation', and a simultaneous weakening of the coherence of nation- and state-bound institutions, called 'globalisation'. Both of these terms have created more confusion than clarification. Taken together, they tend to suggest that social phenomena 'in between' the human beings and the world are disappearing. This, however, is a claim that can hardly be empirically supported. The earlier overemphasis on a coherent social system within the boundaries of a state-bound society finds here its counterpart in a conceptual overreaction in the opposite direction. Significantly, such conceptualisation of the transformation continues to carry implicit assumptions about the driving forces of social change. Whereas in Parsonsian structural functionalism the maintenance of the social system was the key requirement, current revisions tend to see the requirements for the maintenance of the individual in the social order in a competitive environment as the driving force of social change in the 'enterprise culture' of the 'new individualists'. Rather than organising and planning, markets and flexibility are the means towards that end.

As in the earlier period, different theoretical attitudes towards the new situation can be distinguished. The successorship to the affirmative theory of industrial society has been taken over by 'neo-modernisation' theories, which see individualisation as a new expression of the emancipatory promise of modernity. The critical position now considers in the overemphasis on the individual the risk of a breakdown of social order. In older terminology, such a view would have been called conservative. Nowadays, however, it is often known as communitarianism, and it includes many authors who would not want to see themselves as conservatives. A third position – now also associated with the political slogan of the 'third way' – recognises the risks of the loss of 'ontological security' (Anthony Giddens), but finds in the increase of reflexive monitoring of social arrangements also a possible remedy. Accordingly, the approach has become known as the theorising on 'reflexive modernisation' (Beck et al. 1994).

All three positions, which are necessarily presented somewhat schematically here, have one problematic feature in common. They all claim to understand what the ground-rules of the new societal configuration are. Each tries to re-establish intellectual hegemony and, as a consequence, epistemic certainty. In this sense, they mirror the intellectual constellation before the social transformation and they refuse the insight from the experience of the transformation that the ways to sociologically analyse contemporary society may also have to undergo a reflexive turn.

Such reflection on sociological knowledge itself (a question to which I shall return below) needs to address the question of what a sociological diagnosis of the present can achieve, in particular in terms of the possibilities for the future. In my own proposal, I suggested that the demise of organised modernity opens up the perspective of an 'extended liberal modernity'. This would be a societal configuration that, unlike nineteenth-century societies of 'restricted liberal modernity', is fully inclusive, but at the same time needs no longer to rely on the channelling of human desires for the expression of interests and the realisation of selfhood into pre-organised forms. Rather than providing a sketch of a likely – or desirable – future, however, I developed this image to demonstrate basic problématiques of human social life that do not disappear under conditions of alleged 'late modernity'. Major social transformations change the ways such problématiques are addressed; they do not solve them for good.

Convergence or persistent diversity?

It is an understandable desire of human beings to be able to predict the future. However, sociology should not give in to the temptation to satisfy that desire. The former theory of industrial society claimed to know that 'modernisation' was the direction of history, and convergence of societies would be its outcome. This convergence theorem was based less on empirical observations than on the theoretical assumption that superior ways to meet the exigencies of industrial organisation would eliminate inferior ones.

During the Cold War period, the convergence theorem took two forms. Some theorists held that socialism had made some achievements in terms of the conscious organisation of society and that market societies were not unequivocally superior. Convergence would then take place somewhere between the two existing forms of social organisation, though not necessarily in the middle. Others, including Parsons, insisted that socialist societies had not developed a sufficient degree of institutional differentiation and that their inferiority would become apparent once a higher state of development was reached. Convergence would take place towards the Western model, in this view. The collapse of socialism after 1989 is sometimes seen as a confirmation of the latter assessment.

Such an interpretation, however, is superficial, not least because it overlooks both the intellectual change and the social transformation since the 1960s. The convergence theorem resided on the requirement for social systems to functionally cohere. Now, both the social transformations in the West and the collapse of socialism can be interpreted as the breakdown of such coherence. And in its stead, as we have seen above, sociological theory came up with a new driving force and a new functional requirement – individualisation and flexibility – that were now to explain the occurrences, but after the fact. Significantly, this adapted theory contains a version of the convergence theorem, although none would call it by that discredited name. On the one hand, exchange-oriented 'individualisation' is seen as the universal trend to which all collective arrangements have to adapt and which thus will make them all alike. And the outcome is described as 'globalisation', in the very name of which convergence is already presupposed.

If the idea of convergence outlives such major intellectual and societal transformations, should we then accept it as indubitably valid? One reservation is based on the observation that the *telos* of the convergence trend has not remained unchanged over the period in question. In addition, however, we should also ask what it is about this theorem that allows it to outlast those transformations. My answer to that question is that both versions of the theorem are based on a problematic conception of modernity, and it is this conception that tends to limit the possibility of conceptualising societal diversity. In the first version, 'modern society' is the social entity that contains institutional forms of autonomy. At the same time, the differentiation of those institutions allows the effective mastery of the social and natural world in its various aspects. In the second version, 'modernity' is the societal condition under which human beings realise their autonomy and, by doing so, increasingly master and control the world. The main difference between the two versions is the reference-point – a collectivity or social system on the one hand, and the individual human being on the other. Otherwise, the two views work with rather similar understandings of modernity.

The reference to autonomy and mastery, which we find here, is indeed a fruitful starting-point to conceptualise modernity, but it has to be rethought. Following Cornelius Castoriadis (1990: 17–19 and elsewhere; see also Arnason 1989; Wagner 1994: ch. 1), I shall consider modernity as a situation in which the reference to autonomy and mastery provides for a double imaginary signification of social life. More precisely, the two components of this signification are the idea of the autonomy of the human being as the knowing and acting subject, on the one hand, and on the other, the idea of the rationality of the world, i.e. its principled intelligibility. Conceptually, to put it briefly, modernity refers to a situation in which human beings do not accept any external guarantors, i.e. guarantors that they do not themselves posit, of the certainty of their knowledge, of the viability of their political orders or of the continuity of their selves. Despite the enormous variety of specific conceptualisations of modernity, the great majority of them agree in identifying the key characteristic of modernity: human beings think of themselves as setting their own rules and laws for their relation to nature, for their living together and for understanding themselves.

Starting out from some such assumptions, however, most sociological analyses of modernity aim at deriving a particular institutional structure from this double imaginary signification. And this is where they are led to profoundly misconceptualise modern social life. Terms such as 'democracy' or 'market' certainly have one of their points of reference in the idea of the autonomy of human action. But they provide only such general indications as to be almost devoid of content – when, for instance, the political forms of former Soviet socialism are taken to be expressions of collective autonomy and therefore as democratic. Or, on the contrary, they are read in such a limiting way that the current institutions of Western societies are considered to be the only adequate interpretation of the idea of autonomy. Thus, it was the error of large parts of the social sciences during the nineteenth and twentieth centuries to mistake a historically specific interpretation of a problématique for a general problématique of modernity. Sociology tended to conflate the historical form of the European nation-state with the solution to the political problématique, or as it was often called, the problem of social order, which was expressed in the concept 'society'.

To put the conceptual problem in other words: the basic ideas, autonomy and mastery, were taken to be of a universal character, and as such their socio-historical emergence marked the distinction between modernity and 'tradition'. The project of modernity then was the full permeation of the world by this double imaginary signification. Man was to be fully autonomous and in complete control over the world. Modern institutions, such as the democratic polity, the free market and empirical-analytical science, in their ideal form would be completely emptied of any inherited, traditional features. The progress in the building of such institutions was a process of rationalisation. There are many different and overlapping formulations for what ultimately is one single set of issues: modernity was seen as providing universal foundations that transcend all particularities of empirical situations. It can be considered as putting social institutions on a procedural basis and thus overcoming the need for any substantive grounding. And modern societies become thus accessible to a structural analysis, which underlines commonalities across societies, whereas cultural features are what makes individual societies distinct.

Very broadly, such thinking has guided most of the sociology of modern societies, but it has repeatedly led it into dead ends. The basic flaw, to return to my formula above, is that it has been assumed that a modern set of institutions can be derived from the imaginary signification of modernity. The two elements of this signification, however, are ambivalent each on its own, and there is a tension between them. In contrast, one needs to see the relation between autonomy and mastery as instituting an interpretive space that is to be specifically filled in each socio-historic situation through struggles over the situation-grounded appropriate meaning. Theoretically, at least, there is always a plurality and diversity of interpretations of this space (see Skirbekk 1993).

I attempted, as briefly mentioned, to provide historical illustrations for the diversity of modernity. Focusing on Western Europe, I contrasted the West European experience with the modernity of the US, which at most times appeared comparatively more 'liberal', and with the experience of Soviet socialism, which rather consistently appeared more 'organised'. Conceptually, the analysis limited itself to employing basically two registers. The oscillation between historically more 'liberal' and more 'organised' modernities, first, refers to the tension between individualist and collectivist interpretations of autonomy. The second focus was on the relation between procedural and substantive interpretations of collective arrangements, and in particular on the tension between the two main substantive resources for organising European modernity, the cultural-linguistically defined nation and the socially defined welfare state (Wagner 1994).

This conceptual limitation entailed that even this analysis could not fully unfold an understanding of what may be called the cultures of modernity, namely the variety of socio-historical interpretations of the double imaginary signification of modernity and the resources such interpretations draw on and mobilise. Within Western Europe already – e.g. between France and Germany – or within the more broadly defined 'West' – e.g. between Europe and the US – those resources are much richer and much more varied than this attempt of mine showed (see now Zimmermann et al. 1999; Wagner 1999b for complementary analyses). Both richness and variety increase considerably as soon as one focuses on the so-called non-Western societies. Under names such as 'varieties of modernity' or 'multiple modernities', a research perspective has recently developed that aims at analysing the plurality of interpretations of the modern signification (Arnason 1998; Eisenstadt 1998). Such sociologies of modernity break with any reasoning that associates modernisation unequivocally with Westernisation. Without disregarding the problem of the 'specificity of the West', that is, the Weberian problématique, interest is accordingly revived in the comparative-historical study of societal configurations.

Modernity as a problématique

In terms of the analysis of entire societal configurations, this seems to me to be the adequate response, all qualifications in detail notwithstanding, to both the classic-modern representation of society as differentiated into functional subsystems (which is by far not yet fully abandoned) and to the spreading discourse on 'globalisation' and 'individualisation'. The former sees modernity far too unequivocally based on the pillars of an empirical-analytic approach to knowledge, a market organisation of the economy and plural democracy as its political form. It disregards or underestimates the variety of situations and experiences hidden behind those formulae and forecloses the possibility for sociology to grasp that variety. The latter far too often assumes that the increasing density of relations of communication and transport necessarily leads to the overall convergence of societies. In addition, its theoretical emptying of the space between the individual and the globe imposes on singular human beings the burden of continually creating and recreating their relevant connections to others. Thus, it disregards the capacity of 'institutions' to provide relief from the need to act, or at least to guide action. Moreover, its scepticism towards collective concepts is matched by a reverse faith in the individual human being – in theoretical, in normative and in empirical terms. It can hardly otherwise than lead into a view of the world shaped by individualist-rationalist social theorising and then realised by neoliberal policy design. In the former – systemic theorising – there is an *a priori* formula for the set of modern social institutions; in the latter – the rationalist-individualist one – there are no social institutions at all.

Both of these sociological representations of modern society are possible interpretations of the double grounding of modernity in the ideas of autonomy and mastery as the guiding orientation for human social life. In different ways, however, they both overlook – or downplay – the inextricable relation of tension between the two parts of this self-understanding. In contrast, the approaches discussed above as 'sociologies of modernity' underline a basic openness of modernity in terms of institutional forms, a constitutive openness that emerges precisely from the ambivalence of, and tension between, these two basic ideas. Over the past two centuries, sociology and social philosophy have mostly only provided variants of attempts at intellectually handling the advent of modernity by reducing or denying this openness (Wagner 2001: ch. 2); the point, however, is to accept and think through this very openness.

Now, one may object that openness as such is not a virtue. Accepting it as a principle would lead to sociology losing its analytic grip on the social world. It may be possible to convincingly demonstrate that contemporary societies are indeed not driven by technical-organisational requirements or that the rational individual is not the typical form of human being. But does it not remain the task of sociology to develop overarching concepts for all kinds of societies and for the beings that populate them? This is a question to which a full answer cannot be given here, but I sketch out a preliminary approach.

Since the wave of critique, at the end of the 1960s, of a sociological represent-ation of society that tended towards both objectivism and determinism, elements of two alternatives have emerged. Within the tradition of social theory, attempts have been made to bring human agency back in, as pursued in varieties of ways by Margaret Archer, Pierre Bourdieu, Anthony Giddens and Alain Touraine, among others. Mostly from outside the social sciences proper, the linguistic constitution of the social world has been made a key topic. And importantly, the human sciences themselves have been analysed in their form of text and writing by authors such as Michel de Certeau, Jacques Derrida, Michel Foucault and

Claude Lefort, among others. Taken seriously, both strands demand that the question of the intelligibility of the social world be put explicitly on the agenda of the social sciences.

Unfortunately, and here I return to an earlier theme, these works have by and large not had that effect at all. The first strand has basically subsided. Except for replacing the term 'modern society' with 'modernity' and – vaguely and broadly – insisting on the malleability of the world, the call for agentiality has not considerably altered the ways of analysing contemporary societies. Authors from the latter strand have often been accused of making social analysis impossible because of overloading it with concern for its epistemological and ontological conditions of possibility. With few exceptions, they have been too little interested in actual sociological analysis to actively refute that accusation. It is my contention that it is necessary to make and keep the concerns from both strands as central in sociology.

Joining together historical-empirical analysis and philosophical reflection, I advocate that such work on contemporary societal configurations cautiously withdraws from the explanatory over-ambitiousness of the theories of (post-) industrial society and of (late) capitalism. The historical-empirical observation of modernity's variety has its conceptual complement in some constitutive openness of modernity – or of the project of modernity, if some readers prefer this accentuation. It prefers a 'weak' substantive social ontology to the strong ones of earlier sociological analysis.

In this context, the change of terminology from 'modern society' to 'modernity' becomes important. 'Modern society' denotes a social order that gains its modernity from a particular structural and institutional arrangement. Modernity is here seen as a given and identifiable social form. 'Modernity', in contrast, refers to a situation, a condition, which human beings give themselves and/or in which they find themselves. This situation is in need of interpretation; and such interpretation can always be contested. The term 'autonomy', among other connotations, also stands for the human ability for unpredictable beginnings. And the term 'mastery' indicates that there is a relation of human beings to the world and to themselves that is always potentially problematic.

Under conditions of modernity, there is always a range of possibilities, even if some are unlikely. But if the history of modernity reveals both plurality and possibility, can there be a theorising that captures all the present and past diversity as well as the possibilities that are open to the future without itself adopting some mode of plurality and possibility? This question has regularly been answered in the affirmative. Or, even more strongly, the necessity of a single and stable theoretical viewpoint has been asserted as a necessity, for otherwise neither firm analysis nor critique would be possible. The view held here, in contrast, is that the historicity of modernity yet requires the development of modes of theorising that are adequate to the variety of modernities and to the problématiques that the modern condition poses for social life (this argument is more fully developed in Wagner 2001).

In other words, socio-political modernity is constitutively characterised by problématiques that remain open, not by specific solutions to given problems.

Among those problématiques we find, in particular, the search for certain knowledge and truth, the building of a viable and good political order, the issue of the
continuity of the acting person, and ways of relating in the lived present to time
past and time future. Without some assumption of human autonomy – i.e. the
human ability to give themselves their own laws – these questions would not arise.
That is why they are fundamentally modern. But this assumption cannot be taken
for granted, and it does not lead towards solutions. That is why the sociology of
'modern society' unduly limits the variety of possibilities of conceiving these
problématiques.

These problématiques co-emerge with modernity, and they can neither be
rejected nor be handled once and for all by finding their 'modern' solution.
Societies that accept the double imaginary signification of modernity are destined
to search for answers to these questions and to institute those answers. Temporarily
stable solutions can thus indeed be found. But those solutions can always again be
challenged, and then new ways of dealing with those problématiques have to
be elaborated. Hobsbawm's 'most dramatic' transformation was – and still is –
such a transformative crisis of modernity. What the sociology of the contemporary
world needs to take from this experience is that the constitutive problématiques of
modernity will tend to re-emerge and they will always have to be interpreted in
their concrete temporality, at their specific historical location.

NOTES

1 Let me again avoid here the broader philosophical issues and just refer in this respect to my *Theorising modernity* (Wagner 2001), which is in fact a companion volume to this book.

2 For a comprehensive discussion of the impact of such work on social theory and social science see Wittrock (1999); and for implications for the theorising of modernity Wittrock (2000). The analyses in the first part of this book, in particular, owe much to a long-standing cooperation with Björn Wittrock.

3 To avoid misunderstandings, I should add that I do not think that a sociologisation of law can solve the problem of normative political theory, namely the grounding of state action in social theory and political philosophy. This was, of course, the major dispute on law and politics in the inter-war period, with Heller, Schmitt and Kelsen as main participants in German-speaking areas, Duguit an important contributor in France. The legal positivists doubtlessly posed relevant questions, which remain of importance for more liberal states as well. Their legalistic purification, however, was quite obviously not the right direction when searching for answers.

4 Originally used by Pannwitz with reference to Nietzsche's analysis of the crisis of European culture, and later taken up by Arnold Toynbee and Irving Howe, among others, the notion has most extensively been applied in debates in literature, art and architecture; see *Historisches Wörterbuch der Philosophie* (1989: 1142–5). The term became popular, however, really only after Jean-François Lyotard had used it in a prominent place in his *The postmodern condition* (1984a, first in French in 1979). Since then, it has gratefully been received by many social scientists who struggled unsuccessfully with conceptual disorder.

5 The supportive evidence behind this brief exposition of the argument may require a note. On the one hand, I rely on my own work in a political sociology of the social sciences, in which the intellectual discourses on society are analysed in comparative and historical terms; see Wagner (1990) as well as the preceding chapters. If I present my analysis in the following by looking at 'modern societies' through the eyes of contemporary social theorists of the respective periods, I do so to point out the long-term evolution and transformation of certain epistemological and political problématiques (more detail on this in Wagner 2001). On the other hand, however, I want to go beyond a mere comparative intellectual history, as interesting as it is, and try to relate these accounts to the historical transformations of societies (as developed in Wagner 1994). My interest here is twofold: conceptually, it is in the rethinking of categories for the analysis of contemporary society; and epistemologically, it is in the location of discourses with regard to social reality.

6 The term was coined by the social democrat theorist Rudolf Hilferding in 1915; for its more recent analytical usage, see Winkler (1974) and the special issue of *Geschichte und Gesellschaft* 1984.

7 For analysis of this period in terms of early welfare institutions, see de Swaan (1988), Evers and Nowotny (1987), Ashford (1986), Ewald (1986). Some of the contributions to Rueschemeyer and Skocpol (1996) focus on the changes in the self-understanding of turn-of-the-century European societies.

8 Originally a concept of Italian political debates, this notion has been used in a more general sense (see Stone 1983; for Italy see Seton-Watson 1967). It refers to the opening of bourgeois politics to working-class representation or, at least, working-class concerns.

9 A comparative and historical discussion of economic indicators is provided by Maddison (1982). For a historically oriented economic theory of these transformations see Aglietta (1976), Boyer (1979). For a historical approach to the spreading of large-scale technological networks see Hughes (1983; 1989).

10 A classical analysis of such political reorganisation, using the Dutch example, is Lijphart (1975) on the 'metamorphosis of the problem of the masses' (a term suggested by *Masses et politiques* 1988); see, for instance, Kornhauser (1959), Agnoli and Brückner (1968).

11 Baudrillard draws widely and basically affirmatively on Marshall McLuhan's media theory, which is firmly rooted in the intellectual context of the post-industrialist discourse. Lyotard's *Postmodern condition* can be read as a somewhat radicalised version of the theorem of the 'knowledge' or 'information society'.

12 In the 1960s, there was hardly a word about postmodernity. An exception was Talcott Parsons who ended his little book on *The system of modern societies* (1971: 143) by concluding that any 'talk of "postmodern" society is thus decidedly premature'.

13 Again, these observations can be cast either in terms of a loss of both intelligibility and manageability of the world or in terms of an achievement, a recovery of what had been repressed by the imposition of homogenising modernist discourses and institutions on a heterogeneous social world. For the latter version of the argument, see prominently de Certeau (e.g. 1988: 4). See also Maffesoli (1988: 98), who distinguishes a (modern) functionally organised society from a much more open (postmodern) sociality.

14 These statements are not merely *ex post* analytical ones; varieties of them can be found throughout the nineteenth and twentieth centuries in liberal debate about social organisation (see ch. 3).

15 That 'modernisation' is a socially uneven process is, of course, widely accepted. The main affirmative argument would state that people have to forgo present preferences and to subject themselves to externally induced change to reap a better future. The argument is much more difficult, however, not to say impossible in liberal terms, if it has to be assumed that these people have to give up their identity, as it is historically constituted, in favour of a, to them unknown, transformed self of future generations; and that they would do so under the pressure of a hegemonic representation of society. This holds for liberal theories (of 'development' and 'modernisation') as well as for theories of socialist transformation.

16 See, for instance, Jean Baudrillard's (1986) description of the United States, which, all critical elements notwithstanding, does not lack fascination for the object. Another expression of this ambivalence can be found in the high-tech romanticism of Wim Wenders' movies: see (i.e. literally watch) *Bis ans Ende der Welt* (1991).

17 Thus, I concur with Umberto Eco's (1975) remark that the notion of representation has been in crisis from the very day it was coined. More important than the philosophical is the historico-sociological difference in this regard.

18 Wittrock and Lindström (1984). On the extraordinary character of this growth period, one can consult Maddison (1982); on the difficulties of understanding this extraordinary character, see Lutz (1984). A broader – and somewhat different – discussion of the historical experience of modernity is offered in Wagner (2001: ch. 4).

19 But note the remarks made by Michel Maffesoli (1988) on a general need for 'religion' in the broad sense of reconnecting an individual to a social group and a collective representation. Significant also is Alan Wolfe's (1989) argument for a renewed concern for morality and, one could suggest, civil religion. See now Eisenstadt (1998).

20 In this perspective, I propose to talk about a second major crisis of modernity rather than about postmodernity, 'crisis' here denoting a historical period of particularly strong expression of the general ambivalence of modernity (see Wagner 1994).

21 Or at least not for the purposes of my reasoning. Arguably, there are sexual connotations in this proverb as in the other ones in different languages that I will quote below. A consideration of those connotations would make this introductory argument much more complex. Since it seems safe to assert, however, that my line of reasoning would only be further strengthened through their inclusion, I will largely leave them out for the sake of brevity.

22 If this were the case, however, one could also ask why the 'Germans' did not develop or appropriate the much clearer form of 'English' wisdom. As we know, even folk wisdom travels. Those who may be inclined to think that the German form typifies the common obscurity of continental thinking should be aware that there is a version of this wisdom in French which is closer to the English than to the German, at least with regard to the quantitative aspect. In 'Un "tiens" vaut mieux que deux "tu l'auras"', the temporal dimension is explicitly introduced in addition as an aspect of human interaction (bringing in issues of trust). Rational choice theorising is notorious for having difficulties in dealing with future time, since the preferred strategy, namely discounting the future, is open to a number of objections.

23 May it not be the case that these proverbs refer to birds, among the many goods one may want to have, because they are always inclined to fly away, because of the difficulty of durable possession?

24 Eagles as well as doves can symbolise freedom, but possibly the eagle – as a state symbol – stands rather for collective freedom and collective self-determination and the dove for individual freedom.

25 This is, however, far from saying that communication and compromise are impossible, as is sometimes alleged.

26 In the view of its own proponents, the real history of rational choice theory only starts in the middle of the twentieth century, but an insight into its deeper roots or 'predecessors' can occasionally be found. Similarly and significantly, rational choice thinking also lacks a long historical view on the development of Western societies, although it could and should have one, a matter to which I return below.

27 Whatever dissonance there may be between sensations and this image will then be treated as the secondary problem of the relation between theory and empirical observation.

28 But then it may be the cunning of reason rather than its progress of which we find evidence here. From the middle of the twentieth century onwards, we find the earlier European view of America partially confirmed when, even if no overall individualist-rationalist way of life emerges in America, at least its intellectual foundations proliferate at – predominantly – US universities.

29 This issue can obviously not be pursued here. Let it just be noted that approaches that see modernity strongly in terms of the destruction of 'traditions', i.e. of the withering away of common registers of moral-political evaluation, tend to underestimate the human ability to recreate richer forms of social life, even after crises. This is a theme insistently put forward by Hans Joas (1992a; 1996).

30 As doves of rationalism have recently argued: 'In the absence of strong environmental constraints, we believe that rational choice is a weak theory, with limited predictive power . . . The theory of rational choice is most powerful in contexts where choice is limited' (Satz and Ferejohn 1994: 72). The authors, however, move from that insight to arguing for the compatibility of rationalism with 'structuralism' without considering the criticism the latter approach has encountered over the past twenty years. Chapter 7 will show how such resort to structuralism can be avoided.

31 This chapter is dedicated to the memory of Michael Pollak, who contributed to the approach analysed here.

32 Here are early traces of the distinction between conscious and unconscious parts of social life which was to become of great import in structuralism: 'Even when we have collaborated in their genesis, we can only with difficulty obtain even a confused and inexact insight into the true nature of our action and the causes which determined it' (Durkheim 1938: xlv; see also König 1991: 66–8; Schülein 1987: 38). In attempts to bridge this dichotomy, Anthony Giddens (1984) elaborated the concept of 'practical consciousness', Pierre Bourdieu (1979) the one of *sens pratique*.

33 Thévenot (1989: 154) provides a deconstruction of the classical economic assumptions on the coordination of action, counterposing to the three postulates on rationality, on the commodity character of goods and on the market nature of social relations the three open questions as to the competence of persons, the qualities of objects and the forms of coordination.

34 Boltanski (1990: part I), Quéré (1992: 51–2). As in many of the situations that have been studied verbal reasoning was a key element in reaching an agreement, linguistic competences figure strongly in the analyses. However, the French researchers do not merely follow the 'linguistic turn' prominent in much of recent work in the human sciences, but try to link studies of languages of dispute and justification to other resources that may be brought into situations, not least material objects. I shall return to this issue below.

35 See also Boltanski's ambition to overcome the isolation of the 'human sciences of the specific' from those dealing with the general aspects of human life, speaking of a 'separation on which the division into disciplines is built' (1990: 22). In his view, a 'catastrophic distinction [is made] between the disciplines of the collective and the disciplines of the singular, a distinction that cuts deeply through the human sciences – as well as through the institutions to whom these sciences deliver their insights' (1990: 262; see also 255, 323–34).

36 Other examples are the investigation of the formation of the social category of the cadres that had already been published by Luc Boltanski in 1982. Alain Desrosières and Laurent Thévenot have studied the emergence of socio-professional categories more generally in France as well as in

cross-national comparison. Thévenot has looked at Taylor's 'scientific work organisation'; Robert Boyer and André Orléan have read Henry Ford's wage policy as the beginning of new economic conventions. Some studies dealing with the construction of historical phenomena, such as those by Noiriel (1992) and, in a broader understanding, by Charle (1990), may also be ranged under the 'new social sciences'.

37 See also Thévenot (1993: 286): 'This type of explanation provides a good representation of those spaces of action in which a way of qualifying that achieves consensus guarantees the evaluation of behaviour.'

38 Thévenot (1993: 286). This distinction is related to different possible ways of dealing with the unforeseen, namely whether to interpret it as irrelevant 'noise', as an error on the part of the actors which has to be pointed out to them, as a deficiency of a thing or a person in need of durable correction, or – most seriously – as entailing the need to introduce new objects for a general restructuring of the situation; see Thévenot (1993: 280).

39 The concept of safeguarding order by shared belief leads to the cultural approach to social analysis discussed in ch. 8; for the idea of systematic articulation to the concept of society, see ch. 9.

40 Boltanski and Thévenot (1991: 18). The recourse to something general is a typical element of decision-making in the course of a controversy. A denunciation of socially unacceptable behaviour, for instance, has to indicate criteria for what is allowed and what is forbidden and has to create a link between these criteria and the situation in question. Any denunciation is an appeal to some sort of universality (Boltanski 1990: 256).

41 *Cités marchande, inspirée, de l'opinion, domestique, civique, industrielle.* The approach has now been further developed towards a comparison of societally acceptable forms of justification across situations in the US and France (Lamont and Thévenot 2000) and towards a historical analysis of changing modes of justification leading to overall societal transformation (Boltanski and Chiapello 1999).

42 Boltanski and Thévenot (1991: 189). Functionalists – as well as their critics – may want to discover subsystems and their codes here. It seems more appropriate, though, to say that Boltanski and Thévenot try to stand such reasoning on its head; see their use of the term 'complexity', for instance (1991: 57, 266).

43 'Reality, in such a perspective, is exactly the critical space that opens the possibility, available to persons, to move between different worlds, to tie into them, or to deny validity to one of them by making recourse to another one' (Boltanski 1990: 86).

44 See Thévenot (1992), describing objections to Michael Walzer's theory of spheres of justice in institutional terms. I will leave undiscussed here the question of whether Walzer indeed tends to see his 'spheres' as empirically identifiable institutions.

45 Boltanski (1990: 30). Striking parallels to such reasoning can be found in Axel Honneth's recent *Struggle for recognition* (1995 [1992]).

46 To give an example, I may refer to the state of debate on institutions in international sociology. Time and again it is repeated that institutions have to be analysed from a double perspective, as being constructed in human interaction and as pre-existing the human beings whose actions they shape (see Schülein 1987: 40; Göhler and Schmalz-Bruns 1988: 322; Hechter et al. 1990). As a very general statement, this is certainly valid. To rest content with it, however, means to accept and consolidate a basic cleavage in sociology as well as in the other social sciences – a cleavage between theories of interaction and constitution of sociality on the one hand, and theories of societal developments to which individuals are exposed, on the other.

47 Non-French relatives can be found in that tradition of the social sciences that reaches from Max Weber to Norbert Elias to Anthony Giddens and Michael Mann. For my own attempt see Wagner (1994). One thought, appearing only at the margins hitherto, seems to be particularly promising. The emphasis on the situativity of action and on varieties of exigences of coordination makes it possible not only to distinguish historically varying criteria of justification, but also to consider the need for an accord itself in historico-sociological terms. Historical social configurations may be distinct not only with regard to validity and strength of criteria of justification, but also with regard to the extent to which 'situations have to be dealt with in common' at all (Boltanski and Thévenot 1991: 51).

48 Beyond the recent shift which is in the centre of our interest here, both modes of construction

obviously have a long history in the human sciences and the direct comparison of structural and cultural analyses is part of the sociological stock in trade (for a useful recent example see Wuthnow 1992).

49 The key terms we will need are used in confusingly variable ways in the literature. 'Social theory' is meant here in comprehensive terms, referring to every theorising interested in relations between human beings. It specifically includes both of what we call 'structural' and 'cultural' theory.

50 And if there is a reflexive impact of social theory on the world, then, even more perversely, it may be regarded as enhancing the dissolution of its own object, which tends to disappear, not least, under the analytical gaze of the sociologist, to rephrase a common conservative reasoning.

51 In the tradition of structural anthropology, the term more profoundly refers to basic, and mostly unconscious, ways of ordering the social life.

52 The difference between the two kinds of theorising on this point has implications for the role of the theorist, an issue we will only mention but not elaborate on in this chapter.

53 Some readers may want to dispute whether these views on structure and culture are still held. We shall come back to this question. For a general confirmation, one may consult Light and Keller (1985), which is a fairly open-minded sociology textbook. For recent contributions which raise issues related to ours see Sewell (1992) and Emirbayer and Goodwin (1994).

54 For an ambitious critique see Turner (1994). Searle (1995) resorts to biological explanation for 'collective intentionality', which is at the root of bounded social institutions.

55 The relation between political and intellectual positions is never unequivocal. Thirty years ago, the term 'structure' had a rather critical flavour and 'culture' a conservative one. This relation has almost been reversed.

56 For comprehensive discussions see Friese (2001a). What is at stake here, politically speaking, is what could be termed the inevitability of (some kind of) liberalism.

57 We should also at least mention two important kinds of reasoning which do not neatly fit our categorisation. Daniel Bell's *Cultural contradictions of capitalism* (1976) and Fredric Jameson's *Postmodernism, or the cultural logic of late capitalism* (1991) link cultural to structural factors by means of a theoretical reflection on contradictions and affinities. As stimulating as the reading of these works may be, they are but very thinly rooted in empirical observations. In contrast, works such as Pierre Bourdieu's *Distinction* (1984) and, more comprehensively, Michèle Lamont's *Money, morals and manners* (1992) connect cultural to structural phenomena via sophisticated empirical designs and open thus a way to discuss interrelations without imposing the one on the other.

58 For the use of the term 'strength' for a quite similar purpose, there referring to symbolic boundaries, see Lamont (1992: 181–2).

59 One might envisage cultural analysis going the same path of increasing empirical sophistication which has led structural analysis to concepts such as 'contradictory class locations' (Eric Olin Wright), which keep asking the same question – how is structure related to action? – but have robbed themselves of any possibility to answer it.

60 Johan Heilbron argues rightly that the term 'society' in the early social sciences allowed one to relate concerns of moral philosophy, dealing with manners, to political philosophy proper. My own argument could be read as saying that the creation of this relation also entailed some degree of conflation of concerns.

61 To avoid some of the epistemological issues related to attempts to describe an emergent entity before it exists or at times when its existence is in doubt (issues to which Bruno Latour 2000 refers), I shall use the terms 'structure of social relations' as well as 'moral-political order' to denote what often is called 'society'. The former of these terms places the emphasis on the extension, form and nature of connections between human beings. It tries to be less presupposition-rich than related terms (on the theoretical and methodological issues related to such choice of terminology, see ch. 7). The latter refers to the central concern of the 'moral and political sciences', often regarded as the predecessor of the social sciences.

62 Keith Michael Baker (1990), in particular, has emphasised the changes of political language which took place before the French Revolution and, in his terminology, contributed to 'inventing' it. Nevertheless, it was the event of the Revolution that made some intellectual positions almost untenable and thus brought about a considerable shift in the discursive balance. See on this broad topic the works of Michel Foucault and, more recently, François Furet in France; of the Cambridge intellectual historians

around Quentin Skinner in England; and the works on 'history of concepts' around Reinhart Koselleck in Germany.

63 Jacques Donzelot traced the long-term developments in France in his essay under the suggestive title *L'invention du social. Essai sur le déclin des passions politiques* (1984). I should note that 'the social' is synonymous with 'society', when, as is often the case, it is conceptualised as a realm between 'the private' and 'the political'. Other understandings of the 'social', often a result of further differentiations within this discourse, will be dealt with below.

64 As is reflected, for instance, in the title of Hegel's *Philosophy of right*, a term, incidentally, which was still used in Germany in the early twentieth century for quasi-sociological undertakings in the study of 'society'.

65 In response to Mohl as well as to other authors who separate state and society, Treitschke ponders upon why this 'erroneous political theory' of the 'separation of state and society' should have emerged at this time and place, the European nineteenth century, and he finds some reason in the unnatural situation, as in the Germany of the 1850s, where state and society do not match (1927: 88). Significantly, he uses here a sociological mode of explanation (though a rather crude one), by deriving an intellectual state of affairs from a socio-political one.

66 For about half a century, if not longer, Treitschke has to be considered the winner of this dispute in Germany. A re-edition of his *Gesellschaftswissenschaft* in 1927 – in 'the era of sociology' – carries a foreword by Erich Rothacker (incidentally, one of Jürgen Habermas' teachers) who claims Treitschke for a German tradition of the scientific study of societal life which should be preferred to French and English biologism (Rothacker 1927: VII–VIII).

67 A useful first step to determine whether a scientific object is said to exist is obviously a look at codified statements on what the science in question is about, i.e. handbooks and dictionaries. As sociology became somewhat codified and consolidated only after the turn of the nineteenth century, such publications emerged from the 1930s onwards, with a second wave of grand attempts being pursued during the expansion of the discipline at universities in the 1960s. Since then, markets seem to have been big enough for a somewhat steady flow of new works and new editions of old works. The closing decades of the nineteenth century abounded with publications on 'the foundations of sociology' and the like. However, these are rather the proposals and projects of individual authors, trying to assert their own version of sociology, than attempts at comprehensive representation of a consolidated discipline. It would be an interesting study in itself, not to be pursued here, to trace the changes in the characterisation of 'society' in these publications over time, across languages and – given the continued and sometimes deliberate personal imprint of the author(s) in some such works – between authors. The two works discussed are the only two international encyclopaedias of the social sciences up to the present; a new, third one is scheduled to be published in 2001 (Smelser and Baltes in press).

68 This is not necessarily exactly the same as saying that microbes did not exist before their discovery/invention by Louis Pasteur, as Bruno Latour (2000) claims. The existence of 'society' has sometimes been made explicitly dependent on, even shared, human knowledge of it by sociologists. Latour provocatively extends such a viewpoint to the 'natural sciences'. But even in the social sciences, the more conventional approaches insisted on a knowledge-independent existence of scientific objects.

69 Without specification of the term 'social order', which Parsons accepted as a problem inherited from Hobbes through all of the history of social philosophy, this sentence reads tautologically. It was left to American sociological approaches inspired by Simmel and pragmatism to disentangle what social order is and how it comes about; see most recently Strong (1994).

70 I owe the information about Mayhew's position at that time to a personal communication from Neil Smelser. See also Johnson (1961: 10), where society is characterised by '(1) definite territory, (2) sexual reproduction, (3) comprehensive culture, and (4) independence'. Or: 'A society exists to the degree that a territorially bounded population maintains ties of association and interdependence and enjoys autonomy' (Lenski 1970: 9, as quoted in Horton and Hunt 1972: 49). Or: 'The most complex macrostructure is a society, a comprehensive grouping of people who share the same territory and participate in a common culture' (Light and Keller 1985: 93). Other encyclopaedic works consulted include Ogburn and Nimkoff (1947), Mitchell (1968), Lengermann (1974), Geiger (1931), Ambros (1965), Endruweit and Trommsdorf (1989), Reinold (1992), Fuchs-Heinritz et al. (1994).

71 Harry M. Johnson's (1961: 13) remark that 'the concept society, although unrealistic, might have as great scientific interest as, let us say, the concept of perfect competition in economics' is

amazingly blunt about the problematic relation between concepts and experience. In his view 'concepts' seem to refer to some overarching guides for social analysis and/or social life, but – unlike Weber's ideal types, for instance, which are no real socio-historical phenomena either, but whose validity is measured against empirical findings – their relation to reality is not exactly an issue. The concept of perfect competition in economics has at least had the advantage of having acquired strong discourse-organising power, which cannot to the same degree be said about 'society' in sociology (see also Jorland 2000 on the concept of 'value').

72 Significantly, the former is more typically the Scottish-English view, the latter the French one: see Heilbron (1998).

73 My own choice of terminology is guided by the need to avoid those, often more familiar, terms in other views which are strongly shaped by conceptual or historical presuppositions (see ch. 7). The notion of society, for instance, makes an assumption on the coherence of social practices; the (economic) idea of interest makes an assumption of autonomy and rationality shaping the view on self-identity. An analysis of conceptual transformations over time is seriously hampered by maintaining such loaded terms.

74 Parallel to this theorising an alternative approach, the critical theories of mass society, was developed which regarded basically the same phenomenon, namely the closure of modernity, as a threat and a loss; see ch. 5.

75 Politically, the right to diversity – to be different and to handle things differently – is a claim that stems from such reasoning. Other than calls for equality, such claims have proven difficult to deal with under the rules of organised modernity.

76 A major difference between the two situations is that sociological debate proved to be more continuous and persistent in the more recent one. I would attribute this fact mainly to the firm institutional establishment of social science at universities and other academic institutions. Thus, a minimal precondition for the continuity of a discourse was provided. This continuity meant that much rethinking of theories, concepts and methods could and would take place under the broad assumption of the possibility of a social science.

77 See Offe (1989: 755); also Hindess (1991). Elements of the debate among communitarians and liberals have focused on this question, with the communitarians arguing for reinforcing coherence, for building polities on identities. However, some of the most reflective contributions to the debate, such as Charles Taylor's (1989b: 532; 1989a) and Michael Walzer's (1990), have, while accepting the proposition, raised the issue of the degree to which such a strong relation is actually required – as well as normatively defendable. See Frazer and Lacey (1993) for a critical assessment of the debate in related terms.

REFERENCES

(Translations from non-English sources are mine.)

Aaron, Henry J., *The Great Society in perspective* Washington: Brookings, 1978.

Adorno, Theodor W., 'Soziologie und empirische Sozialforschung', in T.W. Adorno et al., eds, *Der Positivismusstreit in der deutschen Soziologie* Neuwied: Luchterhand, 1969.

Aglietta, Michel, *Régulation et crises du capitalisme* Paris: Calmann-Lévy, 1976.

Agnoli, Johannes and Peter Brückner, *Die Transformation der Demokratie* Frankfurt/M: EVA, 1968.

Alchon, Guy, *The invisible hand of planning. Capitalism, social science, and the state in the 1920s* Princeton: Princeton University Press, 1985.

Alexander, Jeffrey C., 'Formal and substantive voluntarism in the work of Talcott Parsons: A theoretical and ideological reinterpretation', *American Sociological Review*, vol. 43, 1978, 177–98.

Alexander, Jeffrey C., ed., *Neofunctionalism* Beverly Hills: Sage, 1985.

Almond, Gabriel A. and Sidney Verba, *The civic culture. Political attitudes and democracy in five nations* Princeton: Princeton University Press, 1963.

Altvater, Elmar, Jürgen Hoffmann and Willi Semler, *Vom Wirtschaftswunder zur Wirtschaftskrise* Berlin: Olle und Wolter, 1979.

Ambros, Dankmar, 'Gesellschaft', in *Handwörterbuch der Sozialwissenschaften* Stuttgart, Tübingen, Göttingen: Fischer, Mohr, Vandenhoeck & Ruprecht, 1965, 427–33.

Archer, Margaret S., *Culture and agency. The place of culture in social theory* Cambridge: Cambridge University Press, 1988.

Are, Giuseppe, *Alle origini dell'Italia industriale* Napoli: Guida, 1974.

Arendt, Hannah, *The human condition* Chicago: The University of Chicago Press, 1958.

Arendt, Hannah, *Between past and future* New York: Viking, 1961.

Arnason, Johann P., 'The imaginary constitution of modernity', in Giovanni Busino et al., eds, *Autonomie et autotransformation de la société. La philosophie militante de Cornelius Castoriadis* Geneva: Droz, 1989, 323–37.

Arnason, Johann P., 'Multiple modernities and civilizational contexts: Reflections on the Japanese experience', unpublished paper, 1998.

Aron, Raymond, *The industrial society. Three essays on ideology and development* New York: Simon and Schuster, 1968.

Ashford, Douglas E., *The emergence of the welfare states* Oxford: Blackwell, 1986.

Asor Rosa, Alberto, 'La Cultura', in *Storia d'Italia*, vol. IV. 2, Turin: Einaudi, 1975.

Aubert, Vilhelm, 'From "Rechtsstaat" and the "rule of law" to the "welfare" or "regulatory state"', *Zeitschrift für Rechtssoziologie*, vol. 6, no. 2, 1985.

Baker, Keith Michael, *Condorcet. From natural philosophy to social mathematics* Chicago: The University of Chicago Press, 1975.

Baker, Keith Michael, *Inventing the French Revolution* Cambridge: Cambridge University Press, 1990.

Barbano, Filippo, 'Sociologia e positivismo in Italia, 1850–1910,' in Filippo Barbano and Giorgio Sola, eds, *Sociologia e scienze sociali in Italia, 1861–1890* Milan: Angeli, 1985.

Bärsch, Claus-Ekkehard, 'Der Gerber-Laband'sche Positivismus', in Markus J. Sattler, ed., *Staat und Recht* München: List, 1972.

Baudrillard, Jean, *A l'ombre des majorités silencieuses. La fin du social* Paris: Denoël-Gonthier, 1982 (English tr. *In the shadow of the silent majorities* New York: Semiotext(e), 1983).

Baudrillard, Jean, *L'Amérique* Paris: Grasset, 1986.

Bauman, Zygmunt, *Legislators and interpreters. On modernity, post-modernity and intellectuals* Cambridge: Polity Press, 1987.

Bauman, Zygmunt, *Modernity and ambivalence* Cambridge: Polity, 1991.

Bauman, Zygmunt, *Intimations of postmodernity* London: Routledge, 1992.

Beck, Ulrich and Wolfgang Bonß, 'Soziologie und Modernisierung', *Soziale Welt*, vol. 35, 1984, 381–406.

Beck, Ulrich, Anthony Giddens and Scott Lash, *Reflexive modernization* Cambridge: Polity, 1994.

Bell, Daniel, *The coming of post-industrial society. A venture in social forecasting* New York: Basic Books, 1973.

Bell, Daniel, *The cultural contradictions of capitalism* London: Heinemann, 1976.

Bénatouïl, Thomas, 'A tale of two sociologies: The critical and the pragmatic stance in contemporary French sociology', *European Journal of Social Theory*, vol. 2, no. 3, 1999, 379–96.

Bendix, Reinhard, 'Tradition and modernity reconsidered', *Comparative Studies in Society and History*, vol. 9, 1967, 292–346.

Berger, Peter, Brigitte Berger and Hansfried Kellner, *The homeless mind. Modernization and consciousness* New York: Vintage, 1973.

Berman, Marshall, *All that is solid melts into air. The experience of modernity* New York: Simon and Schuster, 1982.

Bleek, Wilhelm, *Von der Kameralausbildung zum Juristenprivileg* Berlin: Kolloquium, 1972.

Blume, Stuart S., 'The theoretical significance of co-operative research', in Stuart S. Blume et al., eds, *The social direction of the public sciences* Dordrecht: Reidel, 1987, 3–38.

Bobbio, Norberto, 'Profilo ideologico del novecento', in *Storia della letteratura,* vol. 9, Milan: Garzanti, 1969.

Boltanski, Luc, *Les cadres. La formation d'un groupe social* Paris: Minuit, 1982 (English tr. *The making of a class. Cadres in French society* Cambridge: Cambridge University Press, 1987).

Boltanski, Luc, *L'amour et la justice comme compétences. Trois essais de sociologie de l'action* Paris: Métailié, 1990.

Boltanski, Luc and Eve Chiapello, *Le nouvel esprit du capitalisme* Paris: Gallimard, 1999.

Boltanski, Luc and Laurent Thévenot, eds, *Justesse et justice dans le travail* Paris: CEE-PUF, 1986.

Boltanski, Luc and Laurent Thévenot, *De la justification. Les économies de la grandeur* Paris: Gallimard, 1991.

Boltanski, Luc and Laurent Thévenot, 'The sociology of critical capacity', *European Journal of Social Theory*, vol. 2, no. 3, 1999, 359–77.

Bourdieu, Pierre, 'Structuralism and theory of sociological knowledge', *Social Research*, vol. 35, no. 4, 1968, 681–706.

Bourdieu, Pierre, 'The specificity of the scientific field and the social conditions of the progress of reason', *Social Science Information*, vol. 14, no. 6, 1975, 19–47.

Bourdieu, Pierre, *Distinction. A social critique of the judgment of taste* London: Routledge & Kegan Paul, 1984.

Bourdieu, Pierre, *Le sens pratique* Paris: Minuit, 1979 (English tr. *The logic of practice* Cambridge: Polity, 1990).

Bourdieu, Pierre and Jean-Claude Passeron, 'Sociology and philosophy in France since 1945: Death and resurrection of a philosophy without subject', *Social Research*, vol. 34, no. 1, 1967, 162–212.

Bourdieu, Pierre and Jean-Claude Passeron, *La reproduction* Paris: Minuit, 1970.

Boutmy, Emile, *Quelques idées sur la création d'une Faculté libre d'enseignement supérieure* Paris: Laine, 1871.

Boyer, Robert, 'La crise actuelle: Une mise en perspective historique', *Critique de l'économie politique*, vol. 7/8, 1979, 5–113.

Boyer, Robert and André Orléan, 'Les transformations des conventions salariales entre théorie et histoire: D'Henry Ford au fordisme', *Revue économique*, vol. 42, no. 2, March 1991, 233–72.

Boyne, Roy and Ali Rattansi, 'The theory and politics of postmodernism: By way of an introduction', in Roy Boyne and Ali Rattansi, *Postmodernism and society* New York: St Martin's Press, 1990.

Brian, Eric, *La mesure de l'Etat. Administrateurs et géomètres au XVIIIe siècle* Paris: Michel, 1994.

Brickman, Ronald and Arie Rip, 'Science policy advisory councils in France, the Netherlands and the United States', *Social Studies of Science*, vol. 9, 1979, 167–98.

Brunialti, Attilio, *Le scienze politiche nello stato moderno* Torino: UTET, 1888.

Buchmann, Marlis, *The script of life in modern society. Entry into adulthood in a changing world* Chicago: The University of Chicago Press, 1989.

Burgess, Ernest W., 'Social planning and the mores', in Ernest W. Burgess and Herbert Blumer, eds, *Human side of social planning. Selected papers from the proceedings of the American Sociological Society 1935* Chicago: American Sociological Society, 1935.

Burke, Edmund, *Reflections on the Revolution in France,* ed. L.G. Mitchell, Oxford: Oxford University Press, 1993 (first 1790).

Cassese, Sabino, ed., *L'amministrazione pubblica in Italia* Bologna: Mulino, 1974.

Cassese, Sabino, 'Giolittismo e burocrazia nella "cultura della riviste"', in *Storia d'Italia, Annali 4: Intellettuali e potere* Torino: Einaudi, 1981.

Castoriadis, Cornelius, *Le monde morcelé. Les carrefours du labyrinthe III* Paris: Seuil, 1990.

Charle, Christophe, *Naissance des 'intellectuels', 1880–1900* Paris: Minuit, 1990.

Chateauraynaud, Francis, *La faute professionnelle* Paris: Métailié, 1991a.

Chateauraynaud, Francis, 'Forces et faiblesses de la nouvelle anthropologie des sciences', *Critique,* vol. 47, no. 529–30, 1991b, 459–78.

Clark, Terry N., *Prophets and patrons. The French university and the emergence of the social sciences* Cambridge, MA: Harvard University Press, 1973.

Clifford, James, *The predicament of culture* Cambridge, MA: Harvard University Press, 1988.

Cohen, S.S., *Modern capitalist planning. The French model* Cambridge, MA: Harvard University Press, 1969.

Coleman, James, 'Social theory, social research and a theory of action', *American Journal of Sociology,* vol. 91, 1986, 1309–35.

Collini, Stephan, Donald Winch and John Burrow, *That noble science of politics. A study in 19th century intellectual history* Cambridge: Cambridge University Press, 1983.

Croce, Benedetto, *Conversazioni critiche,* vol. I, Bari, 1942.

Crozier, Michel, *Le phénomène bureaucratique* Paris: Le Seuil, 1963.

Crozier, Michel, 'The cultural revolution: Notes on the changes of the intellectual climate in France', *Daedalus,* Winter 1964, 514–42.

Crozier, Michel, 'Pour une analyse sociologique de la planification française', *Revue française de sociologie,* vol. 6, 1965, 147–63.

Davies, Gareth, *From opportunity to entitlement. The transformation and decline of Great Society liberalism* Lawrence: University Press of Kansas, 1996.

de Certeau, Michel, *The writing of history* New York: Columbia University Press, 1988.

deHaven-Smith, Lance, *Philosophical critiques of policy analysis. Lindblom, Habermas and the Great Society* Gainesville: University of Florida Press, 1988.

de Man, Hendrik, *Zur Psychologie des Sozialismus* Jena: Diedrichs, 1926.

de Palma, Dino, Vittorio Rieser and Edda Salvatori, 'L'inchiesta alla Fiat nel 1961', *Quaderni Rossi,* no. 5, March 1965.

de Swaan, Abram, *In care of the state* Cambridge: Polity Press, 1988.

Derrida, Jacques, 'Structure, sign and play in the discourse of the human sciences', in *Writing and difference* London: Routledge & Kegan Paul, 1978, 278–93.

Desrosières, Alain, 'Histoire de formes: statistiques et sciences sociales avant 1940', *Revue française de sociologie,* vol. 26, 1985.

Desrosières, Alain, 'How to make things which hold together: Social science, statistics and the state', in Peter Wagner, Björn Wittrock and Richard Whitley, eds, *Discourses on society. The shaping of the social science disciplines* Dordrecht: Kluwer, 1991, 195–218.

Desrosières, Alain, *La politique des grands nombres. Histoire de la raison statistique* Paris: La découverte, 1993 (English tr. *The politics of large numbers. A history of statistical reasoning,* Cambridge, MA: Harvard University Press, 1998).

Diesing, Paul, *Science and ideology in the policy sciences* New York: Aldine, 1982.

Dodier, Nicolas, 'Agir dans plusieurs mondes', *Critique,* vol. 47, no. 529–30, 1991, 427–58.

Donzelot, Jacques, *L'invention du social. Essai sur le déclin des passions politiques* Paris: Fayard, 1984.

Donzelot, Jacques, 'The mobilization of society', in Graham Burchell, Colin Gordon and Peter Miller, eds, *The Foucault effect. Studies in governmentality* Chicago: University of Chicago Press, 1991.

Dosse, François, *L'empire du sens. L'humanisation des sciences humaines* Paris: La découverte, 1995.

Drouard, Alain, 'Réflexions sur une chronologie: Le développement des sciences sociales en France de 1945 à la fin de l'année 1960', *Revue française de sociologie,* vol. 23, 1982.

Drouard, Alain, ed., *Le développement des sciences sociales en France au tournant des années soixante* Paris: CNRS, 1983.

Dryzek, John S. and Douglas Torgerson, eds, *Democracy and the policy sciences* Dordrecht: Kluwer, 1993.

Durand, Claude, 'Les ouvriers et le progrès technique: Mont-Saint-Martin vingt ans après', *Sociologie de Travail*, vol. 22, 1980.

Durkheim, Emile, 'Cours de science sociale: leçon d'ouverture', *Revue international d'éducation*, vol. 15, no.1, 1888.

Durkheim, Emile, *The rules of sociological method* (tr. Sarah A. Solovay and John H. Mueller; ed. George E.G. Catlin), London: Collier-Macmillan, 1938 (first in French 1895).

Durkheim, Emile, *Leçons de sociologie* Paris: PUF, 1950.

Durkheim, Emile, 'Sociologie et sciences sociales', in Emile Durkheim, *La science sociale et l'action* Paris: Presses Universitaires Françaises, 1970 (first 1909).

Dyson, Kenneth H.F., *The state tradition in Western Europe* Oxford: Robertson, 1980.

Eagleton, Terry, 'Capitalism, modernism and postmodernism', *New Left Review*, no. 152, July/August 1985.

Eagleton, Terry, *The idea of culture* Oxford: Blackwell, 2000.

Eco, Umberto, *Travels in hyperreality* Orlando: Harcourt, Brace, Jovanovich, 1990 (first 1975).

Eisenstadt, Shmuel N., *Antinomien der Moderne* Frankfurt/M: Suhrkamp, 1998.

Eisenstadt, Shmuel N. and Miriam Curelaru, *The forms of sociology. Paradigms and crises* New York: Wiley, 1976.

Ellwein, Thomas, 'Verwaltungswissenschaft: Die Herausbildung der Disziplin', in Jens Joachim Hesse, ed., *Politikwissenschaft und Verwaltungswissenschaft, Politische Vierteljahresschrift*, special issue 13, 1982.

Elster, Jon, 'Introduction', in Jon Elster, ed., *Rational choice* Oxford: Blackwell, 1986, 1–33.

Elzinga, Aant, 'Research, bureaucracy, and the drift of epistemic criteria', in Björn Wittrock and Aant Elzinga, eds, *The university research system. Public policies of the home of scientists* Stockholm: Almqvist and Wiksell, 1985.

Emirbayer, Mustafa and Jeff Goodwin, 'Network analysis, culture, and the problem of agency', *American Journal of Sociology*, vol. 99, no. 6, May 1994, 1411–54.

Endruweit, Günter and Gisela Trommsdorf, eds, *Wörterbuch der Soziologie* Stuttgart: Enke, 1989.

Engels, Friedrich, *The condition of the working class in England in 1844* Oxford: Blackwell, 1958.

Ernct, Sophie, 'Une rupture avec la sociologie critique?', *EspacesTemps*, no. 49–50, 1992, 33–40.

EspacesTemps, no. 49–50, 1992, issue focused on 'Ce qu'agir veut dire', 5–60.

Etzioni, Amitai, *The moral dimension. Toward a new economics* New York: The Free Press, 1988.

Evers, Adalbert and Helga Nowotny, *Über den Umgang mit Unsicherheit. Die Entdeckung der Gestaltbarkeit von Gesellschaft* Frankfurt/M: Suhrkamp, 1987.

Ewald, François, *L'Etat-providence* Paris: Grasset, 1986.

Fach, Wolfgang, 'Verwaltungswissenschaft: Ein Paradigma und seine Karriere', in Jens Joachim Hesse, ed., *Politikwissenschaft und Verwaltungswissenschaft, Politische Vierteljahresschrift*, special issue 13, 1982, 55–73.

Favre, Pierre, 'Les Sciences de l'Etat entre déterminisme et libéralisme', *Revue française de sociologie*, vol. 22, no. 3, 1981.

Favre, Pierre, 'L'absence de la sociologie politique dans les classifications durkheimiennes des sciences sociales', *Revue française de science politique*, vol. 32, no. 1, 1982.

Favre, Pierre, 'Histoire de la science politique', in Madeleine Grawitz and Jean Leca, eds, *Traité de science politique*, vol. 1, Paris: PUF, 1985.

Ferrarotti, Franco, 'Changement social et sciences sociales en Italie', *Revue française de sociologie*, vol. 7, 1966.

Ferrarotti, Franco, *Roma da capitale a periferia* Bari, 1971.

Ferrarotti, Franco, *Una sociologia alternativa* Bari: De Donato, 1972.

Ferrarotti, Franco, *Introduzione alla sociologia* Rome: Riuniti, 1981.

Fioravanti, Maurizio, 'La scienza giuridica: Il dibattito sul metodo e la costruzione della teoria giuridica della stato', *Il pensiero politico*, vol. 15, no. 1, 1982.

Fischer, Frank, *Technocracy and the politics of expertise* Newbury Park: Sage, 1990.

Foucault, Michel, *L'ordre du discours* Paris: Gallimard, 1971.

Foucault, Michel, *The birth of the clinique. An archeology of medical perception* New York: Pantheon, 1973.

Foucault, Michel, *Discipline and punish. The birth of the prison* New York: Vintage, 1977.

Foucault, Michel, 'Technologies of the self', in Luther H. Martin, Huck Gutman and Patrick H. Hutton, eds, *Technologies of the self. A seminar with Michel Foucault* Amherst: The University of Massachusetts Press, 1988.

Fraisse, Robert, 'Les sciences sociales: utilisation, dépendance, autonomie', *Sociologie du Travail*, vol. 23, 1981.

Frazer, Elizabeth and Nicola Lacey, *The politics of community. A feminist critique of the liberal–communitarian debate* Hemel Hempstead: Harvester Wheatsheaf, 1993.

Freund, Julien, *Pareto. La teoria dell' equilibrio* Bari: Laterza, 1976 (first in French 1974).

Fridjonsdottir, Katrin, 'Social change, trade union politics, and sociology of work', in Stuart S. Blume et al., eds, *The social direction of the public sciences* Dordrecht: Reidel, 1987, 249–76.

Fridjonsdottir, Katrin, 'Social science and the "Swedish model": Sociology at the service of the welfare state', in Peter Wagner et al., eds, *Discourses on society. The shaping of the social science disciplines* Dordrecht: Kluwer, 1991, 247–70.

Friedberg, Erhard and Pierre Gremion, *La recherche administrative et le réformisme politique*, mimeo, Paris: CSO, 1974.

Friese, Heidrun, 'Zitationen der Geschichte: Zur (Re)Konstruktion von Vergangenheit in einem sizilianischen Ort', *Historische Anthropologie*, vol. 2, no. 1, 1994, 39–62.

Friese, Heidrun, *Lampedusa. Historische Anthropologie einer Insel* Frankfurt/M: Campus, 1996.

Friese, Heidrun, 'Geschichte im Alltag', in Jörn Rüsen and Klaus E. Müller, eds, *Historische Sinnbildung* Reinbek: Rowohlt, 1997, 328–52.

Friese, Heidrun, ed., *Identities* Oxford: Berghahn, 2001a.

Friese, Heidrun, ed., *The moment. Time and rupture in modern thought* Liverpool: Liverpool University Press, 2001b.

Frisby, David P., *Fragments of modernity. Theories of modernity in the works of Simmel, Kracauer and Benjamin* Cambridge: Polity Press, 1985.

Frisby, David P., 'Georg Simmel and the study of modernity', in Michael Kaern, Bernard S. Phillips and Robert S. Cohen, eds, *Georg Simmel and contemporary sociology* Dordrecht: Kluwer, 1990, 57–74.

Frisby, David P. and Derek Sayer, *Society* Chichester: Horwood, and London: Tavistock, 1986.

Fuchs, Werner, 'Empirische Sozialforschung als politische Aktion', *Soziale Welt*, vol. 21/22, 1970–1, 2–17.

Fuchs-Heinritz, Werner et al., *Lexikon zur Soziologie* Wiesbaden: Westdeutscher Verlag, 1994.

Furner, Mary O. and Barry Supple, eds, *The state and economic knowledge. The American and British experiences* New York: Woodrow Wilson International Center and Cambridge University Press, 1990.

Game, Ann, *Undoing the social. Towards a deconstructive sociology* Milton Keynes: Open University Press, 1991.

Geiger, Robert L.,'Die Institutionalisierung soziologischer Paradigmen', in Wolf Lepenies, ed., *Geschichte der Soziologie* Frankfurt/M: Suhrkamp, 1981.

Geiger, Theodor, 'Gesellschaft', in Alfred Vierkandt, ed., *Handwörterbuch der Soziologie* 1931, 201–11.

Gentile, Emilio, *Il mito dello stato nuovo dall'antigiolittismo al fascismo* Rome: Laterza, 1982.

Gerber, Carl Friedrich von, *Über öffentliche Rechte* Tübingen, 1852.

Gerber, Carl Friedrich von, 'Über die Teilbarkeit deutscher Staatsgebiete', *Zeitschrift für deutsches Staatsrecht und deutsche Verfassungsgeschichte*, vol. 1, no. 1, 1865.

Geschichte und Gesellschaft, vol. 10, no. 1, 1984.

Ghezzi, Morris Lorenzo, 'Diritto e società nel pensiero socialista', *Sociologia del diritto*, vol. 7, no. 1, 1980.

Giacomoni, Silvia, *Miseria e nobiltà della ricerca in Italia* Milan: Feltrinelli, 1970.

Giddens, Anthony, *The constitution of society* Cambridge: Polity Press, 1984.

Giddens, Anthony, *The nation-state and violence* Cambridge: Polity Press, 1985.

Giddens, Anthony, ed., *Durkheim on politics and the state* Cambridge: Polity Press, 1986.

Giddens, Anthony, *The consequences of modernity* Cambridge: Polity Press, 1990.

Gigerenzer, Gerd et al., *The empire of chance* Cambridge: Cambridge University Press, 1989.

Gilbert, Claude and Marc Guillaume, 'L'acharnement politique ou l'effort de représentation', in François d'Arcy, ed., *La représentation* Paris: Economica, 1985, 89–97.

Gioli, Gabriella, 'The teaching of political economy in nineteenth-century Italy and the characteristics of its institutionalization', in Peter Wagner et al., eds., *Discourses on society. The shaping of the social science disciplines* Dordrecht: Kluwer, 1991, 303–28.

Göhler, Gerhard and Rainer Schmalz-Bruns, 'Perspektiven der Theorie politischer Institutionen', *Politische Vierteljahresschrift*, vol. 29, 1988, 309–49.

Goldmann, Lucien, *Sciences humaines et philosophie* Paris: Gonthier, 1966.

Grauhan, Rolf-Richard, 'Politikwissenschaftliche Forschung zur Verwaltung', *Die öffentliche Verwaltung*, vol. 23, 1970.

Griswold, Wendy, *Cultures and societies in a changing world* Thousand Oaks: Pine Forge, 1994.

Gruber, Helmut, *Red Vienna* New York: Oxford University Press, 1991.

Gruson, Claude, 'Planification éonomique et recherches sociologiques', *Revue française de sociologie*, vol. 5, 1964, 435–46.

Haag, Fritz, Helga Krüger, Wiltrud Schwärzel and Johannes Wildt, eds, *Aktionsforschung. Forschungsstrategien, Forschungsfelder und Forschungspläne* Munich: Juventa, 1972.

Habermas, Jurgen, *Theorie des kommunikativen Handelns* Frankfurt/M: Suhrkamp, 1981.

Habermas, Jürgen, *Der philosophische Diskurs der Moderne* Frankfurt/M: Suhrkamp, 1985.

Hacking, Ian, *The taming of chance* Cambridge: Cambridge University Press, 1990.

Hallowell, John H., *The decline of liberalism as an ideology* New York: Fertig, 1971 (first 1943).

Hannerz, Ulf, *Cultural complexity. Studies in the social organization of meaning* New York: Columbia University Press, 1992.

Harp, Gillis J., *Positivist republic. Auguste Comte and the reconstruction of American liberalism, 1865–1920* University Park, PA: Pennsylvania State University Press, 1995.

Hartwich, Hans-Hermann, 'Einführung', in Hans-Hermann Hartwich, ed., *Policy-Forschung in der Bundesrepublik Deutschland* Opladen: Westdeutscher Verlag, 1985.

Harvey, David, *The condition of postmodernity. An enquiry into the origins of cultural change* Oxford: Blackwell, 1989.

Hawthorn, Geoffrey, *Enlightenment and despair. A history of sociology,* Cambridge: Cambridge University Press, 1976.

Hayward, Jack and Michael Watson, eds, *Planning, politics and public policy. The British, French and Italian experience* Cambridge: Cambridge University Press, 1975.

Hechter, Michael, Karl-Dieter Opp and Reinhard Wippler, eds, *Social institutions. Their emergence, maintenance and effects* Berlin: de Gruyter, 1990.

Heilbron, Johan, 'Les métamorphoses du durkheimisme, 1920–1940', *Revue française de sociologie*, vol. 36, no. 2, 1985, 225ff.

Heilbron, Johan, 'Particularités et particularismes de la sociologie aux Pays-Bas', *Actes de la recherche en sciences sociales*, no. 74, 1988, 76–81.

Heilbron, Johan, *The rise of social theory* Cambridge: Polity Press, 1995.

Heilbron, Johan, 'French moralists and the anthropology of the modern era: On the genesis of the notions of "interest" and "commercial society"', in Johan Heilbron, Lars Magnusson and Björn Wittrock, eds, *The rise of the social sciences and the formation of modernity* Dordrecht: Kluwer, 1998, 77–106.

Heilbron, Johan, 'Natural philosophy and social science', in Theodore Porter and Dorothy Ross, eds, *The social and behavioral sciences* New York: Cambridge University Press, in press (Cambridge History of Science).

Heilbron, Johan, Lars Magnusson and Björn Wittrock, eds, *The rise of the social sciences and the formation of modernity* Dordrecht: Kluwer, 1998 (Sociology of the Sciences Yearbook, vol. 20).

Heller, Agnes, *Everyday Life* London: Routledge and Kegan Paul, 1984.

Heller, Agnes, *Can modernity survive?* Cambridge: Polity Press, 1990.

Heller, Hermann, 'Staat', in Alfred Vierkandt, ed., *Handwörterbuch der Soziologie* Stuttgart: Enke, 1931.

Hennis, Wilhelm, 'Aufgabe einer modernen Regierungslehre', *Politische Vierteljahresschrift*, vol. 6, 1965.

Heun, Werner, 'Der staatsrechtliche Positivismus in der Weimarer Republik', *Der Staat*, vol. 28, no. 3, 1989, 377–403.

Hindess, Barry, 'Imaginary presuppositions of democracy', *Economy and Society*, vol. 20, no. 2, 1991, 173–95.

Hirsch, Joachim, *Parlament und Verwaltung*, vol. 2, Stuttgart, 1968.

Hirsch, Joachim, *Staatsapparat und Reproduktion des Kapitals* Frankfurt/M: Suhrkamp, 1974.

Hirsch, Joachim and Stephan Leibfried, *Materialien zur Wissenschafts- und Bildungspolitik* Frankfurt/ M: Suhrkamp, 1971.

Historisches Wörterbuch der Philosophie, eds Joachim Ritter and Karlfried Gründer, Basel: Schwabe, 1989, vol. 7, 1142–5.

Hoarau, Jacques, 'Description d'une conjoncture en sociologie', *EspacesTemps*, no. 49–50, 1992: 6–25.

Hobsbawm, Eric, *Age of extremes. The short twentieth century 1914–1991* London: Michael Joseph, 1994.

Holloway, John and Sol Picciotto, eds., *State and capital. A Marxist debate* London: Arnold, 1978.

Honneth, Axel, *Kampf um Anerkennung* Frankfurt/M: Suhrkamp, 1992 (English tr. *The struggle for recognition* Cambridge: Polity, 1995).

Hont, Istvan, 'Socialist natural law, commercial society, political economy: A contribution to the idea of social science', paper presented at the conference on 'The rise of the social sciences', Uppsala, June 1993.

Horn, Klaus, ed., *Aktionsforschung: Balanceakt ohne Netz?* Frankfurt/M: Syndikat, 1979.

Horton, Paul B. and Chester L. Hunt, *Sociology* Tokyo: McGraw-Hill Kogakusha, 1972.

Hughes, H. Stuart, *Consciousness and society. The reorientation in European social thought, 1890–1920* New York: Vintage, 1958.

Hughes, Thomas, *Networks of power* Baltimore: Johns Hopkins University Press, 1983.

Hughes, Thomas, *American genesis. A century of invention and technological enthusiasm* New York: Viking, 1989.

Jameson, Frederic, 'Foreword' to Jean-François Lyotard, *The postmodern condition. A report on knowledge* Minneapolis: University of Minneapolis Press, 1984.

Jameson, Frederic, *Postmodernism, or the cultural logic of late capitalism* Durham, NC: Duke University Press, 1991.

Janik, Allan and Stephen Toulmin, *Wittgenstein's Vienna* London: Weidenfeld & Nicolson, 1973.

Joas, Hans, *Die Kreativität des Handelns* Frankfurt/M: Suhrkamp, 1992a (English tr. *The creativity of action* Cambridge: Polity, 1996).

Joas, Hans, 'Von der Philosophie des Pragmatismus zu einer soziologischen Forschungstradition', *Pragmatismus und Gesellschaftstheorie* Frankfurt/M: Suhrkamp, 1992b, 23–65 (English tr. 'Symbolic interactionism', in Anthony Giddens and Jonathan H. Turner, eds, *Social theory today* Cambridge: Polity, 1987, 82–116; and reprinted as 'Pragmatism in American sociology', in Hans Joas, *Pragmatism and social theory* Chicago: University of Chicago Press, 1993, 14–51).

Joas, Hans, 'An underestimated alternative: America and the limits of "critical theory"', in *Pragmatism and social theory* Chicago: University of Chicago Press, 1993, 79–93.

Joas, Hans, *Die Entstehung der Werte* Frankfurt/M: Suhrkamp, 1996 (English tr. *The genesis of values* Cambridge: Polity, 2000).

Johnson, Harry M., *Sociology: a systematic introduction* London: Routledge & Kegan Paul, 1961.

Jorland, Gérard, 'The coming into being and passing away of value theories in economics (1776–1976)', in Lorraine Daston, ed., *Biographies of scientific objects* Chicago: The University of Chicago Press, 2000, 117–31.

Karady, Victor, 'Durkheim, les sciences sociales et l'Université: bilan d'un sémi-échec', *Revue française de sociologie*, vol. 17, no. 2, 1976, 267–311.

Käsler, Dirk, *Die frühe deutsche Soziologie und ihre Entstehungs-Milieus* Opladen: Westdeutscher Verlag, 1984.

Kastendiek, Hans, *Die Entwicklung der westdeutschen Politikwissenschaft* Frankfurt/M: Campus, 1977.

Kern, Horst, *Empirische Sozialforschung* Munich: Beck, 1982.

Kettler, David and Volker Meja, *Karl Mannheim and the crisis of liberalism. The secret of these new times* New Brunswick: Transaction, 1995.

Klingemann, Carsten, 'Heimatsoziologie oder Ordnungsinstrument? Fachgeschichtliche Aspekte der Soziologie in Deutschland zwischen 1933 und 1945', *Kölner Zeitschrift für Soziologie und Sozialpsychologie*, special issue 23, 1981.

Kloppenberg, James T., *Uncertain victory. Social democracy and progressivism in European and American thought, 1870–1920* New York: Oxford University Press, 1986.

König, René, 'Einleitung', to Emile Durkheim, *Die Regeln der soziologischen Methode* Frankfurt/M: Suhrkamp, 1991: 21–82.

Kornhauser, William, *The politics of mass society* New York: Free Press, 1959.

Kramarz, Francis, 'Du marché à l'interaction', *Critique*, vol. 47, no. 529–30, 1991, 479–91.

Lacey, Michael J. and Mary O. Furner, eds, *The state and social investigation in Britain and the United States* Cambridge: Woodrow Wilson Center and Cambridge University Press, 1993.

Lacroix, Bernard, *Durkheim et le politique* Paris and Montréal: Presses de la FNSP and Presses de l'Université de Montréal, 1981.

Lamont, Michèle, *Money, morals and manners. The culture of the French and American upper-middle class* Chicago: The University of Chicago Press, 1992.

Lamont, Michèle and Laurent Thévenot, eds, *Rethinking comparative cultural sociology. Polities and repertoires of evaluation in France and the United States* New York: Cambridge University Press, 2000.

Lanzardo, Dario, 'Intervento socialista nella lotta operaia: L'inchiesta operaia di Marx', *Quaderni Rossi*, no. 5, March 1965.

Lapalombara, Joseph, *Italy. The politics of planning* Syracuse, NY: Syracuse University Press, 1966.

Lash, Scott, *Sociology of postmodernism* London: Routledge and Kegan Paul, 1990.

Lash, Scott, 'Expert systems or situated interpretation? Culture and institutions in disorganized capitalism', in Ulrich Beck, Anthony Giddens and Scott Lash, eds, *Reflexive modernization* Cambridge: Polity, 1994, 198–215.

Lash, Scott and John Urry, *The end of organized capitalism* Cambridge: Polity Press, 1987.

Latouche, Serge, 'La fin de la société des nations', *Traverses*, no. 33–4, 1985, 36–43.

Latour, Bruno, 'On the partial existence of existing and nonexisting objects', in Lorraine Daston, ed., *Biograpies of scientific objects* Chicago: The University of Chicago Press, 2000, 247–69.

Lawrence, D.H., 'The spirit of place', in *The symbolic meaning. The uncollected versions of studies in classic American literature* (ed. Armin Arnold), Fontwell: Centaur Press, 1962.

Lawrence, D.H., *The plumed serpent (Quetzalcoatl)* Cambridge: Cambridge University Press, 1987.

Leca, Jean, 'La science politique dans le champs intellectuel francais', *Revue française de science politique*, vol. 32, no. 4–5, 1982.

Lengermann, Patricia M., *Definitions of sociology. A historical approach* Columbus, OH: Merrill, 1974.

Lenski, Gerhard, *Human societies. A macrolevel introduction to sociology* New York: McGraw Hill, 1970.

Lentini, Orlando, *L'analisi sociale durante il fascismo* Naples: Liguori, 1974.

Leonardi, Franco, 'Italian sociology within the framework of contemporary sociology', in *Contemporary sociology in Western Europe and America. Proceedings of the First International Congress of Social Sciences of the Luigi Sturzo Institute* Rome, 1967.

Lepsius, M. Rainer, 'Die Entwicklung der Soziologie nach dem 2. Weltkrieg 1945–1967', in Günther Lüschen, ed., *Deutsche Soziologie seit 1945*, special issue of the *Kölner Zeitschrift für Soziologie und Sozialpsychologie*, no. 21, 1979.

Lerner, Daniel and Harold Lasswell, eds, *The policy sciences* Stanford: Stanford University Press, 1951.

Light, Jr., Donald and Suzanne Keller, *Sociology* New York: Knopf, 1985.

Lijphart, Arend, *The politics of accommodation. Pluralism and democracy in the Netherlands* Berkeley: University of California Press, 1975.

Lindblom, Charles E., *Inquiry and change. The troubled attempt to understand and shape society* New Haven and New York: Yale University Press and Russell Sage Foundation, 1990.

Loader, Colin, *The intellectual development of Karl Mannheim. Culture, politics, and planning* Cambridge: Cambridge University Press, 1985.

Lorwin, Lewis L., 'Planning in a democracy', in Ernest W. Burgess and Herbert Blumer, eds, *Human side of social planning. Selected papers from the proceedings of the American Sociological Society 1935* Chicago: American Sociological Society, 1935.

Luhmann, Niklas, 'Systemtheoretische Argumentationen: Eine Entgegnung auf Jürgen Habermas', in Niklas Luhmann and Jürgen Habermas, eds, *Theorie der Gesellschaft oder Sozialtechnologie* Frankfurt/M: Suhrkamp, 1971.

Lukács, Georg, *Die Zerstörung der Vernunft* Berlin: Aufbau, 1954.

Lukes, Steven, *Emile Durkheim* London: Allen Lane, 1973.

Lutz, Burkart, *Der kurze Traum immerwährender Prosperität* Frankfurt/M: Campus, 1984.

Lyotard, Jean-François, *La condition postmoderne* Paris: Minuit, 1979 (Geoff Bennington and Brian Massumi, L., tr., *The postmodern condition. A report on knowledge* Minneapolis: University of Minneapolis Press, 1984a).

Lyotard, Jean-François, *Le tombeau de l'intellectuel, et autres papiers* Paris: Galilée, 1984b.

Lyotard, Jean-François, 'Une ligne de résistance', *Traverses*, no. 33–4, 1985a, 60–5.

Lyotard, Jean-François, 'Histoire universelle et différences culturelles', *Critique*, 1985b (English tr. 'Universal history and cultural differences', in Andrew Benjamin, ed., *The Lyotard reader* Oxford: Blackwell, 1989, 314–24).

MacIver, Robert M., 'Sociology', in E. Seligman, ed., *Encyclopedia of the social sciences* New York: Macmillan, 1934, 232–47.

Maddison, Angus, *Phases of capitalist development* Oxford: Oxford University Press, 1982.

Maffesoli, Michel, *Le temps des tribus. Le déclin de l'individualisme dans les sociétés de masse* Paris: Méridiens Klincksieck, 1988.

Maier, Charles S., *Recasting bourgeois Europe. Stabilization in France, Germany and Italy in the decade after World War I* Princeton: Princeton University Press, 1975.

Maier, Charles S., ed., *Changing boundaries of the political. Essays on the evolving balance between state and society, public and private in Europe* Cambridge: Cambridge University Press, 1987.

Maier, Hans, *Die ältere deutsche Staats- und Verwaltungslehre* Munich: Beck, 1980 (first 1966).

Manent, Pierre, *La cité de l'homme* Paris: Fayard, 1994.

Manicas, Peter, *A history and philosophy of the social sciences* Oxford: Blackwell, 1987.

Manicas, Peter, 'The social science disciplines: The American model', in Peter Wagner et al., eds, *Discourses on society. The shaping of the social science disciplines* Dordrecht: Kluwer, 1991, 45–71.

Mann, Michael, *The sources of social power*, vol. I, Cambridge: Cambridge University Press, 1986.

Mannheim, Karl, *Man and society in an age of reconstruction* London: Routledge & Kegan Paul, 1940.

Mannheim, Karl, *Diagnosis of our time. Wartime essays of a sociologist* London: Routledge & Kegan Paul, 1943.

Mannheim, Karl, *Freedom, power and democratic planning* London: Routledge & Kegan Paul, 1951.

Marcuse, Herbert, *One-dimensional man. Studies in the ideology of advanced industrial societies* Boston: Beacon, 1964.

Marin, Bernd, *Die Paritätische Kommission. Aufgeklärter Technokorporatismus in Österreich* Vienna: Internationale Publikationen, 1982.

Martinotti, Guido, 'Il condizionamento della ricerca', in Pietro Rossi, ed., *Ricerca sociologica e ruolo del sociologo* Bologna: Mulino, 1972.

Martinotti, Guido, *L'istituto superiore di sociologia di Milano*, mimeo, Milan, 1984.

Massé, Pierre, *Le Plan ou l'anti-hasard* Paris: Gallimard, 1965.

Massé, Pierre, *Autocritique des années soixante par un Commissaire au Plan* (*Bulletin de l'Institut d'histoire du temps présent*, supplément no. 1, 1981, série 'Politique économique', no. 1).

Masses et politiques, special issue of *Hermes: cognition, communication, politique* Paris: Editions du CNRS, 1988.

Mayer, Arno J., *The persistence of the Old Regime: Europe to the Great War* New York: Pantheon, 1981.

Mayhew, Leon H., 'Society', in David L. Sills, ed., *International encyclopedia of the social sciences* New York: Macmillan, 1968.

Mayntz, Renate and Fritz W. Scharpf, *Planungsorganisation* München: Piper, 1973.

Medick, Hans, *Naturzustand und Naturgeschichte der bürgerlichen Gesellschaft. Die Ursprünge der bürgerlichen Sozialtheorie als Geschichtsphilosophie und Sozialwissenschaft bei Samuel Pufendorf, John Locke und Adam Smith* Göttingen: Vandenhoeck & Ruprecht, 1973.

Messedaglia, Angelo, *L'insegnamento della giurisprudenza nelle Università del Regno* (*Nuova Antologia*, no. 11) 1869.

Meyer, Georg, 'Staats- und Verwaltungsrecht', in W. Lexis, ed., *Die deutschen Universitäten* Berlin: Asher, 1893.

Miceli, Vincenzo, 'La divisione nelle scienze sociali', *Rassegna di scienze sociali e politiche*, vol. 3, no. 55, 1885, 341–56.

Michels, Robert, 'The status of sociology in Italy', *Social Forces*, vol. 9, October 1930 .

Mieli, Paolo, 'I Machiavellini', *L'Espresso*, no. 29, 1983, 66–7.

Mitchell, G. Duncan, *A dictionary of sociology* Chicago: Aldine, 1968.

Mohl, Robert von, 'Gesellschafts-Wissenschaften und Staats-Wissenschaften', *Zeitschrift für die gesammte Staatswissenschaft*, vol. 2, Stuttgart and Leipzig, 1851, 3–71.

Mosca, Gaetano, *Teorica dei governi et governo parlamentare* Torino: UTET, 1982.

Mozzarelli, Cesare, 'Storici, giuristi e stato: Ipotesi sulla cultura delle istituzioni nell'Italia del "900"', *Il pensiero politico*, vol. 15, no. 2, 1982.

Mozzarelli, Cesare and Stefano Nespor, *Giuristi e scienze sociali nell' Italia liberale* Venice: Marsilio, 1981.

Münch, Richard, *Die Struktur der Moderne. Grundmuster und differentielle Gestaltung des institutionellen Aufbaus der modernen Gesellschaften* Frankfurt/M: Suhrkamp, 1984.

Nemeth, Elisabeth, *Otto Neurath und der Wiener Kreis. Revolutionäre Wissenschaftlichkeit als Anspruch* Frankfurt/M: Campus, 1981.

Nettl, J.P., 'The state as a conceptual variable', *World Politics*, vol. 20, 1968.

Noiriel, Gérard, *La tyrannie du national. Le droit d'asile en Europe 1793–1993* Paris: Calmann-Lévy, 1992.

Norris, Christopher, 'Lost in the funhouse: Baudrillard and the politics of postmodernism', in Roy Boyne and Ali Rattansi, eds, *Postmodernism and society* New York: St Martin's Press, 1990.

Nowotny, Helga, 'Knowledge for certainty: Poverty, welfare institutions and the institutionalization of social science', in Peter Wagner et al., eds, *Discourses on society. The shaping of the social science disciplines* Dordrecht: Kluwer, 1991, 23–41.

Offe, Claus, 'Competitive party democracy and the Keynesian welfare state', *Policy Sciences*, vol. 15, 1983, 225–46.

Offe, Claus, *Disorganized capitalism* Cambridge: MIT Press, 1987.

Offe, Claus, 'Fessel und Bremse: Moralische und institutionelle Aspekte "intelligenter Selbstbeschränkung"', in Axel Honneth et al., eds, *Zwischenbetrachtungen. Im Prozeß der Aufklärung* Frankfurt/M: Suhrkamp, 1989, 739–74.

Ogburn, William F., 'Man and his institutions', in Ernest W. Burgess and Herbert Blumer, eds, *Human side of social planning. Selected papers from the proceedings of the American Sociological Society 1935* Chicago: American Sociological Society, 1935.

Ogburn, William F. and Meyer F. Nimkoff, *A handbook of sociology* London: Routledge & Kegan Paul, 1947.

Österberg, Dag, *Metasociology. An inquiry into the origins and validity of social thought* Oslo: Norwegian University Press, 1988.

Oulès, Firmin, *Economic planning and democracy* Harmondsworth: Penguin, 1966.

Panzieri, Raniero, 'Contribution to the seminar "Uso socialista dell'inchiesta operaia"', Turin, 1964, published in *Quaderni Rossi*, no. 5, March 1965, quoted from the reprint in Claudio Pozzoli, ed., *Spätkapitalismus und Klassenkampf* Frankfurt: Europäische Verlagsanstalt, 1972.

Pareto, Vilfredo, *Trattato di sociologia generale*, 2nd edn, Florence: Barbera, 1923.

Parsons, Talcott, 'Society', in E. Seligman, ed., *Encyclopedia of the social sciences* New York: Macmillan, 1934, 225–32.

Parsons, Talcott, *The system of modern societies* Englewood Cliffs, NJ: Prentice-Hall, 1971.

Pasolini, Pier Paolo, *Scritti corsari* Milan: Garzanti, 1975.

Paulsen, Friedrich, *Die deutschen Universitäten und das Universitätsstudium* Berlin: Asher, 1902.

Pinto, Diana, 'La sociologie dans l'Italie de l'après-guerre', *Revue française de sociologie*, vol. 21, 1980, 234ff.

Pinto, Diana, 'Sociology, politics and society in post-war Italy', *Theory and Society*, vol. 10, 1981.

Pisier-Kouchner, Evelyne, *Le service public dans la théorie de l'Etat de Léon Duguit* Paris: Pichon and Durand-Auzias, 1972.

Pollak, Michael, 'L'efficacité par l'ambiguité', *Sociologie et sociétés*, vol. 7, 1975.

Pollak, Michael, 'La planification des sciences sociales', *Actes de la recherche en sciences sociales*, no. 2/3, 1976, 105–21.

Pollak, Michael, *Gesellschaft und Soziologie in Frankreich* Königstein/Ts: Hain, 1978.

Pollak, Michael, 'Paul F. Lazarsfeld: Fondateur d'une multinationale scientifique', *Actes de la recherche en sciences sociales*, no. 25, 1979, 45–59.

Pollak, Michael, *Vienne. Une identité blessée* Paris: Gallimard, 1984.

Popper, Karl R., *The open society and its enemies* London: Routledge & Kegan Paul, 1945.

Porter, Theodore M., *The rise of statistical thinking, 1820–1900* Princeton: Princeton University Press, 1986.

Porter, Theodore M., *Trust in numbers. The pursuit of objectivity in science and public life* Princeton: Princeton University Press, 1995.

Quéré, Louis, 'Le sociologue et le touriste', *EspacesTemps*, no. 49–50, 1992, 41–60.

Quéré, Louis, 'Language de l'action et questionnement sociologique', in Paul Ladrière, Patrick Pharo and Louis Quéré, eds, *La théorie de l'action. Le sujet pratique en débat* Paris: CNRS, 1993: 53–83.

Reinold, Gerd, *Soziologie-Lexikon* München: Oldenbourg, 1992.

Revue économique, vol. 40, no. 2, 1989, special issue on 'L'économie des conventions'.

Riedel, Manfred, 'Gesellschaft, bürgerliche', in Otto Brunner, Werner Conze and Reinhard Koselleck, eds, *Geschichtliche Grundbegriffe*, vol. 2, Stuttgart: Klett-Cotta, 1975a.

Riedel, Manfred, 'Gesellschaft, Gemeinschaft', in Otto Brunner, Werner Conze and Reinhard Koselleck, eds, *Geschichtliche Grundbegriffe*, vol. 2, Stuttgart: Klett-Cotta, 1975b.

Ringer, Fritz K., *The decline of the German Mandarins* Boston: Harvard University Press, 1969.

Rorty, Richard, *Contingency, irony, and solidarity* Cambridge: Cambridge University Press, 1989.

Ross, Dorothy, *The origins of American social science* Cambridge: Cambridge University Press, 1991.

Rossetti, Carlo Guido, 'Sur la sociologie italienne vue par Diana Pinto', *Revue française de sociologie*, vol. 23, 1982.

Rossi, Pietro, 'Presentazione', in Pietro Rossi, ed., *Ricerca sociologica e ruolo del sociologo* Bologna: Mulino, 1972.

Rossi, Pietro, 'La sociologia nella seconda metà del'ottocento: Dall'impiego di schemi storico-evolutivi alla formulazione di modelli analitici', *Il pensiero politico*, vol. 15, no. 1, 1982, 188–215.

Rothacker, Erich, 'Zur Einführung', in Heinrich von Treitschke, *Die Gesellschaftswissenschaft. Ein kritischer Versuch* Halle: Niemeyer, 1927.

Rothblatt, Sheldon and Björn Wittrock, *The three missions. Universities in the Western world* Cambridge: Cambridge University Press, 1993.

Rueschemeyer, Dietrich and Theda Skocpol, eds, *Social knowledge and the origins of modern social policies* Princeton and New York: Princeton University Press and Russell Sage Foundation, 1996.

Sahlins, Marshall, '"Sentimental pessimism" and ethnographic experience, or, Why culture is not a disappearing "object"', in Lorraine Daston, ed., *Biographies of scientific objects* Chicago: University of Chicago Press, 2000, 158–202.

Salais, Robert and Michael Storper, 'The four "worlds" of contemporary industry', *Cambridge Journal of Economics*, vol. 16, no. 2, 1992, 169–94.

Salais, Robert, and Michael Storper, *Les mondes du production* Paris: Editions de l'EHESS, 1993 (English tr. *Worlds of production* Cambridge, Mass.: Harvard University Press).

Salais, Robert and Laurent Thévenot, eds, *Le travail. Marchés, règles, conventions* Paris: Economica, 1986.

Salais, Robert, Nicolas Baverez and Bénédicte Reynaud, *L'invention du chômage* Paris: PUF, 1986.

Satz, Debra and John Ferejohn, 'Rational choice and social theory', *The Journal of Philosophy*, 1994, 71–87.

Scartezzini, Riccardo, 'Il dibattito metodologico in Francia', in Pietro Rossi, ed., *Ricerca sociologica e ruolo del sociologo* Bologna: Mulino, 1972.

Schäfer, Ursula, *Historische Nationalökonomie und Sozialstatistik als Gesellschaftswissenschaften* Wien: Böhlau, 1971.

Scharpf, Fritz W., 'Verwaltungswissenschaft als Teil der Politikwissenschaft', reprinted in F.W. Scharpf, *Planung als politischer Prozeß* Neuwied: Luchterhand, 1973.

Schatz, Heribert, 'Auf der Suche nach neuen Problemlösungsstrategien: die Entwicklung der politischen Planung auf Bundesebene', in Renate Mayntz and Fritz W. Scharpf, eds, *Planungsorganisation* München: Piper, 1973.

Schiera, Pierangelo, 'Amministrazione e costituzione: Verso la nascita della scienza politica', *Il pensiero politico*, vol. 15, no. 1, 1982.

Schiera, Pierangelo, '"Science and politics" as a political factor: German and Italian social sciences in the nineteenth century', in Peter Wagner et al., eds, *Discourses on society. The shaping of the social science disciplines* Dordrecht: Kluwer, 1991, 93–120.

Schorske, Carl, *Fin de siècle Vienna. Politics and culture* New York: Knopf, 1980.

Schülein, Johannes, *Theorie der Institution. Eine dogmengeschichtliche und konzeptionelle Analyse* Opladen: Westdeutscher Verlag, 1987.

Schumpeter, Joseph A., *Capitalism, socialism, and democracy* New York: Harper, 1947.

Searle, John, *The construction of social reality* New York: Free Press, 1995.

Seidman, Steven, *Liberalism and the origins of European social theory* Oxford: Blackwell, 1983.

Seton-Watson, Christopher, *Italy from liberalism to fascism 1870–1925* London: Methuen, 1967.

Sewell, Jr, William H., 'Artisans, factory workers, and the formation of the French working class, 1789–1848', in Ira Katznelson and Aristide R. Zolberg, eds, *Working-class formation. Nineteenth-century patterns in Europe and the United States* Princeton: Princeton University Press, 1986.

Sewell, Jr, William H., 'A theory of structure: Duality, agency and transformation', *American Journal of Sociology*, vol. 98, no. 1, July 1992, 1–29.

Shklar, Judith N., 'Alexander Hamilton and the language of political science', in Anthony Pagden, ed., *The languages of political theory in early-modern Europe* Cambridge: Cambridge University Press, 1987.

Skirbekk, Gunnar, 'Modernization of the lifeworld: Universality and plurality in the process of modernization', in *Rationality and modernity. Essays in philosophical pragmatics* Oslo: Skandinavian University Press, 1993, 215–59.

Smelser, Neil *The problematic of sociology. The Berlin Simmel lectures* Berkeley: University of California Press, 1997.

Smelser, Neil and Paul Baltes, eds, *International encyclopedia of the social and behavioral sciences* Oxford: Pergamon, in press.

Smith, Dorothy, *Everyday life as problematic. A feminist sociology* Boston: Northeastern University Press, 1987.

Smith, Laurence D., *Behaviorism and logical positivism* Stanford, CA: Stanford University Press, 1986.

Sola, Giorgio, 'Sviluppi e scenari della sociologia italiana, 1861–1890', in Giorgio Sola and Filippo Barbano, eds, *Sociologia e scienze sociali in Italia, 1861–1890* Milan: Angeli, 1985.

Stoetzel, Jean 'Sociology in France: An empiricist view', in Howard Baker and Alvin Boskoff, eds, *Modern sociological theory in continuity and change* New York: Holt, Rinehart and Winston, 1956.

Stone, Norman, *Europe transformed 1878–1919* Glasgow: Fontana, 1983.

Strong, Dennis, *The problem of order. What unites and divides society* Cambridge, MA: Harvard University Press, 1994.

Taylor, Charles, *Sources of the self. The making of the modern identity* Cambridge, MA: Harvard University Press, 1989a.

Taylor, Charles, 'At cross-purposes: The liberal–communitarian debate', in Nancy L. Rosenblum, ed., *Liberalism and the moral life* Cambridge, MA: Harvard University Press, 1989b, 159–82.

Taylor, Charles, 'Irreducibly social goods', in *Philosophical arguments* Cambridge, MA: Harvard University Press, 1995, 127–45.

Therborn, Göran, *Science, class and society* London: New Left Books, 1976.

Thévenot, Laurent, 'Les investissements de forme', in Laurent Thévenot, ed., *Conventions économiques* Paris: PUF, 1985a, 21–71 (English version published as 'Rules and implements: Investment in forms', *Social Science Information*, vol. 23, no. 1, 1984, 1–45).

Thévenot, Laurent, ed., *Conventions économiques* (Cahiers du centre d'etudes de l'emploi) Paris: PUF, 1985b.

Thévenot, Laurent, 'Equilibre et rationalité dans un univers complexe', *Revue économique*, vol. 40, no. 2, 1989, 147–98.

Thévenot, Laurent, 'L'action qui convient', in Patrick Pharo and Louis Quéré, eds, *Les formes de l'action. Sémantique et sociologie* (Raison pratiques no. 1) Paris: Editions de l'EHESS, 1990, 39–69.

Thévenot, Laurent, 'Un pluralisme sans rélativisme? Théories et pratiques du sens de la justice', in Joëlle Affichard and Jean-Baptiste de Foucauld, eds, *Justice sociale et inégalité* Paris: Editions Esprit, 1992, 221–53.

Thévenot, Laurent, 'Agir avec d'autres: Conventions et objets dans l'action coordonnée', in Paul Ladrière, Patrick Pharo and Louis Quéré, eds, *La théorie de l'action. Le sujet pratique en débat* Paris: CNRS Editions, 1993, 275–89.

Tönnies, Ferdinand, *Kritik der öffentlichen Meinung* Berlin: Springer, 1922.

Torrance, John, 'The emergence of sociology in Austria 1885–1935', *Archives européennes de sociologie*, vol. 17, 1976.

Torstendahl, Rolf, 'Transformation of professional education in the 19th century', in Sheldon Rothblatt and Björn Wittrock, eds, *The three missions. Universities in the Western world* Cambridge: Cambridge University Press, 1993.

Touraine, Alain, *La sociologie d'action* Paris: Seuil, 1965.

Touraine, Alain, *Le movement de mai ou le communisme utopique* Paris: Seuil, 1968.

Touraine, Alain, *La société post-industrielle* Paris: Denoël, 1969 (English tr. Leonard F.X. Mayhew, *The post-industrial society* London: Wildwood House, 1974).

Treitschke, Heinrich von, *Die Gesellschaftswissenschaft. Ein kritischer Versuch* Halle: Niemeyer, 1927 (first 1859).

Treves, Renato, *Sociologi e centri del potere* Bari: Laterza, 1962.

Treves, Renato, 'Considerazioni sulla sociologia del positivismo italiano', *Quaderni di sociologia*, vol. 29, no. 2, 1980–1.

Turner, Stephen, *The social theory of practices* Chicago: The University of Chicago Press, 1994.

van Doorn, Jacques, 'Die niederländische Soziologie: Geschichte, Gestalt und Wirkung', in Joachim Matthes, ed., *Soziologie und Gesellschaft in den Niederlanden,* Neuwied: Luchterhand, 1965.

van Gunsteren, Herman, *The quest of control. A critique of the rational-central-rule approach in public affairs* London: Wiley, 1976.

von Bergen, Matthias, *Vor dem Keynesianismus. Die Planwirtschaftsdebatte der frühen dreissiger Jahre im Kontext der 'organisierten Moderne'* Berlin: WZB, 1995.

von Gierke, Otto, *Die Grundbegriffe des Staatsrechts und die neuesten Staatsrechtstheorien* Tübingen: Mohr, 1915 (first 1874).

von Oertzen, Peter, *Die soziale Funktion des staatsrechtlichen Positivismus* Frankfurt/M: Suhrkamp, 1974.

von Wiese, Leopold, 'Die Soziologie als Einzelwissenschaft', in *Jahrbuch für Gesetzgebung, Verwaltung und Volkswirtschaft (Schmollers Jahrbuch)*, vol. 44, 1920.

Wagner, Peter, 'Social science and the state in continental Western Europe: The political structuration of disciplinary discourse', *International Social Science Journal*, vol. 41, no. 4, 1989, 509–28.

Wagner, Peter, *Sozialwissenschaften und Staat. Frankreich, Italien, Deutschland 1890–1980* Frankfurt/M: Campus, 1990.

Wagner, Peter, *A sociology of modernity. Liberty and discipline* London: Routledge, 1994.

Wagner, Peter, 'After *Justification*: Repertoires of evaluation and the sociology of modernity', *European Journal of Social Theory*, vol. 2, no. 3, 1999a, 341–57.

Wagner, Peter, 'The resistance that modernity constantly provokes: Europe, America and social theory', *Thesis Eleven*, no. 58, 1999b, 39–63.

Wagner, Peter, *Theorising modernity. Inescapability and attainability in social theory* London: Sage, 2001.

Wagner, Peter and Björn Wittrock, 'States, institutions, and discourses: A comparative perspective on the structuration of the social sciences', in Peter Wagner, Björn Wittrock and Richard Whitley, eds, *Discourses on society. The shaping of the social science disciplines* Dordrecht: Kluwer, 1991, 331–57.

Wagner, Peter, Björn Wittrock and Hellmut Wollmann, 'Social sciences and modern states', in Peter Wagner, Carol H. Weiss, Björn Wittrock and Hellmut Wollmann, eds, *Social sciences and modern states. National experiences and theoretical crossroads* Cambridge: Cambridge University Press, 1991, 28–85.

Walzer, Michael, *Spheres of justice. A defense of pluralism and equality* New York, Basic Books, 1983.

Walzer, Michael, 'The communitarian critique of liberalism', *Political Theory*, vol. 18, no. 1, 1990, 6–23.

Weber, Alfred, *Die Krise des modernen Staatsgedankens in Europa* Stuttgart and Berlin: DVA, 1925.

Weber, Max, 'Die "Objektivität" sozialwissenschaftlicher und sozialpolitischer Erkenntnis' (1904), in Johannes Winckelmann, ed., *Max Weber, Gesammelte Aufsätze zur Wissenschaftslehre,* 4th edn, Tübingen: Mohr, 1973.

Wieacker, Franz, *Privatrechtsgeschichte der Neuzeit unter besonderer Berücksichtigung der deutschen Entwicklung* Göttingen: Vandenhoeck und Ruprecht, 1952.

Winkler, Heinrich August, ed., *Organisierter Kapitalismus* Göttingen: Vandenhoeck und Ruprecht, 1974.

Wittrock, Björn, 'Dinosaurs or dolphins? Rise and resurgence of the research-oriented university', in Björn Wittrock and Aant Elzinga, eds, *The university research system. Public policies for the home of scientists* Stockholm: Almqvist and Wiksell, 1985a.

Wittrock, Björn, 'Social knowledge and public policy: Eight models of interaction', in Helga Nowotny and Jane Lambiri Dimaki, eds, *The difficult dialogue between producers and users of social science research* Vienna: European Centre for Social Welfare Training and Research, 1985b, 89–109.

Wittrock, Björn, 'Rise and development of the modern State: Democracy in context', in Diane Sainsbury, ed., *Democracy, state and justice. Essays in honor of Elias Berg* Stockholm: Almqvist and Wiksell, 1988, 113–25.

Wittrock, Björn, 'Cultural identity and nationhood: The reconstitution of Germany', in Thorsten Nybom and Martin Trow, eds, *University and society: the social role of higher education and research* London: Jessica Kingsley, 1991, 76–87.

Wittrock, Björn, 'Social theory and intellectual history: Towards a rethinking of the formation of modernity', in Fredrik Engelstad and Ragnvald Kalleberg, eds, *Social time and social change. Perspectives on sociology and history,* Oslo: Skandinavian University Press, 1999, 187–232.

Wittrock, Björn, 'Modernity: one, none, or many? European origins and modernity as a global condition', *Daedalus*, vol. 129, no. 1, Winter 2000, 31–60.

Wittrock, Björn and Stefan Lindström, *Den stora programmens tid* Stockholm: Almqvist and Wiksell, 1984.

Wittrock, Björn and Peter Wagner, 'Policy constitution through discourse: State-centered societies in transition', in Douglas E. Ashford, ed., *History and context in public policy* Pittsburgh: University of Pittsburgh Press, 1996.

Wittrock, Björn and Peter Wagner, *Social sciences and societal developments. The missing perspective* Berlin: WZB, 1987.

Wolfe, Alan, *Whose keeper? Social science and moral obligation* Berkeley: University of California Press, 1989.

Wollmann, Hellmut, 'Policy analysis: Some observations on the West German scene', *Policy Sciences*, vol. 17, 1984.

Wollmann, Hellmut, 'Policy analysis in West Germany's federal government: A case of unfinished governmental and administrative modernization?', *Governance*, vol. 2, no. 3, July 1989.

Wright, Terence R., *The religion of humanity. The impact of Comtean positivism on Victorian Britain* Cambridge: Cambridge University Press, 1986.

Wuthnow, Robert, 'Cultural change and sociological theory', in Hans Haferkamp and Neil J. Smelser, eds, *Social change and modernity* Berkeley: University of California Press, 1992, 256–76.

Yack, Bernard, *The fetishism of modernities* Notre Dame: The University of Notre Dame Press, 1997.

Zimmermann, Bénédicte, *Le chômage en Allemagne. Socio-histoire d'une catégorie nationale de l'action publique (1871–1927)* Paris: Editions de la Maison des Sciences de l'Homme, 2000.

Zimmermann, Bénédicte, Claude Didry and Peter Wagner, eds, *Le travail et la nation. Histoire croisée de la France et de l'Allemagne* Paris: Editions de la Maison des Sciences de l'Homme, 1999.

INDEX